The KEVIN WOODS Story

To Fram, Lindsay and family.
With love and so much gratitude for your concern and help over those very long years.
all the best!
from
Kevin
5/01/2008

The
KEVIN
WOODS
Story

In the shadow of
Mugabe's gallows

by

Kevin John Woods

Kevin John Woods

30° South Publishers

First published in 2007 by 30° South Publishers (Pty) Ltd.
28, Ninth Street, Newlands, 2092
Johannesburg, South Africa
www.30degreessouth.co.za
info@30degreessouth.co.za

Cover photo by Joyrene Kramer of Rapport © copyright 2007, Joyrene Kramer/Rapport (Thank you Joyrene)

The song Chikurubi © copyright 2007, Roan Antelope Music, Box 85, Leeupoort 0486 (Thank you John)

Design, origination and cover design by 30° South Publishers (Pty) Ltd.

Index by Mirié van Rooyen

Printed and bound by Pinetown Printers, Durban

ISBN 978-1-920143-14-5

For my children

"He who tells the truth is not well liked"
Bambara of Mali

Storm, Clinton and Dusty

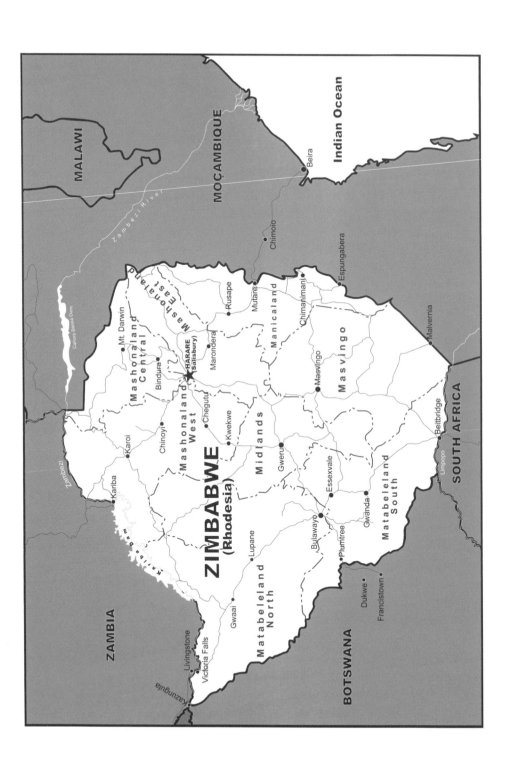

Contents

Acknowledgments

Please bear with me as I take a little writer's licence to include this part: it's important, if only for my soul.

This book is for my children, who must have wondered in their formative years, just why they were different to most of their friends, and did not have a dad.

Thank-you to my GOD for carrying me through purgatory, especially when there was only one footprint in the sand, and for the blessing of my grandson, JJ, born after my release.

There are so many people who prayed and ached for me, all over the world. I know some of you, others I haven't yet met. You know who you are. God bless you all. For special mention I have Father Arthur Lewis, W. Denis Walker, Lolly, Estelle, Wanda, Ethne, Esmé, Nookie, Belle, Lorraine, Jean van H., Miems, Mathilda and your prayer groups.

This book is also for my precious mom, who left for a better place before I could see her again. I love you.

Thank-you also to my special friends, Maria and Phillip, who own a special part of my soul.

Also to Em, Carol and sons, G. C., Margaret Gillespie, Chris Digges, Gordon and Anne Alderson, Lucy and co., Eddie Preston, Val, Dilys, Auntie Beryl and family, Martin and Leana, and Paddy Pereira. Also thank-you to June Hope who was not only a huge support, but who also kept my feet warm each winter for the past fourteen years with an annual pair of woolly socks. Thank-you to farmers Mary-Ann and Unita from Zimbabwe. Thank-you also to Cato le Roux and Don, Eunice and Dr. Paula, Pam Graves, Ann Phillips and Tony, Paul Dubois and Kenneth Heselwood, and Rose and Keith Rudd.

This book would be incomplete and probably would never have seen the light of day without Father Fidelis Mukonori, Judith Todd, Julia and Maggie who saved me and kept me going. Thank-you also to Peta Thornycroft, for the exposure, just when I needed it most.

To Robin Hartley, who was not and is not the stereotypical male lawyer, for all those years, and still, I thank you.

To my brother Mike, my crusader and friend, I say, "You're my bro." Where would I be had you not pushed so much and initiated comms with Judy Todd who brought about my liberty?

Top left: The author with the lady members of the Rat Pack, Joanne Wasserman on the left and Joan Robey on the right.

Top right: My brother, Mike Woods.

Above left: Co-accused Barry Bawden.

Above right: At left John Haswell (police rugby coach 1972) and right Ian MacIntosh (former Sharks and Springbok rugby coach). I was coached by both these fine men during my youth in Bulawayo.

Right: With Michelle. *Photo Ken Swanepoel*

Brian Hayes, you're a beaut. From way back, your help, advice and support have been a mainstay for me. Thank you Ken Gault—you know why. And to Swerve, for the memories that consumed many of the years that the locusts ate. Thank-you to archbishops Desmond Tutu and Ndungane for their prayers and help.

Dankie Esto, and also Rob and Sandy, my old friends.

Thank-you also to the South African high commissioners in Harare, with a special nod to Gordon Ntinsilana for his VIP escort to Beitbridge when I was released.

Thank-you to Australian Senator Ross Lightfoot for all your help, encouragement and concern.

Thank-you to former president Nelson Mandela for his attempts to obtain my release, and after my release for affording me some of his valuable time.

Also, thank-you to JZ for his efforts to obtain my release.

For going the extra mile, I thank Marthinus van Schalkwyk, Hennie Smit and staff, Tony Leon, Dr. Pieter Mulder and James Selfe.

Not forgetting generals Constand Viljoen, Magnus Malan and the late Kat, who never gave up on me.

RIP to former president P. W. Botha who never abandoned me.

Thank-you to F. W. de Klerk and Pik for what you did to help.

Thanks to Ellen, my agent in Jozi, for her faith in me.

Thank-you to Dr. Mitch for everything.

Thank you Dr. Wouter Basson for your advice, concern and help through the years.

Also, thank-you to John and Mary Redfern.

Thank-you to Charles and Sue Montgomery, Linda, Cathy, Bruce, Colin, Ian, Charles T. and their YPO connections for the leg-up.

Thank-you to Michelle for her untiring and diligent work at the keyboard and for showing me that Humpty Dumpties can pick themselves up again.

Thank you Colleen for help with the art and for being a computer whiz.

Craig Bone, also, for some amazing artwork. Thank you.

Thanks to my publishers Chris, Kerrin and Jane, for their encouragement, and especially for their patience. When I was first 'back in the world' soon after my release, I promised them deadlines that I was completely unable to meet.

Thank-you, always, to the late Mike Bullen, wherever you are old china, *Hamba kahle.*

Thank-you Jane Woods, the mother of my girls. I would never have survived death row were it not for you.

And thank-you to my new family—Hettie, Frank, Bel and co.

To my 'connection' Ravi Singh, a real Ford Motors mover and shaker in Durban who got me mobile. I say thanks.

Each of us has an angel in our lives. My Sis. That's you. I love you ... your husband Ken and family too, and especially Natalie, my favourite niece in the whole world!

Top left: With my niece Natalie. *Photo Ken Swanepoel*

Top right: My sister Jo-Ann and her husband Ken Swanepoel.

Middle left: Ravi.

Middle right: Rob and Sandy Hill.

Above left: Maria Radloff and Phillip Albertyn.

Left: Jane.

Above: With Bob and Kim Packer.

Top left: The late Mike Bullen.
Top right: Another member of 'The Rat Pack', ex-SAS sergeant, Terence 'Torty' King.
Above left: With former Chief Superintendent Fred Mason ('The Brylcreem 'Colonel'!! ha! ha! ha!), former Support Unit 2IC.
Above right: John Haswell, Woods and Butch von Horsten.

Thank-you also to Anton de Lange and family.

Fred Punter and Les Burroughs, Liam Hillman and family, Mac Calloway and the BSAP Natal branch, thanks for your help with the bucks.

Dankie to Adolf Malan for his probity, professionalism, fortitude, friendship and support.

Barry Bawden who went through so much with me, before, during, and after jail. Thank you, *boet*.

Thank you Valerie, my son's mother, for everything.

Thank-you to Eugene de Kock, who had enough inner strength to encourage me when I was languishing in a Zimbabwean jail, while in dire straits himself.

Colleagues and associates, and old friends like Butch, Prodder, Felix, Barry Woan, Gus, Lumpy, Alex, Laurie Wasserman, John Steel, Percy Swart and not forgetting 'The Rat Pack' who have shown me so much concern and love since my release. You're the best.

Kevin John Woods
Durban, August 2007

Timeline

1952: Born in Bulawayo, Rhodesia on 5th November.

1969: Completed M' levels at Northlea High School in Bulawayo.

1970: Joined the British South Africa Police (BSAP) aged 18.

1971: Posted as a junior patrol officer to Matobo, in Matabeleland South Province.

1973: Transferred to Bulawayo high-density suburb Western Commonage. Joined Matabeleland sub-aqua section.

1974: Promoted to section officer and later Special Branch attachment to Mount Darwin.

1975: Transferred to Mzilikazi police station in Bulawayo. Joined BSAP SWAT section in Bulawayo. At Mzilikazi, placed at Mpilo Hospital as i/c hospital police post and mortuaries for Mpilo and Bulawayo Central hospitals.

1976: Appointed i/c sub-aqua section and transferred to Bulawayo Central Charge Office.

1977: Transferred to BSAP Support Unit. After troop commander's course appointed i/c Charlie Troop. Promoted to commissioned rank of inspector.

1978: Appointed company commander of Charlie Company, Support Unit. Military deployments to Mrewa, Mtoko, Centenary, Chibi, Tsholotjo, Lupane, Masvingo, Nyanyadzi and Mhondoro/Ngezi.

1979-1982: Transferred to Bulawayo Central as duty inspector in the charge office, then as officer in charge Bulawayo Crime Prevention Unit (CPU). Discoverd ZIPRA arms cache at Filabusi, resulting in detention of ZIPRA commanders Dumiso Dabengwa and Lookout Masuku. Raid on coloured community hall in Barham Green suburb of Bulawayo. Arrests of murderers and armed robbers. Commendation by the Zimbabwe Republic Police commissioner, W. Nguruve.

1982: Joined Central Intelligence Organization (CIO) in Bulawayo and attached to operations desk. Promoted to i/c Operations Matabeleland. Recruited by South African Military Intelligence as a covert double-agent. Promoted to Senior Intelligence Officer. Investigated abduction of six white tourists on the Victoria Falls road, July.

1983-1985: Arms caches discovered on white commercial farms. South African Military Intelligence-sponsored 'Super ZAPU' bandits deployed into Matabeleland. Genocide by the Fifth Brigade in Matabeleland North and Matabeleland South commences. Operational plan for assassination of President Mugabe drawn up on request from Gray Branfield of SA Military Intelligence. Tasked with President Mugabe's close security.

1986: Assisted the operational team, *Juliet*, which was part of the South African Military Intelligence project, *Barnacle*, in SADF attack on ANC facilities in Harare. ANC attacked in Maputo and Lusaka at the same time. P. W. Botha's government admits responsiblilty.

1987: Resigned from the CIO and continued assistance to the SA Military Intelligence operational team in Zimbabwe. Planned attack on Bulawayo ANC facility.

1988: ANC facility in Bulawayo attacked in January. Arrest at residence in Bulawayo. Wife and children arrested. Detained at Luveve police station in Bulawayo. Smith and Bawden arrested. Moved by police vehicle to Harare in February. Detained at Harare Central police station. Remanded in custody to death row cells at Harare Central Prison and then to Chikurubi Maximum. Advised of rescue attempt by South African Special Forces and failure of same in June. Moved to condemned section at Chikurubi. Sentenced to death November/December together with Conjwayo and Smith for the Bulawayo bombing. Imprisoned in Chikurubi, naked.

1989: Second trial with Smith and Bawden. Sentenced to 75 years imprisonment for complicity in the Harare 1986 raids on ANC facilities.

1990: Nelson Mandela released in South Africa on 11th February. Our release supposedly linked to his.

1993: Suffered heart attack while on death row. CODESA talks in South Africa result in the release of political detainees in South Africa. Petitons for clemency to President Mugabe refused. Supreme Court confirms our death sentences. Repair work on gallows at Chikurubi begins. Supreme Court commutes sentence of death to life imprisonment in December.

1994: Moved to general-population cells at Chikurubi in January. Mandela calls on Frontline States to release all South African agents. Mugabe promises leniency, but reneges.

1996: President Mandela state visit to Zimbabwe. Again requests our release, to no avail.

1998: Beahan released. Petitions for clemency to President Mugabe refused.

1999: Bawden released.

2004: Moved to Harare Central Prison. Placed in death-row cells. Mercenaries arrested for planned coup in Equatorial Guinea, detained at Chikurubi. MDC MP Roy Bennett sentenced and imprisoned.

2005: Interview in Harare Central Prison, arranged by Judith Todd and my lawyers, with Father Fidelis Mukonori.

2006: Released 30th June. Deported following morning and crossed into South Africa at 0230 hours, 2nd July.

Preface

This book has been written by a man who is not without sin.

While I doubt that I will ever be able to fully come to terms with some of the things I saw and did while working for Robert Mugabe, I have realized that if I really want to move forward with what is left of my life, it is important for me to document my past.

As I walk this lonely and treacherous path toward self-healing I have written this book, and will do everything else I possibly can, at whatever personal cost toward inner peace, and in the process perhaps also help others who seek to understand events in Zimbabwe, which in some instances directly affected their lives, and to date are confusing and unexplained.

If you are looking for a story of histrionics and heroics, of men running around the bush with daggers gripped between their teeth, or of damsels in distress being rescued in the nick of time, you won't find it here.

This is not a pretty story. This is a book, archetypical somewhat, of Africa north of the Limpopo River. It is a story during which I lived, and nearly died, sometimes in defence of the country of my birth, and sometimes in defence of a racial system in South Africa (apartheid) that I never really believed in, but chose none the less, to aid in its time of need against its perceived communist-inspired enemy.

However wrong society may view extremist action, people often do these things from the best possible personal conviction, belief or motive. But I always knew that my actions would have consequences far down the line, as they did and still do have.

I was born in Rhodesia on Guy Fawkes Day, 1952 and was eventually declared a prohibited immigrant and deported from Zimbabwe after twenty years in jail, on 1st July 2006.

I lived the past nineteen and a half years in a time warp. The world stopped turning for me many years ago. That's why I remember so much from back then with such clarity, simply because I have had such little mental input for so long.

International law is not relevant to Robert Mugabe's Zimbabwe, unless it can be used by his regime to defend his maniacal cause, nor was it relevant during my years in my office, during my imprisonment and on the date of my deportation from the country of my birth.

While jailed in Zimbabwe, and especially during my five years in solitary confinement on death row, I formulated this book in my mind. More numerous than I can recall were the times when I truly despaired at ever having the opportunity of writing it.

However, the wheel turns, time moves on, hope becomes reality and here I am, actually putting pen to paper and reliving many years as a para-military policeman in Rhodesia, as a senior security officer in Robert Mugabe's Central Intelligence Organization (CIO) where I was well placed and had access to Zimbabwe's ultra secrets, and also as a double agent for the South African apartheid government.

The destruction of the ANC (African National Congress) guerrilla's capability to springboard military attacks into South Africa was my mission. To stop them, before they had laid a landmine on a deserted farm road, or placed a bomb on a crowded street or in a shopping centre, was my driving force and motivation.

I am not trying to insinuate that the ANC fighters did only these things—they did attack military targets and government facilities in South Africa, and I suppose it's a fine line and a difficult thing to quantify when a freedom fighter is a terrorist and vice versa, so I took the easy way out and didn't think too much about that.

In the face of much physical danger, I undertook to help the South African government in its fight against its perceived enemy and in the process I know I saved many lives, both black and white.

"What is success? To know that even one life had breathed easier because you have lived" *Ralph Waldo Emmerson.*

I knew only too well the fate that awaited me should I be compromised. As a consequence of my involvement with the South African government and my arrest while doing their work, I am going to relate my almost twenty years' imprisonment in Mugabe's gulag.

The horror of Mugabe's Zimbabwe during the 1980s and South Africa's involvement in cross-border military raids that I have knowledge of, needs to be exposed—and I have attempted to do so in this book.

Since my release from Zimbabwean prison on 1st July 2006 many people have displayed great interest in this book. People who have suffered at Mugabe's hands want to know why; others find the bits of my story that I've told them intriguing; some have wept along with me through my tales; and others want nothing more than the evil that is Robert Mugabe exposed.

Many of my former colleagues, agents, spies and friends fear this book as I remain the only double agent to have been prosecuted and jailed for our activities in Zimbabwe and they don't want to follow in my footsteps! No fuss. No one needs worry. I have no intention whatsoever of divulging any names or other details which will lead to new or further indictments and prosecutions for them or for myself.

Where I use pseudonyms, those involved with me and who were on the inside track, will know who they are. To protect a few other people I have altered their names simply because the Zimbabwean government remains extremely vindictive and paranoid.

The African Union has never been strong in taking pro-active measures in defence of human rights on the continent, and the rest of the world has also neglected its responsibility when it comes to speaking out strongly for people in developing countries. Zimbabwe is just another example of this hypocrisy.

Recent prosecutions of dictators like Charles Taylor and Slobodan Milosevic have only served to seriously encourage people like Robert Mugabe to further dig in their heels and remain in power; no matter what it takes to do so—for the rest of their lives.

There is absolutely no doubt that past and current abuses of human rights in Zimbabwe are part of a comprehensive effort by Mugabe and his coterie to stay in office, and thereby evade any international prosecutions.

My past holds both sordid and good deeds, much like any security-force operator who has lived his life beyond the edge, in the murky world where lines are not always clearly defined, and where you have to be continually alert to every dark and political force operating in and around you—the moral line that is so frequently crossed and where you can find yourself, with huge astonishment sometimes, not knowing how you got there and behaving like the very people you are fighting against.

I purged my soul as I wrote this book and I hope I have delivered what I and many other people have envisioned. I also hope this book will help readers everywhere better understand the evil of the leaders who form the current regime in Zimbabwe.

In it, I aim to give an inside perspective of many events which have occurred in Zimbabwe's past and have to date not yet been factually revealed.

The victors of any war will always rewrite history, and I have obviously placed my life in jeopardy by writing this book, but my life in Mugabe's era covers an astonishing period of African history, and it is important that history is as factual as possible.

I have lost so many years of my life that my future is now behind me. I hope that I have somehow maintained my individual identity. I have overcome most of what I witnessed and did, but the worst is, I cannot forget.

One has to do a lot of forgiving in one's life—no matter who you are. There are so many ways in which life can go wrong and self-pity, for sure, is a one-way street, so please, go slow with thoughts of retribution or hate, against whomever, as you read this.

It's what you learn when you think you know it all, I suppose, that counts in life.

Kevin Woods
Durban, August 2007

Death row cell at Harare Central, sketched by the author. (The death row cells at Chikurubi have no windows.)

A brief background
to Zimbabwe

Zimbabwe lies in southern-central Africa between the Zambezi River to the north and the Limpopo to the south. Toward the end of the first millennium AD, the Bantu peoples migrated southwards from the Congo Basin into central-southern Africa, displacing the indigenous Bushmen. Between AD 1300 and 1450, the empire of Great Zimbabwe was at its zenith, flourishing from trade with the Arab merchants from the east coast of Africa. Inexplicably, but probably as a result of a series of droughts, the empire disintegrated and split into two distinct groupings—the Torwa who migrated west to Khami and the Mwenemutapa who settled in the north along the Zambezi escarpment, to establish what became commonly known as the Kingdom of Monomatapa, consisting of a loose affiliation of clans.

The five main sub-groups, or tribes, of what was later referred to by the white colonizers as the 'Mashona' nation were, and still are, the Zezuru, Mkorekore, Ndau, Manyika and Karanga (the original inhabitants of Great Zimbabwe), the term 'Shona' deriving from the common language of *chiShona*, that was and is used in its various dialects by these five tribes. Other 'non-Shona' tribes that inhabit the region are the Tonga in the Zambezi Valley and the Shangaan in the southeast.

Apart from limited Portuguese intervention, the region enjoyed a period of relative peace and prosperity until the Zulu general, Mzilikazi, established the Ndebele kingdom in Bulawayo in the late 1820s, having fled north from across the Limpopo to escape the ravages of alternately Shaka's Zulu impis, and the Boers. Under Mzilikazi, and latterly his son, King Lobengula, the martial Ndebele (also known as the Matabele) subjugated the Mashona tribes. Matabele impis roamed the country with impunity, pillaging and capturing and assimilating Mashona women and children into the Ndebele tribe. Over a century later tribal friction would again erupt when the Mashona turned the tables on their old Matabele foes.

This all came to an end when Cecil John Rhodes's British South Africa

Company (BSAC), under charter from Queen Victoria, occupied the region in 1890 and raised the Union Jack at Fort Salisbury. The colony became known as Rhodesia.

In 1893, the Matabele under Lobengula rebelled, taking the white occupiers by surprise. After some initial, bloody successes (destroying Major Alan Wilson's 'Shangani Patrol' to a man), the Matabele were ultimately defeated at the Battle of Bembezi by the white men and their Gatling guns. Three years later, the Mashona revolted in what became known as the first *Chimurenga* (war of liberation). In spite of inflicting some notable casualties on the settler population, the Mashona were defeated and their leaders, the women spirit mediums Kaguvi and Nehanda, were hanged for their troubles.

Rhodesia grew and flourished. In 1923, with the BSAC making way for formal colonial administration, a referendum was held (whites-only franchise), with the electortate voting by a narrow margin to become a self-governing Crown colony rather than for incorporation into the Union of South Africa. With the new colony of Northern Rhodesia across the Zambezi River, Rhodesia became Southern Rhodesia. During both World Wars, 'the Rhodesias' contributed considerable numbers of personnel (black and white) to the Allied war effort.

After World War II, the two Rhodesias experienced a phenomenal period of growth and proseperity (mainly because of the copper boom in the north and tobacco production in the south), and experienced a large white immigration from post-war Britain. During this period, to consolidate political and economic control, the white colonial politicians formed The Federation of Rhodesia and Nyasaland. It was during this period of the 1950s that Black Nationalism began raising its head. An economically crippled post-war Britain, in unseeming haste to divest herself of her African colonies, began granting independence to her African colonies, starting with Ghana in 1957. This signalled the demise of The Federation which collapsed in 1963, with Nyasaland being granted independence as Malawi in 1963 and Northern Rhodesia as Zambia in 1964.

Southern Rhodesia dropped its prefix and the conservative white Rhodesian Front Party (RF) came to power in 1964 under Edgar Whitehead and shortly thereafter, Ian Smith. Joshua Nkomo became the leading Black Nationalist and with his Soviet-sponsored Zimbabwe African People's Union (ZAPU) fomented a national campaign of violent civil unrest. The ZAPU Shona faction broke away under Ndabaningi Sithole and formed the Chinese-sponsored Zimbabwe African National Union (ZANU). Both Nationalist parties began dispatching cadres overseas to the Eastern Bloc and China for military training in order to commence the second *Chimurenga*.

In the meantime, Prime Minister Ian Smith and the equally instransigent

British Labour prime minister, Harold Wilson, were deadlocked in talks, with the British insisting upon immediate majority rule ('one man one vote') and Smith demanding a gradual phasing-in of the black franchise. On 11th November 1965, Smith unilaterally declared the country independent (UDI). Britain immediately imposed international sanctions and the Nationalists began infiltrating guerrillas into the country. Robert Mugabe had by now wrested the ZANU leadership from Sithole.

So began a fifteen-year-period of stand-off and conflict with ZANLA (Zimbabwe African National Liberation Army, ZANU's military wing) operating out of Mozambique's Tete Province, supported by the Mozambican liberation movement FRELIMO; and ZIPRA (Zimbabwe People's Revolutionary Army, ZAPU's military wing) operating out of Zambia.

The 'bush war', as it became known, consisted of three distinct phases. Phase One, 1966 to 1971, saw armed incursions from across the Zambezi by both ZAPU and ZANU. These incursions were dealt with easily enough by the Rhodesian security forces in the harsh, sparsely populated terrain of the Zambezi Valley.

Phase Two, 1972 to 1975, saw the guerrillas, particularly ZANLA, changing tactics, using subversion and terror on the local tribespeople to gain local supremacy. The Rhodesians, caught by surprise, opened up Operation *Hurricane* in the northeast of the country, and gradually gained the ascendancy with the introduction of some novel military tactics, like the Fireforce concept. It was during this phase that two events occurred, which were to signal the ultimate demise of the Rhodesians. In 1974, South African Prime Minister John Vorster, using his economic trump card (South Africa kept the Rhodesian economy and war effort afloat with fuel and arms supplies), forced Smith to accept his policy of African 'Détente' (effectively, compliant independent black states north of the Limpopo, including Rhodesia), which entailed a general ceasefire and release of all detained Nationalists. ZANLA, in particular, used the opportunity to lick its wounds and regrouped on the borders. 1975 saw the overnight withdrawal of the Portuguese from Mozambibique, handing over power to an astonished Samora Machel and FRELIMO. In one fell swoop the Rhodesians now found themselves defending a further 1,000 kilometres of hostile border—from the Zambezi to the Limpopo.

Phase Three, 1976 to independence in 1980, saw ZANLA and ZIPRA (to a lesser degree) flooding the country with guerrillas. With South African support dwindling and the country in dire economic straits, Smith and his black-moderate allies, Muzorewa, Chirau and Sithole, were forced to the negotiation table at Lancaster House. Mugabe and Nkomo, with both ZANLA and ZIPRA staring military defeat in the face, were likewise forced to attend the talks as the

'Patriotic Front' (PF), an unholy alliance between the two tribal arch-enemies. To rid himself of the troublesome colony, the British mediator, Lord Carrington, bulldozed through a constitutional 'agreement', clearly biased in favour of Mugabe. A ceasefire was declared in December 1979 and general elections, that were neither free nor fair, were held in early 1980, which Mugabe's ZANU (PF) won overwhelmingly with the vast majority voting for Mugabe simply as a means to end the war.

On 18th April, Mugabe became the first prime minister of Zimbabwe and was heralded by the world as a model of reconciliation and pragmatism. British expendiency was therefore justified. However, it didn't take long for Mugabe to show his true colours. In 1983, using the pretext of a ZAPU insurrection, he sent in his notorious North Korean-trained Fifth Brigade to embark on a systematic programme of genocide against innocent Ndebele tribespeople in Matabeleland.

However, it was only in the late 1990s and early 2000s, with the bloody white-farm invasions, that the world slowly and finally began to appreciate the fact that Mugabe would remain forever a brutal tyrant who would retain power at whatever cost—the ultimate victims being his own people who are today starving and dying.

British South Africa
Police service

"Good is when I steal other peoples wives,
Bad is when they steal mine"
Khoisan/Bushman

I joined the British South Africa Police on my eighteenth birthday, 5th November, 1970 at a time when my world was still innocent. That didn't last long. Our training immediately involved us in the terrorist war that as schoolchildren we had been sheltered from. Of course, with the BSAP being very much a colonial force we were also taught the finer things of life such as washing horses' docks, and much of the actual equitation. This, coupled with mind-numbing foot drill, obstacle courses, study of law and order, musketry, first aid, life-saving and a lot of seemingly irrelevant stuff like running for miles at sparrow each day, turned us out as presentable coppers six months later. Well, that was normally the case for police recruits in Rhodesia. In the case of my intake we got lumbered with the Police Display of 1971, for which we did several months intensive training— basically a glorified circus, but dressed up like cops—vaulting on and off horses, balancing acts on motorcycles and being driven all over the country to perform at different agricultural shows.

Being a bunch of classy horse riders we also landed up forming the mounted escort for the ceremonial presidential opening of parliament in 1971.

My first posting after training depot brought me together with Alan 'Grumpy' Trowsdale, the member in charge of Matobo, a police station whose area incorporated a national park just south of Bulawayo. The number two there was Brian Hayes. All of eighteen years old, I was the number three!

ح ح ح

Alan subsequently became my South African 'handler' many years later when I was heading up Robert Mugabe's CIO (Central Intelligence Organization) in

Matabeleland, as he had moved to South Africa's Military Intelligence. I helped him out with information regarding the activity of the ANC and its guerrillas in Zimbabwe. It didn't take too much convincing by Alan and Gray 'KD' Branfield for me to become one of their clandestine agents in Zimbabwe. As I explain later this was a moral decision I took and was predominantly based on my conviction that the ANC's policy of taking the war to the civilian population in South Africa was indefensible. As a CIO member, Special Branch (SB) officer and in plain clothes as officer in charge of the Crime Prevention Unit (CPU) in Bulawayo, I ran many sources of information. So it was no great shakes to become an informant for the South African military. I already knew the ropes.

From Matobo I served a year or two in Bulawayo's high-density suburbs and played some rugby for the police where I rubbed shoulders with Gray Branfield and 'Rat' (later also to become as spy). My illustrious career as a policeman took me to another high-density station, Mzilikazi, in Bulawayo and thereafter to Bulawayo Central and on to Support Unit, the BSAP's paramilitary arm. I left Support Unit in 1979 and went on to the Bulawayo Crime Prevention Unit, leaving there in 1980 after I had been appointed officer in charge of Bulawayo Central police station, to join the CIO.

Those were heady days. Joshua Nkomo, as minister of home affairs, and Richard Hove, his successor, came and addressed us commissioned officers at the Blue Lamp Hall in Bulawayo and assured us that, in spite of being white ex-Rhodesians, we would not be overlooked for promotion. There would be many black members of the force promoted but we were wanted in the police and would receive our fair share, so we were told. Not so. I had inspectors who had just been promoted from constable, and were now duty officers in the Bulawayo charge office one week and the next were chief superintendents, while I sat as acting chief inspector.

A week later they would be assistant commissioners, sitting in an office next to mine and running the whole of Matabeleland Province.

"Come see here, Mr. Woods," Emilio Svaruka told me, showing off the blue tabs on his epaulettes. "Assistant Commissioner!" And five minutes later he would ask, "Mr. Woods, how do I answer this letter?" or some other duty he had absolutely no idea how to perform. (A few years later Svaruka, as the officer commanding Manicaland Province, committed suicide after being caught with his fingers in the officers' mess till.) I was running Bulawayo Central and covering for two new chief superintendents, who a week before had been non-commissioned section officers, and who were now forever calling me, a few-doors-down, to their offices. It was not only me who was seriously frustrated by this—sanity said, yes, promote these guys, but first teach them how to do the job.

☙ ☙ ☙

Back to the bush war … From the time of my promotion to section officer in 1974 I had daily access to the situation reports (sitreps) and could follow the progress of the war throughout Rhodesia. I was directly involved in the war, as was nearly every other policeman—be it on Special Branch or ground coverage (GC) attachment, PATU (Police Anti-Terrorist Unit) patrols, Support Unit counter-insurgency operations, Riot Squad duties in Bulawayo, SWAT, or just the daily grind as a copper—you were never far from terrorist activity in the city centres and the surrounding suburbs.

Many was the time that I would fraternize with blokes from the other forces, be they SAS, Selous Scouts, RLI (Rhodesian Light Infantry), air force and so on, and their hair-raising stories of the action and adrenaline on 'externals' (pre-emptive raids on ZANLA and ZIPRA guerrilla bases in Zambia and Mozambique) was enough to have me drooling with envy as I would have dearly liked to have gone on such raids. No such luck though—as Support Unit we were confined to within Rhodesia. Actually, there were enough 'gooks' inside the country to keep us more than busy.

Late in 1974 I was attached to Special Branch for a couple of months. This was soon after I was promoted to section officer. A couple of days training at Red Bricks, the Special Branch headquarters in Salisbury, was all that was deemed necessary to turn me and a bunch of other new section officers into Special Branch operatives.

I was then deployed to Mount Darwin, in the Operation *Hurricane* area northeast of Salisbury. This was the main anti-terrorist operational area in the country. At Mount Darwin I was posted to a place called Bveke. Don't rush to find Bveke on a map. It consisted of a police camp (a few tents surrounded by a defensive earthen wall) and an Internal Affairs camp about 100 metres away, which was also nothing but a few tents and an earthen wall. And that was it. Nothing else. To get there I had to travel along a thin dirt road as far as Dotito, a small village some 40 kilometres north of Mount Darwin, then turn right toward Rusambo and Marymount Mission along an even thinner dirt road, which was pockmarked every few kilometres with landmine holes. Testing fate on too many occasions, I'd leave the forces' canteen at Mount Darwin after a skinful of Castle beer and against all regulations, try and beat the fading light to get back to Bveke before total darkness. Passing these massive blast holes in the road always had a sobering effect on my alcohol-induced bravado.

As you will appreciate, getting to and from Bveke was quite dangerous and sometimes amounted to running the gauntlet. I was sitting at camp one rainy day just before Christmas 1974, when a lone Rhodesian Army Sabre vehicle pitched up. The Sabre was a 2.5-litre semi-truck, about half the size of a five-ton troop-carrier and had no pick-up sides or roof. For some reason that's the way it turned out after the army workshops had had a go at the vehicle with their cutting torches. I was quite surprised to see that the vehicle was unaccompanied but more worrying was the fact that there was only one person in the Sabre—the driver—no one else. I walked over to the vehicle not really knowing what to expect. There were no Rhodesian detachments deployed near Bveke at that time, so I wondered where this lone ranger had come from.

Imagine my astonishment when the driver jumped down and he turned out to be none other than my brother Mike.

"What the fuck?" I blurted out, incredulous that he had pitched up in the middle of nowhere, but more so I was seriously angry with him at the risk he had just taken. Driving around that part of the country was dangerous enough with an escort—let alone when by yourself.

It transpired that he was three sheets to the wind with a half-empty case of beers behind the seat, which in itself was crazy, as glass in the vehicle is not that good for your health when you hit a 'biscuit tin'. Mike was deployed with the Military Police at Bindura, about a hundred miles away. So after a skinful at the corporals' mess earlier that day, he'd decided to 'borrow' the Sabre and visit his younger brother at Bveke.

It was pointless berating him for being such a fool and taking such a risk. It was a quiet day after all, so we retired to my tent, where we sat for the rest of the day and well into the night, doing some serious damage to our livers with a few crates of beer.

Around 7.00 p.m., and with both of us inebriated into total irresponsibility, we saddled up in the Sabre and drove the couple of hundred miles to Salisbury—alone and with no escort. We visited a few nightspots, caused trouble at some of them and got into a punch-up at the Khaya Nyama drive-in restaurant at the Park Lane Hotel. Before the cops arrived we ducked back on to the Bindura road, dragging ourselves in a boozy haze all the way back to Bveke, arriving there well after sunrise. As we drove into Bveke we heard a contact taking place to our north, where the Selous Scouts were doing their thing, and simultaneously heard the deep boom to our east, where some poor sod had just hit a landmine.

Our guardian angels were working overtime that night, that's for sure.

A couple of hours later I gave him a two-vehicle escort back to the tar road at Mount Darwin. After a couple of *regmakers* (lit. 'right-makers', i.e. more beers) and a magnificent hamburger from the volunteer ladies at the forces' canteen I drove back to Bveke, escorted and unscathed.

I don't know if the ladies who volunteered to provide us *skelms* (rogues) with 'the best meals on the run' in the country, ever realized just how much we valued their efforts and culinary delights. These ladies, wives of men who were on military call-up throughout the country, would spend months out in the loneliest places, in their caravans-cum-kitchens, or at sports clubs and community halls, working hours every day and night, for absolutely nothing, to provide us with something to eat. They were always there, always with a warm welcoming smile, and were loved and treasured by us all. Just as Sally Donaldson was the 'Forces Sweetheart', with her Saturday-afternoon 'Forces Requests' programme on the radio where she would read out greetings from our wives and girlfriends. Sally had such a lovely voice and used to manage so much feeling into each message that there weren't many of us without a lump in the throat and an embarrassed smile when our eagerly awaited message came over the air.

While at this Godforsaken place, literally in the middle of nowhere, the South African Prime Minister John Vorster, forced a ceasefire upon the Rhodesian government and pushed through his policy of 'Détente' for a negotiated settlement in Rhodesia which would lead to majority rule within two years. Détente set us on the back foot in no small way. We had to obey the ceasefire and stop killing the gooks. The gooks didn't operate by the same rules and used Détente as a massive re-supply, re-training and re-equipping opportunity.

Any Charlie Tango (CT, i.e. Communist Terrorist) seen walking with his rifle over his shoulder was suddenly 'royal game' and untouchable as he walked his way out of the country to safety. And of course they continued their terrorist activity at full thrust, all the while blaming any events on 'rogue elements' within their ranks. It was a bit of 'extra time' to relax while out in the bush and so all we Special Branch attachés and regulars would drive hundreds of kilometres, be it to Mukumbura where the underground pub facing the minefield and border with Mozambique was called The Mukumbura Surf Club, to Centenary or Sipolilo, and even down the escarpment to places like Gutsa and Mushumbi Pools which lay in the sweltering heat of the Zambezi Valley.

It was on one of those 'booze cruises' in a Special Branch mine-proofed Land

Rover, and with a tame young baboon called Bobo, strapped in my passenger seat, that I detonated my first anti-vehicle landmine. Luckily I was going uphill so I was well within the safety speed limit and there wasn't much ado other than the left-front wheel and the engine being blown to smithereens. Bobo, who had been sitting there dozing, as he liked a few sips of Castle beer himself, was not amused. He was rudely awoken from his drowsy state by a massive *crack-boom* which threw the remains of the Land Rover about ten metres down the treacherous slope we had just navigated. The last I saw of Bobo was him sitting in a small tree a few metres off the road, screaming his indignation before galloping off into the bush. He was quite a character and was missed back at the base camp. Maybe he managed to link up with one of the baboon troops that used to abound in that area, and lived happily ever after. I hope so.

It was standard procedure at Special Branch to randomly pick up local tribespeople for interrogation regarding the whereabouts of any gooks. Soon after my Land Rover's destruction on the escarpment road, which for some reason was called 'Alpha Trail', I was issued with a brand-new Isuzu five-ton pick-up. This was a huge, cumbersome vehicle but was all that was to hand while I awaited a replacement pick-up. It wasn't a week later, and with a full load of Mkorekore tribesmen in the rear, whom I had spent the day arresting for interrogation, that I clobbered my second (and thankfully my last) landmine of the war. Maybe I had a guardian angel because I certainly did some serious mileage on the dirt roads of Rhodesia. There was only one casualty in this second blast—a tribesman from Pachanza Kraal, a large hamlet on the main dirt road from Dotito to Mukumbura. I had picked him up earlier that day and he, as with all the others in the rear of the vehicle, had denied ever hearing of any *gandangas* (gooks). A winch I had been carrying in the back of the vehicle had crushed his head in the fallout following the *gandanga*-laid landmine. He was just in the wrong place at the wrong time. Fate is something else.

৵ ৵ ৵

Because of our inaction and the massive ZANLA and ZIPRA re-grouping exercise on the borders during the Détente ceasefire, the government was subsequently forced toward the end of 1975 to open further operational areas throughout the country—*Thrasher* (in the east), *Repulse* (in the southeast) and *Tangent* (in the west). Prior to Détente, the Rhodesians had the enemy in big trouble. They numbered less than 100 within the country, were ill-equipped and running scared—as were their recruits and trained fighters in the camps in Zambia and Mozambique. Rhodesia was so close to finishing off the terrorist menace in late '74 and early '75, but the whole initiative was lost with the 'ceasefire' charade.

Add to this Samora Machel's Frelimo Party being handed power on a plate in Mozambique by the Portuguese in mid-1975, and suddenly Rhodesia's eastern frontier increased by over 1,000 kilometres—from the Zambezi to the Limpopo. From a mere 100 guerrillas 'in-country' in mid-1975, by early 1976, over 2,000 ZANLA cadres had infiltrated the Op *Thrasher* area alone.

In addition, in many rural areas the tribespeople were (forcibly) moved by the Rhodesian authorities into large collective camps called 'protected villages', or PVs, where water, sanitation and other basic amenities were provided—in order to deny succour to the guerrillas. Theses PVs or 'keeps' as they were euphemistically called were a failure, simply because they were too large to effectively police. Lack of finance precluded proper development in the villages which the insurgents were able to take full advantage of with their more effective propaganda. The gooks were eventually able to use the PVs as places of refuge for themselves, and where they even conducted political meetings—so lax was PV security—the domain of Internal Affairs and Guard Force. (The PV system was eventually dismantled in 1978 as a political move designed to bolster the image of Bishop Muzorewa, the incumbent Zimbabwe-Rhodesian prime minister.)

To gather intelligence in, and to police, this environment became an increasingly difficult task, coupled with a sharp rise in guerrilla atrocities. The 'hearts and minds' pendulum had swung—ZANLA's way—as the *povo*, the masses, were subjected to a reign of communist terror which the Rhodesians simply didn't have the stomach to match.

ৼ ৼ ৼ

After my promotion to section officer and my subsequent Special Branch attachment to Bveke, I was posted to Mzilikazi police station in western Bulawayo's high-density suburb. I recall listening with astonishment to the South African prime minister's efforts to force a political settlement in Rhodesia. Apart from the Détente ceasefire débâcle, he withdrew all South African troops from Rhodesia, and worse, he forced Smith to release all political detainees (Mugabe, Nkomo, Sithole et al) from jail, thereby ultimately sealing the country's fate. It was at this time that I got involved in SWAT.

The mid-'70s were the years of passenger-aircraft hijackings and hostage-takings in the Middle East. They were years of terrorism and bombings across Europe by extremist organizations such as the Red Brigade and Al Fatah. Police forces all over the world were forming Special Weapons and Tactics teams to counter this new global threat. In Rhodesia we were no exception and SWAT teams were formed from serving and reserve police officers in Salisbury, Umtali, Gwelo and Bulawayo.

As with a lot of things in the force in Rhodesia, finance was critically short and as SWAT we struggled obtaining really sophisticated equipment. We obviously never had helicopters and the like, so we relied on our wits and on basic weaponry like CZ 9mm pistols, Uzi sub-machine guns (ideal for urban combat), plus we had a couple of Schulz & Larsson sniper rifles which fired the same NATO 7.62 round as used in our FN rifles.

We taught ourselves to abseil, how to enter cramped buildings, unarmed combat and most of all how to shoot accurately, quickly and with both hands, with CZ pistols, and with Uzi sub-machine guns.

Fighting against armed guerrillas in crowded and cramped township houses, always occupied by innocent civilians, was no joke, so split-second and accurate shooting became an imperative.

We trained for hours on end day after day, before deploying into the high-density suburbs, together with Special Branch, looking for guerrillas, month after month. Most of us as uniformed policemen never saw the inside of a charge office for many months as Special Branch seemed to have an unending list of houses to raid and pick-ups to make.

During many of these raids it was a serious problem trying to capture or kill the guerrillas and at the same time avoid wailing mothers and children among whom the gooks had no compunction in hiding. It was always a downer when an innocent civilian was killed or wounded in the cross-fire which frequently erupted during these urban cordon-and-search operations.

We had bullet-proof vests. They were cumbersome things which we eventually cast aside, preferring the mobility of being without them to the possibility of being shot with them on. And anyway, it was a sad day when we discovered that the vests were useless against an AK-47 bullet. They did provide some protection against grenade blasts, but that was about all they were worth.

Another aspect of police life in Rhodesia where we were self-taught was sub-aqua. I started diving for the Bulawayo sub-aqua section in 1972. Salisbury had a diving section of their own which covered eastern Rhodesia, while we in Bulawayo were responsible for the west. Our equipment was good enough for the job we had to do, but was nowhere near what we would have liked. We never had access to decompression chambers, for instance. We only had wet suits. A dry suit for diving in sewage tanks for example would have been far more pleasant than swimming among the turds in a plain wet suit.

Each year there were many drownings throughout western Rhodesia. Most of the time the people drowning chose the most unpleasant or frightening place to drown. Just outside Bulawayo there is a beautiful granite-bottomed dam, Inyankuni. The water is crystal-clear and wonderfully fresh. No one drowned there—they chose the sewage dams of Bulawayo North or the stagnant pools that abound throughout the province. Failing that it was a farm dam with underwater barbed-wire fences. And diving in Rhodesia often involved black water. You could never, other than at Inyankuni, see your hand in front of your diving mask. An underwater light, which we didn't have anyhow, would not have worked in those sediments.

Without doubt, and I can speak for all other divers, my worst was diving down wells. And I'm not talking of a nicely dug well with concrete sides. I mean mud-wall wells with all sorts of shit down the bottom—snakes, sticks, bottles, wire and just about anything else. Children always love playing near wells, don't they? They spend their lives chucking all sorts of things down them, just to hear the splash. I dived down so many wells in Bulawayo and especially in the rural areas where kids had fallen in. They were always very sad dives.

Once I dived in a reasonably clear dam in the Matopos National Park, south of Bulawayo. The guy who had drowned was a South African. He and a friend had been diving together in a couple of metres of water where for some reason he panicked and drowned. Maybe he'd come across a croc under the water, I don't know. I recovered the body simply by free-diving, and didn't need to don the scuba compressed-air tanks—that's how important it is not to panic when under water. This guy had beautiful equipment, which I tested and found in perfect order. He could have sat on the bottom for an hour if he'd wanted to. I will never forget grabbing the body by the arm and kicking my fins to get us back to the surface as I saw the diver's watch on his hand showing 10.20 a.m. I will never forget that. Clear as you like, 10.20 a.m. We didn't have a diver's watch on the Police sub-aqua section. A diver's watch not only shows you the time you've spent under water but also displays the depth you are at, which is very important to know, especially when you have no decompression chambers on hand.

It would have been so easy to slip the watch off his wrist and incorporate it with the other gear we had on the Bulawayo sub-aqua section. We really needed a diver's watch. And who would know? If this oke's (chap's) buddy had asked about the watch I could just say it must have fallen off in his underwater panic.

I never took it. Over the years that I dived, in dangerous water and without a depth gauge or watch, I regretted it so often. But now, after so many years, so much older and perhaps a little wiser, I feel a small glow within me when I recall that I never, not once, crossed that line.

↩↩↩

There are many occasions as a policeman where the opportunity to take something offers itself. Be it at a car accident where the occupant is dead, or has been taken to hospital and you can help yourself to whatever remains in the car, or at a break-in where the accused have already departed, probably never to be arrested and have dropped valuables or have left a store or factory open—and as a cop you can just walk in and do as you please. As with all police institutions there were occasions where a colleague fell to this temptation, sometimes for something of such little value, that you would wonder what had overcome the man. The disgrace that comes with that sort of thing, when you get caught, is just too sad to witness.

I had a friend who was a member of the BSA Police in Bulawayo. We were in the same squad when we joined the police force in 1970. He used to steal cash from our clothes in the rugby changing rooms. The CID blokes among the players set a trap for the thief, using fluorescent-activated powder. He was caught, but no big prosecution or anything followed. His utter devastation and shame was punishment enough.

The same bloke was subsequently hanged in Harare Central Prison for the murder of his adulteress wife and her mother.

↩↩↩

It wasn't all work and no play. Chilobi, Mike Bullen and I formed the Bulawayo police third league snooker team. We never got too far until Mike was placed in charge of an intelligence-gathering station in the high-density suburbs and I was made the member in charge of the police post at Mpilo General Government Hospital. In that position I had a small staff who oversaw all post mortems at the hospital which was the second-largest referral facility in Rhodesia. The brass left me alone. As long as the paper work was done, no one checked what I was up to, mainly because my office was a mortuary. This was really cool, no pun intended, as I could delegate and then abscond to the police camp snooker room, where I'd meet up with Mike, who also had an unaccountable job, and Chilobi, who was a traffic motorcyclist. He would hide his bike behind the snooker room, pretending he was out on motorcycle patrol, and most afternoons we would get in some serious snooker. We ended up as Matabeleland third league champions!

I've done my three in the BSAP
And that's enough for the likes of me
Kum a kye, aye, aye, aye, aye
Kum a kye, kum a rookie, kum a kye

ممم

In 1977, I transferred to Support Unit, the military arm of the BSAP, where I became company commander of Charlie Company. The war was really hotting up and I felt I had a greater chance of seeing action in the BSAP's frontline unit. We worked closely with the RLI and the Rhodesian African Rifles (RAR) on their Fireforce operations throughout the country. But Fireforces were wholly dependent on helicopters, military 'luxuries' which were always in short supply.

Sitting out there in a forward Support Unit base camp during 1977/78, maybe at Mtoko, Nyakasoro, Shangani, or wherever, it became quite frustrating having no helicopters at your disposal. No Fireforce, and the worst, no medical evacuation because the choppers were forever being used by the army on their 'externals'. Having 120-men-per-company deployed under my command, at times with four companies in one base—with daily firefights and sightings of gooks, never mind the normal everyday problems associated with running the war across huge swathes of Rhodesia—but having no air cover was a huge worry. I'd have to uplift call signs from all over the place and organize my own Fireforce using Land Rovers and troop-carrying vehicles to attack guerrilla camps sighted by my observation posts.

I was at Mtoko a few times during my tour as Charlie Company commander. Quite often I'd have the Fireforce there on hand, covering an external operation out of the galvanized-iron Selous Scout fort at the base, or with the RLI commandos on stand-by at the air force base. That was heaven. Any action or a sighting and I'd have choppers at my beck and call within five minutes.

On other occasions the choppers were nowhere to be seen or heard. I'd be lucky if I had a single Police Reserve Air Wing (PRAW) Cessna four-seater civilian aircraft at my disposal. And what could you do with that? Improvise is what. The pilot and I, both gung-ho chaps, would have the rear passenger door off in a flash and I'd sit in the back with an MAG machine gun loaded with tracer. We had successes too, shooting the shit out of everything that moved on the ground, well … nearly everything.

ممم

One occasion, while I was deployed at the Mtoko Fireforce base, an Internal Affairs (Intaf) armoured Land Rover, a 'Rhino', detonated a landmine near Mudzi. These Intaf *okes* were not the best trained and were certainly at the bottom of the food chain when it came to equipment. But they would just not listen. When it came to vehicle landmines they seemed to have a death wish, roaring all over the bush at top speed.

This particular incident involved the Rhino and a full-speed rear-wheel detonation, which flipped the Rhino easy as you like onto its roll-barred roof. The roll bars, constructed of a few steel pipes, were made to protect the vehicle during a sideways roll—not head over tail. So the vehicle flipped onto its roof and the roll bars collapsed, entombing the six Intaf occupants in the back.

On each side of the Rhino was a large 100-litre fuel tank. In a few seconds the fuel was pouring out the damaged fuel tanks, and of course with the vehicle smoking-hot from the landmine, it immediately caught fire, roasting the six men who must have been frantically trying to undo their seatbelts and escape the inferno.

When I arrived, the vehicle had been burned to a black, tyreless hulk of molten, sizzling rubber and metal. One of the occupants had managed to squeeze himself out the rear door, a second was halfway out, and the others had burned to black twisted lumps of crackled meat in their vehicular oven. The only identification possible was from a watch on the driver's wrist which had a steel strap—otherwise you wouldn't have known they were human remains, so badly had they been charred.

Don't for a moment think the chap who had squeezed out was fortunate. He had suffered the most horrendous burns imaginable. His legs and arms were burned-off stumps—no feet, no hands; his face had no eyes, no nose, no mouth, no ears. How he was alive I don't know. He was a bare form of a human—pink, brown, black peeling skin, nothing else, except the pulse of his heart that refused to stop beating.

My medics managed to get about six drips into different parts of his charred body, which was not an easy task with his skin grilled to a crisp, cracking through to the underlying meat at the gentlest touch, while I frantically tried to get a chopper to casevac (casualty evacuation) this poor creature.

There was no way I could take him anywhere in my Land Rover. Over rough bush roads he would have fallen to pieces much like the leftovers of a roasted pig does when picked to the bone and thrown to the dogs.

A chopper eventually arrived and took him away, after I had nearly gone beserk, swearing at all and sundry over the radio trying to impress upon those in control the urgency of the man's condition. He died a few hours later, mercifully

I suppose. But his driver, the white *oke* with the watch, shouldn't have been going so fast … and we needed more choppers.

I took the remains of the five Intaf blokes back to Mudzi, all jumbled up in the rear of my Land Rover much like bits and pieces of burnt firewood, where I made a huge show of trying to impress the dangers of fast travel to the Intaf base personnel—and to my own Support Unit drivers.

Clear as day, I recall about a week later, travelling along the same road, I cursed in disbelief as another Intaf troop-carrier came hurtling past me in the opposite direction. I checked—the vehicle was from … guess where? … Mudzi!

The South African Police, when they were in Rhodesia, also had a bunch of drivers who were lunatics. "Going fast you miss the blast!" they would yell out.

The Support Unit deployment plan for the whole of Rhodesia included four senior superintendents who each had an operational area of the country to oversee. As company commanders we used to run the war in our own areas, just as we wanted, and reported to the senior superintendent every now and then, as he would continually traverse the allocated sector. Fred Mason was one of these senior men. He had a landmine-proofed Land Rover, as we all did, but had gone a step further and had it armoured against small-arms fire as well.

The result was quite impressive, and we all ended up adding little bits of extra steel plate to our Land Rovers, plus doubling up on conveyer belting, especially after attending vehicle ambushes where we had seen AK bullets slice through belting like a knife through butter. Fred's Land Rover carried many such scars from the various ambushes he had survived. We all had twin AK rifles mounted just behind the driver's cab facing left and right with another one inside the engine compartment, facing forward. In an ambush you just needed to hit two solenoid buttons in the driver's cab for all three AKs to let fly with a full magazine of 40 rounds, sideways and front. It was quite effective too.

I can testify to Fred utilizing his AKs on many occasions. Once, while driving about twenty metres in front of me in the Chiduku Tribal Trust Lands, the gooks opened up on us and Fred's vehicle automatically, or so it seemed, turned into a mobile Gatling gun. With his magazines filled with tracer, just for effect, it was a sight to behold. Fred was posted at Rusape's Support Unit base for many years and his solidness was such a reassuring factor that sat constantly in the back of our minds.

He had excellent rapport with the army commanders and the air force too, which was wonderful as, when in trouble, it was always nice to know that an aircraft could be found, somewhere, somehow. And he was good at that, as were the other senior superintendents, upon whom we all relied so much, to sort out the many things that can mount up and almost overwhelm you as a company commander out in the field. Small things like extra medical supplies, extra fuel, replacement of rifles and machine guns that Support Unit Headquarters sometimes were a little slow in procuring—Fred was the man!

As a Support Unit company commander, while deployed in the Selukwe area, we had to supply guards at Prime Minister Ian Smith's farm. Obviously this was a sensitive task, not only because of his standing in Rhodesia, but also because the gooks were always sniffing around his farm looking for an opportunity to crank off a few shots at him. We always made sure our most responsible troop commanders and details were posted in and around his farm. And it was a very frequent necessity to check on the blokes deployed there, especially when the PM was at home.

It was always a morale-boost to visit the troops at the farm even though we didn't have to visit the farmhouse itself. Ian Smith would always know when we company commanders were on the farm and every time we were summoned to the kitchen for a cup of tea and a chat. Ian Smith would insist he make and pour the tea himself, for us lowly coppers! It was quite nerve-wracking on occasions as he would want to know what we felt, and what was going on at ground level. Trying to drink tea with your back ramrod stiff is quite a feat.

It is amazing (and occasionally incredibly frightening) how fate will play its part in your life. When something is going to happen, no matter what the odds, if fate decrees it, it will happen. In late 1978, I was deployed at the Support Unit base in Mrewa, about a hundred kilometres north of Salisbury. A fellow company commander, Tony Dawson and I were sitting having a quiet chat late one evening in our command tent, when a Special Branch operative from Mrewa popped in to request an escort to accompany him the following morning on an early pick-up raid in the communal area.

Tony was on his last deployment with Support Unit and we had been talking of his hopes and dreams, his pregnant wife, and the fact that he was seriously relieved to have come through nearly two years in the bush. He was a huge, strong man and played rugby for Rhodesia.

We listened to the request from Special Branch and I was just about to give the order to my sergeant-major to organize the escort when Tony suggested to me that we go along in our command Land Rovers as the escort. This would entail a departure time of about 3.30 a.m. so I was a little reluctant at having to creep out of my sleeping bag at such an unearthly hour, but I grudgingly agreed.

At the agreed time, we got going. Special Branch were in a Land Rover bringing up the rear, with Tony in his Land Rover close behind me in the front Land Rover. About half an hour into our little trip we were ambushed, from the right-hand side of a small dirt road, just as it entered a rural business centre. A group of gooks had been there at the business centre having a party, and emboldened by the booze they had plundered from the bottle store, gave our little convoy a squirt as we drove slowly through the scattered buildings in the dark. We immediately hit our gunship buttons, sending hundreds of AK rounds flying off left and right, not as a killing machine, but as a deterrent to the enemy whom we couldn't even see. They had fired at us from about a hundred metres off the road before withdrawing.

We drove through the ambush position and stopped about a hundred metres thereafter to regroup. We hadn't brought any troops along with us though—after all, this was a simple escort duty. Tony had been sitting in the left front seat of his Land Rover. Next to him was a Special Branch sergeant who would have done any sumo-wrestling tournament proud, he was a massive fellow. One of Tony's drivers was at the wheel.

When we stopped the vehicles and got out to have a natter about this unexpected turn of events we were devastated to hear from Tony's driver that Tony had been hit. We couldn't believe it. The gooks had only cranked off a few rounds and had fled. I rushed to Tony's vehicle and found him, strapped in, and peacefully still.

Fate had played its hand. Our little convoy had been struck with one bullet from the gooks. The round had entered through the rear right of Tony's vehicle, passed neatly through the conveyer-belt mine-proofing, missed the driver, missed the obese Special Branch operative in the middle by a whisker, and struck Tony. One fucking bullet strike on the whole convoy. One wonderful man dead.

Amai na baba
Musandechema
Kanandafa
Ne hondo

A Support Unit song, always sung in chiShona but which translated into English, means:

Mother and father
Do not cry
If I die
In the war

ง ง ง

As 1979 ground to its inevitable and bloody climax, I was transferred to Bulawayo Central police station as duty inspector in the charge office. The Lancaster House talks too were grinding toward an inevitable conclusion—that of 'democratic', 'fair' elections to be held in early 1980 and that would embrace all the belligerents. The country was war-weary and the *povo* would do anything to stop it—even if that meant voting in Mugabe and ZANU (PF).

I wasn't in the charge office long before I was promoted to officer in charge of the Bulawayo Crime Prevention Unit.

The interesting bits were just around the corner …

Crime Prevention Unit and
Central Intelligence Organization

"The fly that has no one to advise it,
Follows the corpse into the grave"
Nigerian

On 18th of April 1980, the Union Jack was lowered and Robert Gabriel Mugabe was sworn in as the prime minister of the newly independent republic of Zimbabwe.

I now had a new boss.

❧ ❧ ❧

It was very interesting, as officer in charge of the Bulawayo Central Crime Prevention Unit, watching the gooks at Entumbane high-density suburb in Bulawayo shooting the hell out of each other. Added to this excitement was the carte blanche we all had as members of the security forces to blast anyone walking around the high-density suburbs who looked like a gook and who was carrying a gun.

Former Rhodesian pilots flew the same helicopter gunships they had used in the Rhodesian war, this time siding with the ZANLA gooks of Robert Mugabe on the ground in their fight against the ZIPRA fighters. The guerrillas from both liberation armies who were in the Bulawayo area had inexplicably all been housed right next to each other in new housing blocks in Entumbane Township, soon after they had been moved from the assembly points they had reported to after the ceasefire of December 1979. Very few former fighters had been integrated into the new Zimbabwean army (the ZNA, the Zimbabwe National Army) and simply sat around in their respective camps, armed to the teeth with nothing much to do for over a year. It was a recipe for disaster … mainly for the ZIPRA gooks.

A convoy of ZIPRA armoured personnel carriers that had come into Bulawayo from an assembly point near Essexvale to support their comrades, was ambushed by the former Rhodesian Armoured Car Regiment as it entered the outskirts of Bulawayo. It was totally destroyed. For a few consecutive nights the sky was lit up with tracer bullets and zooming RPG rockets as the two arch-enemies let fly at each other. It made for exciting times, without a doubt. Such were the ZIPRA casualties in Bulawayo that the mortuaries at the main hospitals could not cope and refrigerated wagons from the railways had to be used to store all the bodies before they could be incinerated.

It was only after direct addresses to the gooks by Joshua Nkomo himself that the unrest died down, only to flare up again a few months later. We went through the whole rigmarole again—sky shouts calling for a ceasefire from Dakotas that were fired on from the ground, circling helicopters, tracers, rockets, illuminating flares and mortars all over the place. This time the railway wagons were in place when the shooting started. The disturbances between the former armies of Mugabe and Nkomo occurred all over the country, and in every case former Rhodesian soldiers who had chosen to stay on with the Zimbabwean army climbed in and ZIPRA got clobbered.

I would drive around the suburbs cranking off a few shots here and there at the gooks from my open Land Rover with a couple of my white CPU staff who were good shots sitting in the back with FN rifles. I would provoke a firefight by shooting out the driver's window with my CZ revolver at a bunch of ZIPRA gooks who would then skirmish and return fire. My boys would then pop their heads up and let fly. I had a few sandbags lining the inside of the Land Rover behind which we all took refuge once or twice a day when the gooks returned fire a little too accurately or hotly.

This deliberate reaction against them by the new ZANU (PF) government led to many ZIPRA soldiers deserting from the army and from the assembly points for fear of reprisal, before fleeing into the rural areas of Matabeleland. Most took with them their liberation-war AK rifles and other war matériel that they had not handed in at the ceasefire. They also had numerous weapons caches throughout the province from which they could replenish themselves. This was the start of the dissident problem in Matabeleland.

ও ও ও

The Crime Prevention Unit comprised normal police officers who worked in plain clothes. The nice thing about CPU duties was that you covered all crimes. If a policeman was attached to the CID for instance, he became a specialist in homicide, or law and order, car theft or whatever, whereas in CPU you could sniff around the edges of any offence. And there was not too much paperwork either—just an arrest form, the suspect detained and off you went. As CPU we lived our lives close to the edge and mainly among the scum of humanity—among the thieves and housebreakers, rapists and murderers—that's where you would find us.

My staff made some incredible arrests while I was officer in charge of the unit—sometimes through excellent police work and sometimes through sheer luck. I had my own fair share of luck. My staff worked three shifts whereas I did as I pleased. I came and went any hour of the day or night. A perk of the job was free admission and usually free beer from the nightclub owners of Bulawayo. It was all quid pro quo because if you had a bunch of *skollies* (lads) from CPU in your bar you really didn't need to hire bouncers or call the cops when fights broke out as the boys were right there.

I was fortunate enough to be awarded a commendation by the Commissioner of Police for the work that my men and I had done. In early 1980, because of the general amnesty announced after independence, which had seen the jails nearly emptied of crooks and criminals and with all the former guerrillas sitting around with nothing to do, there were armed robberies taking place on a daily basis. Banks, service stations, you name it—anywhere where there were rich pickings, was being robbed. One day an emergency call came through on the police 999 line about an armed robbery taking place at a building society while I was driving around in my unmarked CPU vehicle. I rushed to the building society branch and quickly found out that the three robbers who had just been in there with FN rifles appeared to be coloureds. I had a number of coloured informers and managed to establish the name and address of a coloured man, recently returned from Botswana who drove a vehicle similar to the one used in the robbery as the getaway car. With a little luck and a bit of graft I had arrested the three coloureds within the hour, and recovered the cash and the motor vehicle. Being in the right spot at the right time also helped.

I don't have anything against coloured people (in southern Africa, people of mixed race). I had many good friends among the coloured community. I had arrested many black *okes* and white *okes* too, but this next story coincidentally relates to Bulawayo's coloured population, especially the unruly section. Some individuals had been getting out of hand for a few months in the Bulawayo area, and generally making nuisances of themselves at nightclubs and other licensed premises.

Every time there was a minor commotion, a gang of aggressive coloured *okes* would turn the issue into a huge fracas, and even got to the stage of overturning a police Land Rover filled with riot squad details.

I spoke to the Officer Commanding Bulawayo Central about the attitude of this gang and their disregard for law and order and obtained authority to discipline them a little. This 'discipline' took the form of a police drugs raid on a hotel and bar right in the middle of a coloured area, Barham Green, in mid-1981. I planned the raid to look as much as possible like a legitimate police operation which was essentially to cordon and search the bar and community centre on a Saturday night, during one of their serious *jols* (parties).

The result was policemen from all over Bulawayo joining in the fun as about a hundred of us climbed into the, mainly male, coloured guys in the bar, with batons and police dogs. There wasn't much of a cordon and search. It was simply a thorough bit of discipline. And it worked too. I can safely say that the ruffian faction among the coloured community of Bulawayo never again, after that night, misbehaved.

There was quite a fuss as some of the people that were clobbered got a kitty together and hired lawyers to prosecute the police for malicious injury and damage. It was a nervous time for me too as I had been the person in charge of the raid. I had incredible cover from the Officer Commanding Bulawayo Central and also in fact from the Provincial Officer Commanding the Province— thankfully, or else I might have been in deep trouble.

I had a few section officers on CPU. They were supposed to be in charge of a different duty section each, but sometimes, being bachelors, they teamed up and worked together. Many was the time that I came into the office to find that these youngsters had made some sort of cock-up and a frantic time would be had by all to try and cover it up before the brass upstairs got wind of it. On one occasion two of my section officers erroneously released from custody a person wanted for multiple counts of housebreaking and rape. I was fuming as it had taken considerable effort to catch the bugger. I told them exactly what I thought of them, gave them a vehicle and said that I didn't want to see them again until the same accused was back in the stocks. This was not easy for them as the crook was a habitual criminal and wily to police ways, but they got him eventually. No sleep for three days and nights before they finally pitched up and reported the fellow was once again safe behind bars, after scouring the high-density suburbs following different scents for more than seventy hours. Just for good measure, I sent them straight back on duty too. My record while in charge of the CPU was reflected in my Commissioner's Commendation as having accounted for more arrests than any other police section operating in Bulawayo, and this was mainly due to the diligent work of my junior officers, supervised by my young section officers, John W, Craig V, Rob H, Doug B, Phil M, and the rest, including the patrol officer 'skates', Dave, Chris, Ian et al. We worked hard and played hard.

My successes with CPU hadn't gone unnoticed and in 1982 I was lured into the CIO. Life was to become even more interesting ... and so much murkier.

ల ల ల

The Central Intelligence Organization saw its genesis in Rhodesian Prime Minister Sir Edgar Whitehead's brain in 1962. At that stage the idea was to form a state intelligence and security organization to replace the FISB, the Federal Intelligence and Security Bureau of the Federation of Rhodesia and Nyasaland. The FISB comprised a loosely knit security organization working in the Federation but had become defunct with independence in Malawi (formerly Nyasaland) in 1963.

Winston Field replaced Sir Edgar Whitehead and in January 1964, implemented the now-modified original Whitehead plans for a Rhodesian security organization. This new department, called the CIO, was to fall under the Prime Minister's Office and was known in inner circles as 'The Department of the Prime Minister' with its own (unaudited) budget. The then BSAP Deputy Commissioner, Ken Flower, was tasked by Field to get the CIO up and running and remained as its head until a few months after independence in 1980. The Rhodesian BSAP Special Branch formed the nexus of the CIO but remained within the BSAP at regional and district police-station level.

The BSAP Special Branch was responsible for internal security, while CIO, which had access to all Special Branch material, dealt with safeguarding national security and co-ordinating all intelligence acquired from internal, external and other sources.

The CIO consisted of a number of branches. Branch 1 (Internal) was in essence the BSAP Special Branch. When I transferred from the BSAP to the CIO, I was attached to Branch 1 (Internal).

The other branches dealt with external operations, military intelligence, telecommunications, and the close security of government officials. Throughout the Rhodesian war the Special Branch operated throughout the country, usually in close support with all other armed forces, including the Support Unit, the SAS and the Selous Scouts.

After independence and subsequent to the addition of thousands of appointees from the liberation movements, the majority of whom were untrained and mainly from Robert Mugabe's ZANU (PF), the CIO slowly but surely mutated into the government's strongest right arm and operated with general impunity, especially during the state of emergency, which guaranteed the organization everlasting fame as the most feared organ of state security in Zimbabwe.

In the Central Intelligence Organization we infiltrated every facet of civilian life. I had sources of information just about everywhere. From waiter-listening to bar gossip in Bulawayo's clubs, bars and night spots, to spying in its factories and commercial areas—in fact everywhere. Nothing was sacrosanct. Everything was intelligence and needed to be documented and filed away. We entered other people's lives by the back door. It's like continuous adultery. You lose sight after a while as to who is prying into whose lives. And in the CIO, as it is with most government security organizations all over the world, you continually watched your own back, not knowing who to trust. It was best, ultimately, to trust no one. The CIO has an enormous computerized library and almost everyone who lived and breathed in Bulawayo is in there somewhere.

୬୬୬

During the early 1980s and because of my position in the CIO, I was ostracized by the white community in Zimbabwe. I was feared and most white people regarded me as a sell-out for working for Mugabe. This attitude was blatant when my back was turned, but the same accusers would fawn when talking to my face. And yet I didn't abuse my immense authority. I used to attend commercial farmers' clubs throughout Matabeleland where I would go off the record and give the farmers a bit of a security briefing. I would supply them hundreds of bullets for their government-issue FN rifles to help protect themselves. These bullets were to supplement the meagre supply they received and I also assisted with their weapons training that they carried out among themselves. Many was the time that my life was in great peril, following up on murderous dissidents for instance, when not one word of gratitude came my way. It was difficult for my wife and children to live in Zimbabwe following my arrest as many of these back-stabbers suddenly lashed out—as I was now locked up and helpless—to publicly denigrate me and my family. Amazingly, since my release, the number of people who used to flood the Internet with vicious words about me has almost dried up completely.

୬୬୬

Relations between the governments of Zimbabwe and South Africa were always strained—Zimbabwe as a Frontline State was supporting MK (Umkhonto we

Sizwe, the military wing of the ANC) and the fact that as the CIO we had information of South African military assistance to the dissidents in Matabeleland did not help matters at all—the perception being that everything in South Africa was white-sponsored and -driven, military intelligence included. This was totally corroborated in December 1983 when a group of ZAPU dissidents were deported from Botswana.

During their interrogation we were delighted to come upon a ZIPRA commander, Hillary Vincent Nkomo. He gave us full details of numerous supply missions of military equipment from South Africa, for use by former ZAPU terrorists in Matabeleland. These supplies included landmines, which thankfully were never used.

The landmine was a popular and deadly piece of equipment used by both liberation armies during the Rhodesian war. However, they weigh about seven kilograms each and carrying these things long distances was not fun. Most landmines were therefore planted near the border areas. But I do know that we never recovered any landmines from dissident caches in Matabeleland, and I know for a fact that they were issued quite a few of them. Maybe the mines are still on islands in the Limpopo where they were initially cached after issue by the South Africans. The South Africans were not shy about issuing weapons either. Among the other stuff they gave the former ZIPRA guerrillas were RPG rocket launchers and rockets, 60mm mortars, RPD machine guns with thousands of rounds of ammunition, hundreds of hand grenades and so on. Enough to carry on with a small war, which they did.

Every year Zimbabwe hosts an International Trade Fair held in Bulawayo, which used to be Rhodesia's industrial hub. Exhibition stands are hired by hundreds of Zimbabwean companies as well as by several foreign companies. Some countries, like South Africa and the UK, own permanent buildings at the Trade Fair where they hold their annual exhibitions. In the first years of Zimbabwe's independence numerous countries that had never exhibited in the country arrived, and from 1981 onwards the Trade Fair really did become an international event. In latter years the number of international stands has dwindled to single figures due to the economic and political situation in Zimbabwe, where there really is not much of anything to trade anymore.

However, back in the early '80s everything was still rosy. The Russians decided to exhibit at the 1983 Trade Fair. This was of immense interest to us in the intelligence world. The Russians had supported Joshua Nkomo's ZIPRA military wing during the liberation war, and it was assumed that ties between ZAPU and the Russians remained strong, and therefore needed monitoring.

All credit must go to the CIO technical branch which, upon being advised that the Russians had reserved the entire second floor at the Bulawayo Holiday Inn, bugged it without ever being detected. It was a huge operation in which all the existing furniture in the second-floor rooms was replaced with new lounge and bedroom suites by the CIO for the duration of the Trade Fair and then removed after the exhibition. The beds and chairs all had listening devices fitted prior to moving them into the rooms. Even the management at the Bulawayo Holiday Inn was not aware that there was something going on. Maybe the Russians brought their technicians along but they never picked up the devices, or maybe they thought that Zimbabwe, which they had helped liberate, wouldn't slap them in the face, or maybe they were just clever and found the devices but said nothing and if they'd had anything sensitive to talk about they did it elsewhere.

The People's Democratic Republic of China was also exhibiting at the Trade Fair. The Chinese had supported Mugabe during the liberation war. They were not spied upon at all.

The founding director of the CIO, Ken Flower, seems to corroborate this policy of distrust toward the Russians in his book *Serving Secretly*, where he says: "Mugabe had returned from exile in Mozambique as a professed Marxist—but the term is relative. ZANU (PF) had sought aid wherever they could, but had been rejected by Russia in favour of Joshua Nkomo's ZAPU. This no doubt explains the early advice I received from Mnangagwa—to accept foreign missions as friendly or non-aligned until proved otherwise, but in the first instance to make life as difficult as possible for the Russians. The principle of non-alignment obviously appealed, in enabling the new rulers of Zimbabwe to choose as friends those who responded most readily to their appeals for aid."

A lot of things happened in Zimbabwe which for one reason or another there was no resolution. I'm talking of murders, sudden deaths, 'accidental' deaths and the like. The bombing of the independent press and media houses in Harare are also cases of these incidents in which the police never found a culprit or displayed little interest in the investigation.

The attack on ZANU (PF) headquarters in Manica Road in Harare in 1981 was one case that was always suspect in the corridors of the CIO Headquarters. There was never a prosecution for this attack, which in my opinion, due to its clumsiness, was a result of internal squabbles within Robert Mugabe's establishment that were already tearing it apart, even at that early stage of his rule in Zimbabwe.

The Zimbabwe Congress of Trade Unions (ZCTU) is where the current Movement for Democratic Change leader, Morgan Tsvangirai, emerged from. In the early 1980s, the government took over the running of most socio-economic organizations and the ZCTU was one of these. The government appointed Robert Mugabe's cousin Albert as ZCTU president.

Albert was a highly intelligent man and a bit of an independent thinker, which was not exactly what the government wanted in a position like that. He fell out of favour after a few embarrassing strikes. His wife found him dead in the swimming pool of his suburban home one evening. This was not in itself suspicious as he could have easily drowned, being a man who was known to like his drink. The suspicious aspect was that he was fully dressed in a three-piece suit. Everybody at CIO headquarters walked around with that sly 'you know something about this' look in their eyes for quite a while after that—especially as there had been rumours that the deceased had been getting a little too close to the president's wife, the late Sally Mugabe. I will add, these rumours were never substantiated, but were rife, nonetheless. No foul play was ever established in his death.

Sydney Malunga was a ZAPU member of Robert Mugabe's coalition government. In 1982, he was accused of associating with the ex-ZIPRA fighters in the bush in Matabeleland and also with the dissidents. There was not too much evidence of this but he was a bit of a loose cannon and that was what got him into trouble. He died after his government Mercedes sedan was involved in a head-on collision with an armoured military vehicle on Glenville Drive, an unlit road just outside Bulawayo. There was no prosecution of the driver of the military vehicle.

In 1985, Eric Roberts was a detective superintendent in the CID in Bulawayo. He had remained in the police force after independence and was an exceptional investigator who seemed loyal to the Zimbabwean government, as far as doing his job as a policeman was concerned. He was murdered at the gate to his home in Waterford suburb, east of Bulawayo. I attended the scene on the morning his body was discovered where it had been dragged behind the dustbin at the main gate entrance. A detective chief superintendent from Bulawayo CID was drafted in as the chief investigating officer and I liaised closely with him and reported the progress, or lack thereof to CIO headquarters in Harare.

Roberts had been shot a number of times in the head. Ballistic examination subsequently revealed that a number of .32 bullets had penetrated his skull, probably killing him instantly. The investigation showed that two or more people had waited for his arrival by hiding behind the front hedge of his residence. From the investigation, it appeared as if Roberts was shot as he was closing the manual gates after driving his vehicle into his yard, and thereafter had been dragged out of sight behind the dustbin.

The pistols used were an enigma to the ballistic people because the slugs removed from his skull and the cartridge cases showed lands and grooves which they had never seen before. Quite a few arrests were made in connection with this murder but to no avail; no prosecution was ever successfully mounted. Roberts had recently been involved in arresting a couple of South African Military Intelligence liaison officers at Beitbridge who used to frequent the pubs in the border town of Messina across from their office on the South African side. The only assumption we could make was that his over-zealous attitude had irritated someone on the South African side, resulting in his elimination.

The destruction of Zimbabwe's air force at Gweru's Thornhill air base also never produced any successful prosecutions even though the regime arrested and brutally tortured some white air force officers into confession. I have no doubt that this was a South African Military Intelligence operation and was part of South Africa's policy of destabilization of the Frontline States, but exactly which branch of the Military Intelligence, and who, if any agents inside were used, is anybody's guess. 'KD' has admitted complicity in that attack but not to me.

So there you have it—the region was now set for some nasty scenes that would shortly be acted out. The players in this macabre setting were Robert Mugabe and his ZANU (PF) government; Robert Mugabe and his Fifth Brigade killers; Joshua Nkomo and ZAPU, Joshua Nkomo and 'his' ZAPU dissidents; South African Military Intelligence and their 'Super ZAPU' dissidents; the white Zimbabwean farmers; the Matabele people; the Frontline States; the CIO ... and in the middle of all this —me—maintaining a delicate balancing act in the mire of sleazy politics, double-dealing, murder, assassination and genocide.

Genocide in
Western Zimbabwe

"If you look into the eyes of a dead body you will see a ghost"
Ghanaian

In the early 1980s President Robert Mugabe, perhaps with foresight, but almost certainly consumed by paranoia and with evil in his heart, ordered that a new full Zimbabwe National Army brigade be formed consisting only of his staunch supporters—erstwhile ZANLA guerrillas from the liberation struggle, many of whom were still housed in the Tongogara Assembly Point, and very strictly screened young men of the same tribe as himself, who were still to be trained.

They were to be placed under the authority of North Korean military officers for training and political education purposes at a Zimbabwe National Army battle camp in the Rusape area. Their instruction consisted of basic military tactics taught by the North Koreans and considerable brain-numbing ideology drummed in by Mugabe's political indoctrination staff. Upon completion of their five-month training they emerged as brainwashed zombies, armed to the teeth, and with blood-lust in their eyes. All they then needed was a convenient target and a venue to be set loose upon.

When commissioning the Fifth Brigade in December 1982, Prime Minister R. G. Mugabe (as he was then) had said, "The knowledge you have gained here will make you work with the people, plough and reconstruct. These are the aims you should retain." Fine words until you realized that they were meant for the chosen few dignatories and journalists who attended the pass-out parade. Initially the intention to form a new brigade had been mentioned by Mugabe in 1980, saying that, "former guerrillas would form a new militia who would be fully trained to combat malcontents who were causing mayhem in Matabeleland."

Mugabe then entered into an agreement with the North Korean leader, Kim Il Sung under which the North Koreans, who had long supported Mugabe's liberation army, ZANLA (Zimbabwe African National Liberation Army, ZANU's military wing) were to train and equip the new brigade.

Joshua Nkomo, whose former ZIPRA (Zimbabwe People's Revolutionary Army, ZAPU's military wing) guerrillas made up most of the dissidents in Matabeleland was very wary of this new brigade, and complained in parliament that Zimbabwe already had sufficient men under arms to deal with any problems that could arise. His sentiments, though well founded, were ignored and the Fifth Brigade was formed.

The Fifth Brigade commander, Colonel Perence Shiri, was quite clear when he told them at their pass out, "From today you will start dealing with dissidents. Wherever you meet them, deal with them, and I don't expect a report back."

Mugabe announced that his new brigade would be called *Gukuruhundi* which is a Shona expression basically meaning 'the early rain that washes away last year's chaff'.

They were called the Fifth Brigade and were destined to become Zimbabwe's most notorious unit. With their smart camouflage uniforms, in a pattern different from the other army battalions, their red berets, new AK rifles and gleaming new Korean-supplied vehicles and equipment they looked impressive. They used Korean-supplied radio transmitters so that they would in reality be a separate unit from the rest of the Zimbabwe National Army (ZNA). It was not unusual to hear them say, "We do not follow ZNA command and control or discipline. Our commander is President Mugabe. We are his army. We are not Zimbabwe soldiers' army." (Catholic Commission for Justice and Peace, CCJP, report on the disturbances in Matabeleland.)

Tragically, their first deployment where they would "plough and reconstruct" on behalf of their commander-in-chief turned out to be the long-suffering Ndebele people of Western Zimbabwe, who Mugabe had had his eye upon for a long while. Conveniently there was some armed dissident trouble in the Ndebele part of the country and that gave him the excuse to unleash his storm troopers.

Enter the Fifth Brigade. Contrary to rumours at that time that their instructors deployed with them, they deployed on their own, and were not accompanied into the field by the North Koreans.

By late 1983, the dissident situation in Matabeland was going nowhere, with the gooks and the security forces playing cat and mouse with each other. The people taking the most strain were the local Ndebele peasants and the Matabeleland commercial farmers.

This was not good enough for the political elite in Harare. Mugabe couldn't resist the urge to decimate the Ndebele, as they were obviously (according to the propaganda machine) aiding the dissidents. This provided the perfect excuse for some heavy-handed action and must have had him and his Shona security force commanders drooling in anticipation of avenging past wrongs when the

Ndebele nation had overwhelmed and terrorized Mugabe's Shona tribe a short century before, and for their spurning of Mugabe's current chosen path of socialist politics.

And who could blame him? These dissidents were a huge embarrassment to him. He was Africa's new shining star that had dazzled the West with his policy of reconciliation at independence a few short years earlier. The bandits were stymieing commercial and tourist growth in Western Zimbabwe, and were a bit of a thorn in its side.

So, on Mugabe's instruction, it was decided at Combined Operational Headquarters in Harare to implement a full curfew in Matabeleland North. This curfew was supposed to aid the security forces in their hunt for the dissidents by limiting any vehicle or pedestrian movement by the locals between the hours of 1800 and 1000 hours the following morning—all livestock was also confined during these hours, every day—the object being 'shoot on sight' anything and everything moving during the curfew hours, in the hope of seriously damaging the sixty or so dissidents who were creating havoc in the Matabeleland North area. A hard time was coming for the cats, dogs, cattle, donkeys and chickens of Matabeleland North as the indiscriminate shooting started, never mind what was in store for the people!

The troops available in Matabeleland at the time to enforce the curfew included Zimbabwe National Army 1 Parachute Battalion under the command of a white colonel, Lionel Dyck, who was a remnant from the Rhodesian African Rifles, and who had somehow hung on with Mugabe. Give him his due though; Dyck was a good soldier and a strict disciplinarian. His troops were well disciplined and feared him greatly. As in many ZNA units, discipline was sometimes swift and brutal with no recourse by the junior ranks to their hierarchy in the event of over-zealous enforcements of pack drill, flogging, etc. Despite their presence, and that of a few companies of the police para-military Support Unit, the dissident kill rate just wasn't up to the political mandarins' expectations in Harare.

Dissident deaths were actually few and far between, and a great song and dance was afforded each kill by Mugabe's propaganda machine. The bandits and the regular forces were exceptionally fast to take to the hills at the first whiff of gunpowder. Any kills were generally the result of the first few shots of a gunfight, or when a small group of three or four dissidents accidentally walked into a large contingent of ZNA troops, and one or two from either side were killed in the shooting frenzy that followed, before both sides fled in different directions. This sounds a little cowardly, and certainly was, but this 'fight and run away, and live to fight another day' tactic, if you can call it that, was ingrained in many of these soldiers' and dissidents' minds from their days as guerrillas in the Rhodesian war, where very few actually stood their ground when in contact with Rhodesian forces. To have done that would have been suicide, and life preservation is a hard instinct to override.

More troops were needed "to saturate the curfews area and eliminate the bandits"—simple as that! My opinion at the time was that if the troops on the ground were dedicated and willing to close with the enemy (which they were not) this task could have easily been accomplished with those already deployed in Matabeleland, which also included a company of horse-mounted soldiers based at Gwanda, a small village south of Bulawayo, and air force helicopters at 1 Brigade headquarters at Brady Barracks, in Bulawayo. To enforce the curfew, vehicle movement in and out of Matabeleland North, including on the major roads, was stopped. All vehicles using the roads were vigorously searched at police and army roadblocks and were sometimes detained for weeks on end at the roadblock, while the soldiers in attendance enjoyed the spoils of war in the form of everything that was being transported in those vehicles—women included.

Untold suffering for the rural people, now into their second year of drought, was the result of this measure alone, as all food supplies to rural stores was vehicle-borne and most travel by commuter bus. Vehicles of all kinds, and even ox- or donkey-drawn carts were banned from the curfew area for the full three-month duration of the curfew, with only passenger cars on their way to Hwange and Victoria Falls being allowed through the roadblocks.

Vehicles that had transported food into the curfew area prior to the clampdown were subsequently confined to the curfew zone, and not allowed to return to Bulawayo even though they had no load whatsoever left to carry. Food aid to the curfew area donated and transported by non-governmental organzations and international aid organizations was also denied.

In preparation for the curfew I did a security briefing at the Bulawayo Joint Operational Command centre—1 Brigade at Brady Barracks. This briefing was chaired by Brigadier Dominic Chinenge (as he was then), later to become general in command of all Zimbabwean forces after changing his name to Constantine Chiwenga.

(A point to note is that most of the major role players in the security forces involved with the Matabeleland security operations and curfews changed their names soon after the curfews had been lifted, be it due to fear of the spirits of those slaughtered, or traditional voodoo beliefs … or just attempting to duck responsibility, who knows?)

෴ ෴ ෴

The fact is they all altered their names with the notable exception of Perence Shiri, the commander of Fifth Brigade at the time, and who is now the air force commander. This briefing was also attended by the CIO Director of Political Affairs, Edison Shirihuru (subsequently involved with and accused of murdering his girlfriend, Rashiwe Guzha, in Harare). The security minister Emmerson Mnangagwa (rumoured to be Robert Mugabe's personal banker and financial advisor) was also in attendance, together with regional commanders from all branches of the security forces. General Gava, the ZNA chief of staff was also there (he was later elevated to the position of Zimbabwe Commander of the Defence Forces with his name changed to Zvinavashe, and subsequently after retirement, when everyone thought he would be rewarded with a foreign ambassadorial position to the United Kingdom, so the rumours went, he became a ZANU (PF) (Zimbabwe African National Union (Patriotic Front)) member of parliament).

Perence Shiri kept his name, but he did apply for compensation from the War Victims' Compensation fund some years later. He was paid nearly a 100,000 Zimbabwe dollars (a substantial amount at a time when his monthly salary as air force commander was in the region of Z$10,000) for 'Mental Stress Disorder'. Whether this mental disorder was as a result of the *Gukuruhundi*, or his days as a guerrilla in the fleshpots of the Mozambican capital, Maputo, is debatable.

The 'medical doctor 'who assessed his disability was none other than Chenjerai Hunzvi, a former ZAPU (Zimbabwe African People's Union) combatant with a very dubious war record and academic credentials who had been given the role of assessor of all war veterans' disabilities. The different wounds or scars all carried a percentage which, when added up, defined the total disability and hence the total payout.

True to form the fund was totally abused by the ruling elite, and Hunzvi, devious and totally corrupt as always, played the pivotal role of assessor. Having gained this foothold with the war veterans he rapidly climbed the ladder to become chairman of the War Vets' Association. Some of the injuries assessed and confirmed by Hunzvi were ludicrous. Anything from a scar on the knee, loss of a finger or even of a toenail warranted and received compensation! Three months and 1.5 billion dollars after the fund was initiated it had been looted so thoroughly that all payments had to be ceased.

The police started fraud investigations, but they went nowhere. President Mugabe's brother-in-law, Reward Marufu (brother to Grace Mugabe, who later helped herself to some of the housing fund, set up to supply cheap loans for war vets to build houses, and made herself six billion Zimbabwe dollars after selling the mansion she built with money from the fund), received Z$822,000 after Hunzvi declared that 'a scar on his leg and ulcers' qualified him for 95 percent disability. Marufu was quickly transferred to the Zimbabwe High Commission in Canada when the police started their investigations and was therefore 'unavailable' for questioning.

Hunzvi was the icing on the cake in this scam though. When you think that a person who is assessed as 100 percent should be dead, he pronounced himself as being 117 percent disabled and received over a million dollars from the fund. He was the only one to be charged by the police, but by then he had ingratiated himself so totally with the war vets that they would not permit his court hearing to proceed by creating such an uncivilized ruckus in court and jumping on the counsels' and judge's benches, singing revolutionary songs and shouting abuse at the judge, while the police looked on, to such an extent, that every time he was summoned, the case just could not proceed.

Hunzvi lies at Heroes Acre in Harare, after dying of 'a long illness' and having done his thing as leader of the commercial-farm invasions in Zimbabwe, during which he drove around in a new government Pajero SUV. Ah! Life in Zimbabwe!

Most funds that were legalized by the Zimbabwean parliament especially for the war veterans were looted, thoroughly and entirely by the ruling party's elite. So much in fact, that even the independent press on occasions sympathyized with the war veterans, who were otherwise forever misbehaving outside the law, to try and get just reward for their suffering in the struggle.

For instance, in August 1997, the *Zimbabwe Independent* said, "Like the rest of the population, the war veterans and other liberation war heroes are victims of a corrupt system that clearly does not have public concerns at heart. Long ago the politicians lost the drive to solve problems that the public experiences, particularly if there is no personal gain for them in those pursuits. The nation finds itself in a desperate power vacuum as those vested with the power and authority fail to exercise it to the benefit of the electorate. The politician's main preoccupation is self-enrichment and everything else comes later."

Is there really anyone out there who believes that the Zimbabwean government's foray into the Democratic Republic of the Congo in support of Laurent Kabila's regime was based on defending the soverignity of a friendly neighbour? Or was it simply the road to riches for the elite in Zimbabwe, at the total expense of the Zimbabwean economy, its military resources, and its people? The United Nations has already investigated that little scenario and had deemed the Congo's mineral wealth and other riches were thoroughly looted by the Zimbabwean government elite, with people like Emmerson Mnangagwa lining his pockets at the vanguard.

భ భ భ

Meanwhile, back at the Bulawayo JOC (Joint Operations Centre), Mugabe decide to deploy the ace that he had up his sleeve, based on the intelligence reports he was given, and after being advised that a full curfew was necessary in Matabeleland. His specially prepared (for just this occasion?) storm troopers of the Fifth Brigade, became the main force on the ground in Matabeleland, ostensibly to play the leading role of enforcing the curfew. At full strength the Fifth Brigade numbered 2,000 soldiers, not 5,000 as rumoured. Their actual deployment into Matabeleland North and their setting-up operation were efficiently carried out. Thereafter the wheels fell off and any semblance of disciplined and civilized military activity flew out the window. Let no one be under the illusion that the Fifth Brigade, consisting only of the Mugabe's Shona tribe, were sent to the Ndebele regions of Zimbabwe to eliminate the dissidents. Apart from their specialized North Korean military training they were politically brainwashed to fully and completely devote their skills and expertise to Mugabe.

They had been equipped by the North Koreans and could therefore operate outside of the confines of the Zimbabwe National Army for their supplies, stores and so on. They had been drawn, mostly from the Tongogara Assembly Point in Eastern Zimbabwe, and in the initial stages of training, any members who were not of Mugabe's Shona tribe were weeded out.

Fifth Brigade was deployed to destroy Joshua Nkomo's political and military movement in ZAPU and to politically re-orientate the way the Matabeleland people thought, with gloves off, no rules, at whatever cost, and with absolute impunity. Pure and simple—and if they killed a few dissidents along the way that would be an added bonus.

Within a few days of their deployment I received radio messages from my CIO operatives who were based at isolated police stations in the rural areas of Matabeleland that the Fifth Brigade had cut the telephone lines, and were slaughtering innocent people. They told me the brigade was randomly shooting people, and were displaying no interest in anti-dissident operations, which was supposed to have been their primary role.

Whole families were being butchered and to avoid the hassle of digging graves, families were forced into grass-thatched huts which were then locked and torched with anyone trying to escape the burning huts being shot. I compiled full reports on all these messages from my field operations, and every report went to CIO national headquarters in Harare.

Ultimately thousands of people were murdered, others were disfigured for life and mutilated after having body parts, such as ears or noses, sliced off with bayonets or ripped off with pliers. Hundreds suffered broken arms and legs after being beaten with heavy logs. Rape of any Ndebele girl was their forte, regardless of age.

Fifth Brigade was simply a bunch of murdering thugs. In addition to performing these grisly deeds with apparent relish, they also had their orders, pure and simple: "Re-orientate the Ndebele people of Western Zimbabwe."

A tradition of inter-tribal warfare has existed between the Shona (Mugabe) and Ndebele (Joshua Nkomo) tribes dating back nearly two centuries. Indeed, during the liberation war the two factions, although fighting for the same cause, distrusted and hated each other to the extent that when they met in the bush, they did their damndest to kill each other.

The Shona people had lived in what is now Zimbabwe for centuries before the Matabele arrived from South Africa. The Matabele, led by Mzilikazi had fled South Africa after being chased from Zululand by the fierce Zulu chief, Shaka and then again by the Boers on the Highveld. Fleeing north over the Limpopo, they immediately engaged the Mashona in open warfare, killing their warriors, and stealing their cattle and women. The Matabele measured their wealth in cattle, and were not skilled farmers like the Mashona. The depredations wreaked upon the Mashona by the Matabele do not feature in contemporary history books in Zimbabwe, but those memories, handed down by generations certainly do. And in Zimbabwe, as in most countries of Africa, old wounds heal slowly.

Meanwhile, "Cut off the head of the snake" was one cliché Mugabe seemed partial to using during the early 1980s, specifically when referring to Joshua Nkomo, who he had recently fired from his cabinet after the ZIPRA arms caches were discovered in Matabeleland, and Nkomo and his lieutenants had been suspected of plotting a coup.

Then at a ZANU (PF) rally, Mugabe declared that "Nkomo will never be a part of this government again," thereby apparently seeming to make the break with ZAPU final.

In early March 1983, during the Matabeleland North curfew, Nkomo escaped by the skin of his teeth from being assassinated by the Fifth Brigade and CIO in Bulawayo's high-density township of Pelindaba. About a month before that I stood at Bulawayo International Airport and watched the immigration people confiscate his passport as he was trying to leave on a flight to the UK. The police supervised the confiscation while we in the CIO stood by and watched. Nkomo created a bit of a fuss—with some of his bodyguards getting quite anxious, resulting in their arrest and detention under the emergency regulations. They were held in Stops Camp for a couple of months before being released. Nkomo was not detained and was driven off in a huff a couple of hours after his passport was seized. Under orders from Minister Herbert Ushewokunze, a month later, the police sealed off Pelindaba while the Fifth Brigade soldiers searched for Nkomo, who was well aware that his life was in great danger and frequently altered where he slept at night.

As his passport had been seized a month earlier he couldn't go anywhere, so he had to be in town. He was a very well-known man, and because of his enormous 130-kilogram frame he found it impossible to disguise himself.

When the soldiers discovered that Nkomo was not at home and after searching his house, during which they destroyed as much property as they could, they went crazy, shot three people, and smashed the windows of Nkomo's vehicles which were parked in the driveway. His chauffeur, Yona Ncube, was one of those killed. The Fifth Brigade platoon who searched Nkomo's house said that Ncube had pulled a gun on them soon after they broke the front door down, but the driver's blood-splattered bed in a side room told a different story. Another person, a pedestrian who was simply walking past the house and happened to be in the wrong place at the wrong time was also shot dead.

Pelindaba's high-density township falls in the police area of Western Commonage. Nkomo's house is probably two kilometres as the crow flies from Western Commonage, whose officers refused to attend the shooting and murder of the driver and his friend at Joshua Nkomo's house that night.

Earlier that day I sat, with other senior officers from the Bulawayo CIO office, while the CIO provincial head briefed us on the upcoming operation to nullify Joshua Nkomo. This briefing was in the PIO's (Provincial Intelligence Officer) office in CABS Building, Bulawayo and I recall the room, which wasn't very large, being crammed nearly to overflowing. The two ZR Police (Zimbabwe Republic Police) senior assistant commissioners commanding Matabeleland North and South, including Bulawayo, and their deputies were present, (their presence was to ensure the police at Western Commonage were given instructions not to react to the incident at Joshua Nkomo's house) as was the JOC commander Brigadier Chinenge (now the Zimbabwe Defence Force commander General Constantine Chiwenga). A colonel and a few majors from Fifth Brigade plus some CID, PISI (Police Internal Security Intelligence) and ZR Police Support Unit officers (with whom I shared a few warm words afterwards as I had been a company commander in the Support Unit in the last two years of the Rhodesian war and had a lot in common with them) were also present.

The PIO outlined the objective of that night's operation, which was the apprehension and detention of Joshua Nkomo. These orders, he said had come from the Minister of State Security, Emmerson Mnangagwa.

After a lot of talk about logistics and so on the Fifth Brigade, police and other armed representatives went off to 1 Brigade JOC where there were adequate maps and other necessary facilities to fully plan the operation.

We CIO officers remained to discuss the issue for a while and it became very evident to me that the whole reason for this cordon and search was the elimination, once and for all, of Joshua Nkomo. You didn't need a college degree to fathom that one out. Why involve Fifth Brigade as the force to approach Nkomo's house and pick him up—normally a straightforward role?

The Provincial Intelligence Officer's parting shot was, "If Nkomo's there tonight, he is dead!"

Joshua Nkomo obviously had some sympathetic people infiltrated into the CIO, army and police, and somehow got wind that Mugabe's threats against him were very close to being carried out. He consequently decided to flee to Botswana. That night Nkomo was driven to Plumtree where he managed to cross the dry Ramakwebana River on foot and despite his enormous bulk, he squeezed through the three-strand barbed-wire fence which served as the border between Zimbabwe and Botswana. There were rumours, which the government propaganda machine went crazy about, that Nkomo had escaped detection dressed as a woman, but that was not true. The vehicle conveying him to the border simply used back roads and avoided the main Bulawayo–Plumtree road which was policed with permanent roadblocks, and which would have picked him out in a second, dressed as a woman or not.

In Botswana Joshua Nkomo was a hot potato for the Botswanan President Ketumile Masiri. Nkomo was only allowed to stay there for a week while his friend Tiny Rowland, head of the mining giant Lonrho in the UK arranged an aircraft to convey him to Johannesburg where he was plonked on a British Airways flight to England. The British high commissioner to Botswana had visited Nkomo in Gaborone, and it is assumed he arranged some sort of travel document to enable the departure from Botswana and the flight from Johannesburg.

In the interim the propaganda circus in Harare was in overdrive, accusing Botswana of supporting fugitives from justice and that they should have picked him up (*The Star*, Johannesburg 10/3/83 and *The Citizen*, Joahnnesburg 10/3/83). Security Minister Mnangagwa, accompanied by the CIO political affairs guru Shirihuru, and the commander of the Zimbabwe National Army arrived in Bulawayo a day or two after Nkomo had fled Zimbabwe. They were escorted into Botswana by a huge delegation from the Bulawayo office to see Nkomo, which they did in Gaborone, where they tried to convince him to return to Zimbabwe. Nkomo declined their offer and assurances of his safety and they returned after a night at the Holiday Inn in Gaborone, empty-handed. Thereafter, rumours abounded that Nkomo had sought political asylum in Botswana and Zambia, both of which were refused. During the Rhodesian war both countries had supported Nkomo's ZIPRA fighters, more so Zambia, and the latter especially had been seriously damaged as a result of this support. Zimbabwean–Zambian relations under Kaunda were not great, but not so bad as to allow Kaunda to afford Nkomo asylum.

While in the UK, Nkomo gave press conferences where he accused the Zimbabwean government of trying to assassinate him, and of atrocities in the rural areas of Matabeleland. This seemed to displease Rowland enormously, especially as Lonrho had vast ranching, mining and other business ventures running in Zimbabwe. It was no secret that Tiny Rowland placed his bets well all through that era, and Mugabe's ZANU (PF) was continually funded by Lonrho, in addition to the support he gave Nkomo. Surely this was mostly a business decision as Rowland would have suffered great financial loss with a destabilized Zimbabwe, so keeping things as calm as he could by buttering both sides of his bread seemed an astute decision to make. However, with the press conferences from Nkomo, which unfortunately coincided with a Catholic bishop's report on the Matabeleland atrocities, Rowland flexed his muscles and tightened the purse strings on Nkomo.

In the meantime Mugabe was telling the world that he had no designs on Nkomo's scalp. "I am not an assassin. I don't know if he intends to stay in Botswana, but he is welcome back home," (*The Star*, Johannesburg 11/3/83) while Mugabe's home affairs minister was screaming at all who would listen that Nkomo should be arrested for contravening, the Law and Order Maintenance Act, for supporting terrorism, dealing in diamonds and for leaving the country illegally (*The Guardian*, UK 11/3/83). And at the same time the Zimbabwe ZANU (PF)-dominated parliament started making noises of stripping him of his parliamentary seat because of his absence.

It was only some months later that Nkomo, under a negotiated deal with Mugabe that guaranteed his personal safety, was allowed to return to Zimbabwe. But while he was absent his house in Pelindaba was searched again, in May of that year, during a cordon and search exercise in the western areas of Bulawayo. Nothing of interest to the CIO was ever found at Nkomo's house; he was too wily for that, and no one was killed this time round.

୬ ୬ ୬

This is the self-same Joshua Nkomo, whose ZIPRA guerrillas had shot down two civilian passenger aircraft just outside the Rhodesian resort town of Kariba a few years earlier during the Rhodesian war. For the first time ever, civilian aircraft were shot down using ground-to-air missiles. During these episodes, and not being satisfied with murdering innocent passengers by downing the first Viscount, named *Hunyani*, on 3rd September 1978, his ZIPRA fighters sought out the wreckage of the aircraft and raped and butchered the survivors as they lay injured and suffering on the ground. The second Viscount was shot down near the same place, once again with a Soviet heat-seeking SAM-7 missile. This act revolted the Rhodesians, especially when Nkomo, sanctimonious as always and live on international television, chuckled, and admitted his men had been responsible, but denied that they had murdered the survivors of the *Hunyani*. Joshua Nkomo's own man at the United Nations, Dr. Callistus Ndhlovu, in a common breakdown of communications, admitted that ZIPRA had killed the survivors, "for being in a ZIPRA area". Three people did in fact survive the aftermath of the *Hunyani* atrocity by hiding in the bush as the guerrillas approached and opened fire with automatic weapons. They tell a very different tale of the cold-blooded murder of the other survivors by Nkomo's ZIPRA 'freedom fighters'. He and his movement later tried to disguise this barbarity by claiming they had information that the Rhodesian army supremo, General Peter Walls, had been on the aircraft, which of course, was not true. They only came up with this excuse after it had been revealed by the Rhodesian Broadcasting Corporation that the general did on occasions fly to Kariba, using Rhodesian civilian airliners.

The Viscounts were simply soft targets—soft targets where there was not much danger of retaliatory fire, as favoured by both Nkomo's and Mugabe's armies. No danger to yourself if you fire a heat-seeking missile at slow and low-flying civilian aircraft, you see?

The SAM-7 is a Russian-made, shoulder-fired, heat-seeking missile that would have easily picked up and homed in on the heat trail of the Viscount's engines. The Viscounts were attacked about ten minutes airborne and as they climbed out of the resort town, at a height of probably no more than 1,000 metres

In his sermon called, *The Deafening Silence*, preached by the Dean, The Very Reverend. J. R. da Costa of St. Mary and All Saints in Salisbury, Rhodesia, on Friday 8th September 1978 at the service for those who died and were massacred in the Viscount air disaster Sunday 3rd September 1978, the dean said, "Clergy are usually in the middle, shot at from both sides. It is not an enviable role. Yet times come when it is necessary to speak out and in direct and forthright terms, like trumpets with unmistakable notes. I believe that this is one such time. Nobody who holds sacred the dignity of human life can be anything but sickened at the events attending the crash of the Viscount *Hunyani*. Survivors have the greatest call on the sympathy and assistance of every other human being. The horror of the crash was bad enough but that this should have been compounded by murder of the most savage and treacherous sort which leaves us stunned with disbelief and bring revulsion in the minds of anyone deserving the name 'human'. This bestiality, worse than anything in recent history stinks in the nostrils of heaven, but are we deafened by the voice of protest from nations which call themselves civilized? No we are not! As it is, we are bypassed by the world as if it is irrelevant. The ghastliness of these ill-fated flights from Kariba will be burned on our memories for years to come. For others, far from our borders it is an intellectual matter, and not one that affects them deeply. There lies the tragedy."

ʮ ʮ ʮ

And there was Joshua Nkomo with his selfish concern for his own skin before returning to Zimbabwe while his Ndebele people were stuck in Matabeleland trying to live through the genocide. Just prior to independence in Zimbabwe, Ian Smith is on record as saying that, "Between Nkomo and Mugabe, Nkomo was the lesser of the two evils," which is not such a great recommendation for Mugabe, is it?

Volatile anti-ZAPU statements at that time were not limited to Mugabe himself with many ministers and members of parliament, at some stage or other, trying to outdo themselves with their histrionics, and thereby ingratiate themselves with Mugabe. For instance, when Joshua Nkomo alleged in parliament in February 1983, just before he fled to Botswana that, "Fifth Brigade was murdering civilians," Minister of Defence Sekeramayi acknowledged in his response, "that innocent people could well be suffering and that this was acceptable. Can Nkomo identify a dissident, a dissident supporter or an innocent civilian?"

Not to be outdone in this field, another of Mugabe's members of parliament, Enos Nkala, told civilians at a Matabeleland South rally that if they continued supporting ZAPU dissidents "you shall die or be sent to prison." (The fact that there had been ZIPRA-inspired attacks, although poorly planned and executed, on the Harare homes of both President Mugabe and Enos Nkala in June of 1982 didn't help either.) This statement also implied that by supporting ZAPU you supported dissidents.

Mugabe was his normal unsubtle self: "Where men and women provide food for dissidents, when we get there, we eradicate them ... We don't differentiate when we fight because we can't tell who is a dissident and who is not."

After receiving news of the Fifth Brigade activity from my men on the ground and in conjunction with the reports I forwarded to CIO headquarters, I was told by the CIO provincial commanding officer to report what was going on to the JOC commander, Brigadier Chinenge. I drove to the JOC and as always obtained admission to his office with no problem. I was a frequent visitor to the JOC and well known by all the staff there. I told him that things had gone wrong in the curfew area. Chinenge was not perturbed with my news and told me not to worry, but to include these aspects in my normal weekly security briefing which at the next occasion was to be attended by Mugabe, CIO minister Emmerson Mnangagwa, Edison Shirihuru the CIO political affairs big wig, Perence Shiri, Fifth Brigade commander, and the then ZNA chief of staff, General Gava.

Whenever Mugabe went to any event such as this briefing, the room was wall to wall with political and military wannabes; he was always crowded by a retinue of ministers, aides, bodyguards and other loyal functionaries all trying to catch the Commander in Chief's attention with the right contribution, joke or action. It was later that week, and again at the JOC with President Mugabe and his normal entourage in tow that I gave them the run-down, as far as the situation was up till then. I voiced my concern at the murder of civilians that was now, according to my staff on the ground, reaching very alarming levels.

I was sure there would be international repercussions and told the briefing this, to which, amid great mirth, Shirihuru told me and the whole gathering, that he would personally deal with any international hassles and that I should stay out of their war, and that my job was simply to brief the JOC meetings on dissident numbers, tactics, and weaponry. In other words, I should stick to basic intelligence work.

That comment by a luminary such as Shiriuru, while sitting there in Mugabe's presence, obviously compounded the perception of support for their activities that the military commanders felt. Their blood-lust was flowing together with their intent to increase their efforts and outdo each other to please their military and political master. Among them sat the Fifth Brigade officers who were directly responsible for the murdering and who were going straight back to their bases in Matabeleland to continue with their mandate.

I could see that Robert Mugabe, despite all the buffoonery going on around him at the JOC, was giving some thought to something I had said, and the following morning I was told by the CIO Provincial Intelligence Officer to prepare a report on the Fifth Brigade activity, specifically for Mugabe, with special emphasis on the 'so-called' atrocities I had mentioned to the day before.

Mugabe had apparently told the JOC commanders after my departure that he had been receiving serious complaints and reports on the alleged atrocities from people such as the Catholic Commission for Justice and Peace in Harare, the

Catholic bishops themselves, Amnesty International, and from that which he was reading about in the foreign press (which he diligently perused every day).

He obviously wanted to know exactly what Fifth Brigade was doing—either to egg them on to greater effort or to try and wind them in—I just don't know. There was certainly no evidence of Fifth Brigade slackening off; rather, they simply became more circumspect with the disposal of their victims in the bush.

I contacted my team bases in the field, who in turn reported to Bulawayo for a full briefing on these reports that were now required by the president. It would have been lethal if I had just advised them by phone (if they were working) or radio that they were required to submit TOP SECRET reports on Fifth Brigade activity in their areas of operation. They would have simply joined the victims down the mineshafts if Fifth Brigade got wind of what they were doing.

The ASDIN Ops (Assistant Director Operations for CIO throughout Zimbabwe) and the CIO Provincial Intelligence Officer had to attend the briefing I gave the field teams, because even though I had the rank, I was still a white man, and this was serious stuff. In essence, spying on the Fifth Brigade was very detrimental to one's health, to put it mildly. The CIO heads were there to give them the assurance that these reports would always be treated as TOP SECRET and were required by the president himself.

Some of the team leaders were aghast at this, simply because it was going to be very tricky living and working with the Fifth Brigade and then smuggling reports on their murderous activity out. There were so many loopholes where the information of these new reports could slip through. I could sympathize with these field commanders. With different factions and back-stabbers around every corner you just never knew when you were on solid ground and as there was nothing in writing from the president in which he ordered these reports, it could always be denied if the shit eventually hit the fan.

The field teams were on slippery ground when it came to Fifth Brigade even with the police out there in the middle of nowhere. They lived and drank together. These reports would have to be completed by the team leaders and hand-delivered to my office three times a week without the knowledge of their juniors who were very loose-tongued when drunk.

The CIO provincial boss, the PIO, was in control of CIO for the whole province. Also stationed in Bulawayo was the CIO operational commander for the whole country, who carried the title of Assistant Director Operations (Zimbabwe). He called me in and made it absolutely clear during this briefing that the president was not overly concerned with the odd murder of white farmers; what he wanted was reports on the massacres and genocide he was hearing about.

This was a priority assignment and within a few days I began submitting

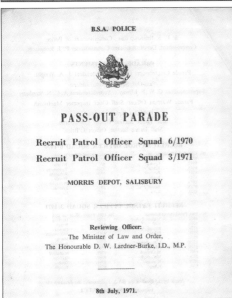

Top left: Junior school football team, Bulawayo. The author is seated centre with the ball. Top right: BSAP recruit, 1970. Centre: BSAP passing-out parade programme, 1971. Above left: Police recruits, 1970. Left to right: Niemand, Keyser, U/K, Woods, Wright. Above right: Matobo, 1971. First station posting as a patrol officer.

Top left: Police Display write-up in the BSAP *Outpost* magazine, August 1971. Author vaulting horse in display.

Top right: Bveke Keep, Mount Darwin.

Centre left: Author aged 22 at Bveke Keep, Mount Darwin. Special Branch attachment, Christmas 1974.

Above: Author on SWAT training, Bulawayo 1975.

Left: Author at Mount Darwin, 1974.

Top left: Fred Punter's Land Rover after a landmine detonation.

Top right: BSAP Support Unit landmine-proofed vehicles—'Kudu' in the front with a 'Hyena' behind it.

Above: A 'Pookie' landmine-detecting vehicle.

Centre right: Support Unit volleyball game in progress—always a great distraction.

Above: Fred Mason's armoured Support Unit Land Rover in the foreground.

Left: Support Unit APC 'Crocodile' having detonated a landmine in the Chibi Tribal Trust Lands, 1977.

Top left: Support Unit's Shabani base camp, 1977.

Top right: Support Unit deployment, Rusape area, 1978.

Above left: Support Unit vehicle at Chibi, 1978.

Above: Another landmine, this time in the Mtoko area, 1978.

Centre left: Support Unit base camp, Rusape, 1978.

Left: Fred Mason, 2IC Support Unit, briefing his patrol commanders, Rusape, 1978.

Top: Support Unit battle camp, Shamva area, 1978.

Centre left: Brian Hayes, c. 1978.

Centre right and above: The author receiving the Police Commissioner's Commendation, 1981.

Above right: This fine drawing by artist Peter Badcock, illustrates Support Unit personnel resting on arms reversed at a military funeral.

BRITISH SOUTH AFRICA POLICE

Certificate of Service

𝕿𝖍𝖎𝖘 𝖎𝖘 𝖙𝖔 𝕮𝖊𝖗𝖙𝖎𝖋𝖞 *that* ___Kevin John WOODS___ *was*

appointed in the B.S.A. Police on the ___5th___ *day of* ___November___ , 19 ___70___ ,

that he served for a period of ___9___ *years and* ___242___ *days and left the Force*

on the ___3rd___ *day of* ___July___ , 19 ___80___ ,

Force No. ___8531___   *Reason for leaving* ___On Pension___

Rank ___Inspector___

Date ___3 July 1980___   *Conduct* ___"VERY GOOD"___

for   Commissioner, B.S.A. Police.

Member's Signature _____

Decorations, Medals or Commendations awarded while serving in the B.S.A. Police.

Rhodesia General Service Medal
Zimbabwe Independence Medal

An impression by Craig Bone. This is Bobo prior to the landmine.

An impression by Craig Bone.

my reports, compiled from submissions from my teams all over the province. Because of this new role and its sensitivity, I started making more frequent trips to my rural base stations to collect the reports myself, such was the fear of my subordinates to convey this deadly information themselves. Further they would only reduce their reports to writing immediately prior to my arrival so that there was nothing lying around for any length of time that could have accidentally been spotted, or seen by the ever-prying eyes of the different political forces, evident even within the CIO.

At that time I was driving a CIO Mercedes SUV and had a secret panel fitted under the dashboard where I could hide the sheaves of paper and which would have taken a comprehensive search of the vehicle to find. I did not want to be found in the middle of nowhere by Fifth Brigade with reports like those in my pocket, or briefcase. (Incidentally, I later used to use the same compartment to smuggle ANC documents and maps and so on across the border when going for a briefing with my South African handlers.)

Needless to say there were no duplicate copies and no carbon paper was ever used. About the only precaution not taken was to change typewriter ribbons immediately after a report. I can remember dropping off an increased amount of ribbon cartridges, just in case they ever felt the need though!

It was no big deal for my CIO teams to be present when the Fifth Brigade were doing their thing and, following on that, as most of the Fifth Brigade commanders on the ground knew and trusted me, I could accompany my teams to scenes where Fifth Brigade had committed atrocities or were busy burning huts filled with charred bodies.

As long as I wasn't walking around with a clipboard and camera, there was no problem. It is amazing how one's brain can accept only so much horror before everything you try to remember becomes a blur.

I have spoken of many scenes and cases I attended and witnessed, and maybe it's because of the repetition that they have stuck in my mind. I've related some of these horrors to CIO colleagues, to my South African handlers and to other colleagues, maybe in the pub or wherever, or I remember them after lying sleepless in my bed. Subsequently, after years of solitary contemplation on the cold concrete floor of my cell in Chikurubi, I have visions of bloodshed and murder engraved on my memory forever. I suppose some of the cases remain with me because of their exceptional brutality, or their excessive overkill, or other more poignant mental triggers, such as one where there was a small child standing outside the flaming wreck of her grass-thatched rural hut which had just been torched by Fifth Brigade soldiers, with her whole family locked screaming inside.

In order to ensure reality to the weekly briefings I was now avidly documenting the atrocities. I frequently travelled the length and breadth of the curfew area in order to visit the CIO outposts that fell within my control, and while there I would be taken to murders, recently committed, and villages left desolate after the brigade had moved on. I was sent to St. Pauls Roman Catholic Mission where teachers had been murdered. My sole task was to exonerate the Fifth Brigade who swore blind the dissidents had killed the teachers. I wasn't sent there as part of the investigation, but simply to try and establish the innocence, or otherwise, of the Fifth Brigade. I had built up an extensive ballistic record of cartridge cases recovered all over Matabeleland and no match could be found regarding the teachers' murders. While that was not entirely conclusive, it did provide the suspicion that this crime could have been attributed either to other dissidents or a new supply of AKs to the Fifth Brigade.

I was in Lupane in February 1983 during the curfew when reports of a large massacre reached the CIO office there. I went and had a look, together with my Lupane team. Just to the north of Lupane and among the gutted and smoking ruins of the thatched huts of a large village, like something out of *Apocalypse Now* or *Dante's Inferno* lay scores of dead and wounded people who had just been shot by Fifth Brigade. But this was very real, not a movie.

In my report I told the plain truth, that the Fifth Brigade were responsible. At the same time, and referring to the same incident, Mugabe's ministers were denying it and blaming the dissidents, while refusing any independent observers into the curfew area to establish just what had happened. By refusing such an investigation the government proved it had something to hide.

The majority of the mission schools and hospitals throughout Matabeleland, and the rest of Zimbabwe, as it is throughout Africa, are run by the Catholic Church. On 16th March 1983, a Catholic delegation which included two bishops and the chairman of the Catholic Commission for Justice and Peace presented Mugabe (who grew up in the Catholic faith and attended Catholic schools and colleges, and who, to this date swears by his faith) with a comprehensive dossier which detailed the activity of Fifth Brigade. They also delivered a pastoral letter that they intended reading at the following weekend's Easter services throughout the country.

In their report they accused the army of conducting a "reign of terror" which included indiscriminate killing of men, women and childres, mass rapes, beatings and the burning of homes and villages. The report concluded that this "had brought about the death and maiming of thousands of innocent people who were neither dissidents nor collaborators."

Mugabe's response was predictable. He contemptuously brushed aside their protestations, dismissing their complaints as a "pack of lies". He described the

Catholic priests and bishops (who, don't forget, had nurtured and educated him in his youth) as "sanctimonious prelates who were playing to the international gallery". He added that, "They were not their own masters but are mere megaphonic agents of external manipulative masters, and in those circumstances their allegiance and loyalty to Zimbabwe becomes extremely questionable. The Church of Zimbabwe, whatever the denomination, must forever abandon the tendency to play marionette for foreign so-called parent churches whose interests and perspectives may, and often will be at variance with the best interests of the people of Zimbabwe, and they should attune themselves to the realities of the New Zimbabwe".

In late February 1983, while I was in charge of CIO operations for Matabeleland, I was ordered to reply to a letter which CIO headquarters in Harare had received from the Roman Catholic Bishop of Bulawayo, Henry Karlen. The bishop's letter, dated 12th February, had been addressed to the President's Office and had an annexure attached to it of eye-witness reports of atrocities as reported to him including an eye-witness report which had been compiled by another Roman Catholic priest, Father Pius Ncube. Both reports detailed murders, rapes and beatings by Fifth Brigade soldiers in the Lupane and Gwaai areas of Matabeleland North, which were under curfew at the time. Both reports also detailed the suffering caused by strictures placed on the movement of food using any sort of wheeled transport.

I can recall instructing my CIO officers from Lupane and Nyamandhlovu to visit each place detailed by the two bishops and report back to me with their findings on the gound. A few weeks later I did the reply to CIO headquarters in which I had to confirm that the complaints made by the bishops were true facts of what had happened to the people they had spoken to. CIO headquarters would have then done a report to the President's Office, who may or may not have replied to the bishops. I never got to see the reply by CIO HQ or the letter, if there even was one from President Mugabe's office. It would be interesting to see just what the reply was that the bishops might have received, especially as I clearly recall corroborating their complaint.

You may wonder how, amidst all the reports and atrocities, I can specifically remember these complaints by the two bishops? I was recently handed copies of documents dating back to that era, and the second I glanced at Bishop Karlen's and Father Ncube's letters I had instant recall to that time and place.

In March of 1983, the Fifth Brigade again murdered more than fifty men and women on the banks of the Cawale River in the Lupane area. This was early in the curfew when there was no subterfuge on the part of Fifth Brigade and the bodies lay for days in the broiling sun, being preyed upon by wild animals and vultures before soldiers from a nearby camp gave the authority that they be buried.

I went there, a day or two after the massacre, and I documented the whole thing in my report to the President's Office. Just as I did with the case of about ten men who were dragged off a bus at a Fifth Brigade roadblock, just south of Bulawayo in January 1983. The men were taken into the bush, shot and then buried in shallow graves. I attended the roadblock, saw the graves, and returned there some years later when they were re-discovered by some local herdsmen in the area.

The murder of large groups of people by Fifth Brigade was restricted mostly to the Matabeleland North curfew. By the time they got to the south of Matabeleland they were a little more cautious, obviously under instruction, and their murders were seldom in excess of ten people at a time.

I have memories, as reported to me from both curfew areas, and which I documented and forwarded to the President's Office, of Fifth Brigade forcing whole villages to dig mass graves into which they would force randomly selected people, shoot them and, dead or living, order the graves be filled in by relatives who were frequently forced to watch, but who dared not refuse to cover in the holes.

It was impossible for me to visit every atrocity; there were just too many and too widespread. But each and every Fifth Brigade atrocity that I did confirm was documented and went up through the channels. Those records still exist, I expect, somewhere. I could go on a little more, and relate other murders I attended, and those reported to me, but I think now its 'enough unto the day'. I feel I've painted the picture sufficiently clearly. Suffice it to say, Mugabe and his coterie of security ministers knew exactly what was going on in the curfew zones.

I also attended most of the commercial farmers' murders. I collected cartridge cases, took photographs and produced an extensive file. This was part of my role as an intelligence officer, but as many of the commercial farmers and their families who were murdered were friends, it became a personal mission. I have the ghastly scenes of blood-splattered remains of so many friends and their wives and children imprinted on the inside of my skull, that I know I will never erase, or forget. At other places in this book I refer to my sanity or lack thereof and sometimes I wonder if any of us who lived through that era in Zimbabwe are completely all there. Can you live a life with all that butchery and cope?

❧❧❧

In a separate chapter I do expose the 'Super ZAPU' terrorists who were trained, equipped and deployed into Zimbabwe by the South African Military Intelligence. These dissidents were infiltrated with a mission to cause mayhem and disruption from within Zimbabwe, but, and I was assured this at the time, and have had it reconfirmed by the people in South Africa who ran the operation, that Super ZAPU were given strict instruction not to kill commercial farmers. On quite a few occasions, attending and investigating commercial farmer murders I would be able to establish quite definitely whether the culprits were normal ZIPRA dissidents, Fifth Brigade (because they too murdered commercial farmers), or Super ZAPU.

There wasn't much I could do about the first two—if it was a dissident murder I could ensure some sort of military follow-up was initiated. Fifth Brigade went into my weekly report to the presidency, even though I'd been told there was not too much interest at national level if a commercial farmer was murdered. Super ZAPU was, however, a different matter.

After I had established that their recruitment and training was taking place in South Africa, I then had a conduit, via my own handlers, to get messages to the Super ZAPU controllers. They had methods of getting messages to their dissidents who were on the ground within Zimbabwe. However, as this communication was by courier it would take a little while, a week or so for instance, for a message to reach their gooks in the field. I collected cartridge cases at all the murders I attended, and it was easy to identify Super ZAPU empty casings by the 22/80 stamp on the base. Whenever I established Super ZAPU were the killers I would forward the casings and a summary of the intelligence I had through my runners to the Super ZAPU controllers in South Africa who would usually recall the responsible dissident from the field "for consultation, debrief, and rest" and if necessary a thorough thrashing to get his mind back on track. Or worse; if it were deemed he was beyond reconditioning, he would be shot. This sort of response to my reports from Zimbabwe has been told to me, since my release from prison last year, by those who were involved in it.

The Super ZAPU controllers had a full ballistic database on the weapons they had issued to their dissidents, so it was quite easy for them to identify who had been issued the weapon used in the specific murder I was referring to.

Never once did I find the same Super ZAPU weapon being used at a subsequent commercial farmer, or any other, murder for that matter, after I had made a report on the rogue activity to the South Africans, and I am assured, whole-heartedly, by ex-Colonel Mac, that none of the rogues were re-deployed. Their fate I will leave up to the reader's conjecture, but there was a war going on and discipline, especially when dealing with rogue elements who would not listen, had to be very harsh, and was needed to dissuade others from doing their own thing. Obviously, on occasions, the dissidents would not heed their recall. This would lead to Mac having to dispatch other Super ZAPU to either go and fetch them or, if the recall was still ignored, eliminate them in the Zimbabwean bush.

There were many reasons for the Super ZAPU to have gone rogue and kill commercial farmers and other people such as priests, who were also supposed to be left alone. Mainly these murders were carried out at the behest of the locals in the farmer's area who were having problems watering their livestock on his land, or the farmer was giving them trouble because they were snaring his game and cattle, or perhaps a headman asked for the murder to show his followers he had clout with 'the boys in the bush'. The fact is that it was very difficult for the South Africans to keep a tight rein on their dissidents once they had crossed the Limpopo into Zimbabwe.

୬ ୬ ୬

Fifth Brigade were not shy when it came to dressing up like dissidents, visiting a rural homestead for food, and then returning the following day to check if any 'strangers' had been around. And of course the locals, being terrified of reprisals from the dissidents would deny any such thing, and be killed on the spot for supporting them.

I can recall many villages, sometimes a single thatched hut ablaze, other times the whole village of three, four, or even more burning, each with the pungent 'burnt pork' smell that the human body gives off when burned, thick in the air.

The Nkayi, Lupane and Tsholotjo areas, perhaps because of their exceptional remoteness, were favoured by the Fifth Bridage for this way to kill whole families, thereby not leaving too much evidence behind. The grass-roofed huts burn fast, with immense heat intensity and not much is left, especially after a grenade is lobbed into the ashes afterwards, just to spread things out a bit.

Meanwhile on the propaganda side and never to be outdone in public, especially by his cabinet ministers, Mugabe himself continually let his feelings be known in his speeches at rallies and comments in the government newspapers, "We will show evil ZAPU our teeth, we can bite and will certainly bite—ZAPU is destined for destruction." Just in case his followers misunderstood his sentiments.

Joshua Nkomo tried to bring the Fifth Brigade murders up in parliament many times and on one occasion, the response he obtained from the Home Affairs minister, Herbert Ushewokunzwe was quite revealing—that Nkomo, "would win a Nobel Peace Prize for fiction".

To try give truth to the lies that claimed there was nothing going on, most certainly not massacres, Mugabe's propaganda machine forced people to attend a rally in the small rural business centre of Kezi, a few months into the

Matabeleland North curfew. Kezi is about 100 kilometres south of Bulawayo, while the Fifth brigade curfew was in operation about 30 kilometres north of Bulawayo. I attended the Kezi rally in my official CIO capacity and listened to Mugabe's Director of Information, Justin Nyoka, as he challenged the gathered international journalists to find and produce proof of the "full-scale war they were telling the world about, which is just a figment of your imagination, planted in your minds by the colonial powers".

The security minister Mnangagwa (who at one time sat in Rhodesia's death cells on charges of terrorism, but managed to skip the noose due to his age, and who probably holds the title for being the most evil of Zimbabwe's elite, and who also, in latter years, especially during Zimbabwe's ill-advised intervention in the Democratic Republic of the Congo, was there with his hands in every venture he could as generalissimo and carpetbagger), during the curfew, told the crowd that had been forced to attend, "Blessed are they who will follow the path of the government's laws but woe unto those who choose the path of collaborating with the dissidents, for we will surely shorten your days." This was said to great merriment to the assembled security force members, who included the Red Berets of the Fifth Brigade, and a contingent of us from the CIO Bulawayo office. Mnangagwa liked these parodies of the Scriptures. In jail many years later he told me, "If you want to speak to God [meaning Mugabe] go through his son [meaning himself]."

A few years later the ever-militant Enos Nkala, who now is an outcast from Mugabe's tent after being caught up in a little corruption, but who was then home affairs minister, said on National TV and radio, "We want to wipe out the ZAPU leadership. You've only seen the warning lights. We are not yet at full speed. ZAPU is a murderous organization and its murderous leadership must be hit so hard!" This was soon after the 1985 general election where Nkala was made to look an utter fool after being annihilated by a newcomer from ZAPU in a Matabeleland constituency, and where ZAPU had made a clean sweep, despite *Gukuruhundi* and years of suffering at the hands of the ZANU (PF) government, which was supposed to have 're-oriented' them.

Thereafter reports of the murders and other atrocities by the Fifth Brigade increased dramatically. The dissidents were also doing their fair share of butchery in order to maintain some sort of 'patriotism, support and discipline' among the people living in the rural areas—who really were caught between two evils.

During the liberation war the civilian population knew the Rhodesian security forces would beat and shock the living shit out of them, but the gooks would kill them to obtain information or to maintain a hold over their hearts and minds. That distinction, after 1980 and especially in the curfew area, suddenly disappeared, with the *povo* (the people) findng themselves being killed by both the soldiers and the gooks.

I can state with as clear a conscience as I can, that to the best of my knowledge, CIO did not fall out of its tree and wantonly murder civilians left right and centre, as has been reported in the past and is currently spoken of when referring to the dissident era …

A month or so into the curfew, with no results other than a few lucky pot shots at the bandits, and with news of the butchery thoroughly leaked from the bush to the international community, I again spoke to the CIO provincial head, Sam Chitava, and he didn't even have the decency to blush as he quoted Shirihuru, and told me, "Do not worry, Mr. Woods. This is not your war."

&&&

Meanwhile Fifth Brigade had no qualms about leaving their victims where they died, be it in the bush, at their kraals, alongside roads, wherever. Any graves that were dug were rushed affairs in shallow ground done by the deceased's families, or simply anybody who happened to come across some human remains, as mostly the people were denied permission to bury their families. It's a simple fact that Fifth Brigade felt no need to cover their dastardly deeds.

Their perception of indemnity and sanction for their acts and their impunity was always reinforced. For instance, during the curfew, there is the case of a rape and murder of an off-duty ZNA lieutenant, his wife and two passengers, dragged from their car on the Victoria Falls road in February 1983. Their bodies were found in a shallow grave, with hands tied behind their backs, and the women showing evidence of gang rape.

The four Fifth Brigade members who were responsible were taken into Fifth Brigade 'custody' and subsequently found guilty of four counts of pre-meditated murder in a show trial. The trial was supposed to give the internatonal community the impression that Mugabe's regime would not tolerate this sort of misbehaviour by its troops and that the rule of law would follow its course, without fear or favour.

The trial judge had subsequently found their murder exceedingly cruel, as the victims had been sexually abused and repeatedly stabbed with bayonets. He sentenced all four Fifth Brigade soldiers to death for pre-meditated murder.

All four were immediately pardoned by President Mugabe and returned to full duty. Why the government went to all the fuss of a show trial is anybody's guess, because the immediate pardon by Mugabe, which exposed the whole charade, did more international and local damage to Zimbabwe's reputation than no trial at all would have.

The four Fifth Brigade accused who were pardoned by Mugabe had not spent a single hour in detention, military prison or otherwise. Far from hoodwinking the international community, this show trial and pardon resulted in immense exposure of the evil the Mugabe regime had become. Despite huge local and international outcry, Mugabe and his security chiefs maintained the curfew in Matabeleland North until the end of 1983 when Fifth Brigade was finally withdrawn for re-training.

In early 1984, the curfew was moved to Matabeleland South—and not because of its success in eliminating the dissidents in the north to be sure! But certainly as part of Mugabe's stated mission to eradicate "evil ZAPU", to re-orientate the Ndebele people, and of course to thumb his nose at the rest of the world who were whining about human rights abuses and the recent horrific events that had reportedly occurred in Matabeleland North the previous year.

Upon deployment, the Fifth Brigade immediately recommenced their madness. This time round they were a little more discreet regarding killing and disposal of their victims. They still favoured the torched-grass hut scene, but also had the locals dispose of their relatives down mine shafts, which abound in the area.

On certain occasions when there were no locals on hand to do the disposal, Fifth Brigade used covered military vehicles to convey bodies to Turtle Mine near Kwekwe, hundreds of kilometres away in the centre of Zimbabwe where a conveniently very deep, derelict mineshaft was available, off the beaten track.

Mugabe has always denied the existence of mass graves, mineshaft disposals and so on—and if ever they are located and exhumed, he blames them on Rhodesian forces disposing of people they had murdered during the liberation war era. Yet after some exhumations of mass graves in the curfew areas, Zimbabwean coins minted after 1980 were found on some of the recovered bodies, clearly indicating that they died after the end of the Rhodesian war.

The Matabeleland South curfew was just as ruthless and cruel as that in the north, with vehicles carrying food supplies to the rural stores being prevented entry into the curfew area despite yet another failed rainy season and most of the people's grainaries being empty. Buses and private cars, commercial vehicles and animal-drawn carts were detained within the curfew area, and there was no movement whatsoever allowed by any civilian transport. They remained where they were inside the curfew boundary for three months. Limited passenger-vehicle traffic only was allowed on the main Bulawayo–Beitbridge and Bulawayo–Plumtree roads, and every vehicle on the main arteries into Zimbabwe was subjected to repeated searches at police and army roadblocks.

In a change of tactic for Matabeleland South, the Fifth Brigade gathered large numbers of the rural people into camps, where they could rape, torture, maim, politicize and kill as they pleased.

At the end of the Zimbabwe liberation war, the forces of Mugabe (ZANLA) and Nkomo (ZIPRA) were housed in hastily erected brick-under-asbestos barracks throughout the country, in what were to become known as assembly points. Some of these structures remained more or less intact in Matabeleland South.

Balagwe at Antelope Mine near Kezi was one such large establishment where the Fifth Brigade did their thing. Four years after its use as an assembly point, and completely in disrepair, Balagwe was totally run down with very little infrastructure still functioning, other than a few ramshackle buildings here and there. No sanitary facilities, no bedding, no medical aid—nothing.

Food, which comprised one meal a day (sometimes not even one meal a day), of maize porridge cooked in 200-litre drums over open fires by the detainees was all that was provided. The people in these camps died like flies. Men and women were detained together, with the latter being a source of enjoyment for the troops. The reason given by the Fifth Brigade for raping the Ndebele girls was to create a generation of youngsters whose blood would then be Shona.

These former assembly points were now used as holding centres for people, supposedly, who had been aiding and abetting the dissidents throughout Matabeleland South. This had not happened in the north. The idea was to give the impression to the foreign media, who were forever sniffing at the edges, that some sort of programme of supervised and civilized interrogation was going on, and that it would lead the regular ZNA forces to dissident camps and routes.

In fact, the holding camps were no more than torture centres, not dissimilar to the Nazi extermination camps of World War II. There have been reports by the Catholic Commission for Justice and Peace (CCJP) of sophisticated methods of interrogation and torture being used, such as using rubber tubing bound around the victim's genitals and so on.

The Fifth Brigade did not waste time and energy with sophisticated methods of interrogation and the death of the victim was not an issue. Victims were simply thrashed with sticks or leather whips used for rounding up cattle, or the detainees were forced to beat each other, sometimes to death. Ironically, not once was intelligence obtained from detainees that led the security forces to dissidents and resulting in their death or capture.

Schools were closed during both curfews. Teachers were detained and killed to disrupt education of the Ndebele child. Hospitals, clinics and mission schools were also closed. To alleviate boredom, and not as a system of re-education, or re-orientation of the Ndebele, many all-night *pungwes* were held at which the soldiers gorged themselves on butchered cattle, goats and chickens taken from the locals, and on beer looted from rural bottle stores or which had been locally brewed. At a time when the rural people were struggling through their third successive drought, and were already on their last legs, coupled with the food embargo imposed as part of the curfew, this pillage of their remaining livestock was immeasurably cruel and insensitive.

At these *pungwes,* the Ndebele had to sing as loud as they could all night long—Shona liberation songs and scream and shout derogatory messages about Joshua Nkomo.

This curfew in Matabeleland South was maintained for about three months, and just like the one in the north, achieved absolutely nothing as far as combating the dissident menace was concerned.

Despite the savagery, grief and fear that the people of Matabeleland had been subjected to, they refused to be re-orientated and in the subsequent 1985 general election not a single seat in Matabeleland was won by Mugabe's candidates. Hearts and minds? Re-orientation? In the run-up to these elections, the ZANU (PF) youth brigades had been terrorizing the locals and forcing them to purchase ZANU (PF) membership cards. Being found without a ZANU (PF) card was inviting a good hiding, or even worse. The police watching these events made no attempt to intervene and the youth did as they wished.

Scores of ZAPU councillors and officials, as many as 350, were abducted, as a prelude to the elections, and some of them have never been seen since.

On the eve of the election, Mugabe, while addressing an election meeting in Bulawayo, made himself very clear with a thinly veiled threat, "Where will we be tomorrow? Is it peace or war tomorrow? Let the people of Matabeleland answer this question." The genocide, abductions and intimidation again did not work. The Matabeleland people still voted overwhelmingly for ZAPU.

Mugabe then appointed a new home affairs minister, Enos Nkala, who was well known for his hatred of ZAPU and Joshua Nkomo. This was just after Nkala had been trounced in the election. Within a few days of his appointment, the police had arrested numerous ZAPU officials, councillors and five newly elected members of parliament. Nkala made himself clear: "My instincts tell me that when you deal with ruthless people you have to be ruthless. I have locked up a few members of parliament and I think that they will have to rest for a long time before they reappear to continue with their dissident activities." Nkala made it very clear to the ZR Police that they worked for a ZANU (PF) government, and accordingly would have to be loyal to ZANU (PF) (and not apolitical, as was the case with the Rhodesian BSAP and most police forces worldwide).

Nkala continued with his clampdown on ZAPU, ignoring all local and international protests. He banned all ZAPU rallies and closed their offices. "ZANU (PF) rules Zimbabwe, and if you dispute that then you are a dissident," Nkala said, which dispelled any pretence by the government that the aim had been to crush the dissidents; rather it was ZANU (PF)'s intention to destroy all opposition in Zimbabwe.

It will be nigh impossible to accurately determine the number of Ndebele killed in the two curfews. Many died in the bush, unseen and left as carrion, many fled to Botswana and South Africa or to the western areas of Bulawayo where they could melt into the high-density suburbs. CIO estimates are that close to 10,000 people were killed in the North curfew and 8,000 in the South. Not one prosecution for any crime committed by any member of the security forces was effected; in fact Mugabe, after the Unity Accord was signed between himself and Joshua Nkomo, granted an amnesty to all security forces, dissidents and Super ZAPU for the full period of the dissident era. And that was that—more or less.

For many years, human rights organizations were barred from investigating the atrocities of that era, and people were not allowed to exhume mass graves, which still abound both in the north and the south or to try to reclaim victims from mineshafts.

The CCJP document, *Breaking the Silence*, which is a very dedicated and comprehensive document on Fifth Brigade atrocities in the two areas which fell under the curfews, created quite a fuss when it was published in 1998, but it must be read with an objective mind simply because it is only one side of the story. Hopefully one day a more comprehensive story will emerge, but certainly not while ZANU (PF) is in power in Zimbabwe.

ﻉﻉﻉ

From late in 1984, in the run-up to the 1985 general election, the government deployed ZANU (PF) Youth Brigades into Matabeleland. They were nearly as bad as the Fifth Brigade, and would have been, had they been allowed to carry firearms. Their task was widespread intimidation of the rural people so that they would "vote correctly".

And these brain-washed youths, who today of course, form part of Zimbabwe's current adult population, went about their task vigorously and maliciously, with mass beatings, school closures, rapes, village burnings, and murder. (None have ever had to face justice for any of this.)

They were modelled on the Chinese Red Guard and were supposed to work on 'National Development' which clearly means different things to different people. To them, it meant forcing people to buy ZANU (PF) cards and attend ZANU (PF) rallies, and woe betide anyone who had a ZAPU card or who wanted to listen to a ZAPU candidate speak.

It didn't work then, and doesn't work now, with the Matabele people continually voting for anyone but ZANU (PF) including Jonathan Moyo, who used to be one of Mugabe's most passionate enemies before becoming his fast-rising star and beloved minister of information. Interestingly, he is now a ZANU (PF) discard as an independent member of parliament in Tsholotjo, where he is a firm opponent of the government's insane policies, and a vocal supporter of redress for the Matabeleland people who suffered so during *Gukuruhundi*.

᪣᪣᪣

Throughout the dissident era Joshua Nkomo went through the motions of trying to distance himself from the bandits. At every opportunity he profusely wept and complained that he had no control over them. "Whoever you are, stop it and stop it now" was just one such piece of showmanship by Joshua Nkomo (*Bulawayo Chronicle,* 29th April 1982 and 26th June 1982).

In 1987, as part of the Unity Accord, and after only a few rallies where he called on the dissidents to, "lie down their arms", magically, they listened and around 120 gave themselves up!

Their total number in the bush including hangers-on at the time of the Unity Accord was probably closer to 200, but many just mingled back into society in the crowded high-density suburbs of western Bulawayo and elsewhere in Matabeleland—not trusting the ZANU (PF) government. Some of the South African-sponsored Super ZAPU dissidents who were still there, made their way back to their training base near Messina in South Africa.

The Unity Accord, celebrated with a public holiday each year on 22nd December, was signed in 1987. It was a sleight of hand on Mugabe's behalf and one of his wisest political hoodwink tricks of his career. With one signature he brought the dissident era to an end (a war in western Zimbabwe that he could not win militarily, and which he had to end, at whatever cost). The war was draining the country's military budget, and critically damaging the tourist trade—Hwange (Wankie) Game Reserve, which used to be one of the worlds greatest animal preservation areas, falls within Matabeleland, as does Victoria Falls.

It was Mugabe's unity plan to incorporate Joshua Nkomo into the government, along with a couple of his followers in ministerial positions, as a means to end the conflict, and thereafter allow the ZAPU elite to enrich themselves on his gravy train, which they immediately did, so that any future thoughts of insurrection would fade away and be obliterated by the luxury of plush leather seats in their latest Mercedes.

And to this day, if people like Dumiso Dabengwa and his cohorts think Mugabe has forgiven their original treachery, they are dreaming. The Unity Accord was a means to an end, initiated in desperation by Mugabe when he failed to destroy ZAPU militarily and its people by genocide. Just as it is a dream for Mugabe to think the Ndebele people of Matabeleland will ever forget the genocide he dealt them.

Dabengwa had been released from indefinite detention as part of the unity negotiation process that culminated in the Unity Accord at the end of the dissident troubles. At the same time, most of Joshua Nkomo's vehicles that were held in Stops police camp in Bulawayo were returned to Nkomo, together with many properties and farms that had been seized after the original arms caches had been found on ZAPU land.

I kept the keys to Nkomo's fleet in my desk drawer in CABS Building, along with the keys for a CIO office on the same floor as mine where the ZIPRA archive was stored after being found in a barn at Nest Egg Farm in Bulawayo.

The archive, consisting of about twenty four-drawer steel cabinets full of individual files, was a treasure trove for us during the dissident era. The files in the archive held detailed information on most of Nkomo's ZIPRA guerrillas and we used them extensively to keep an eye on the homes of dissidents who originated from ZIPRA and whom we had identified through captures and other sources. Numerous were the occasions when just watching a dissident's home, instead of chasing him through the bush, produced results. Just like any human being, even the ZIPRA dissidents longed to feel the warmth of a home fire and meet their families once in a while, and that was the downfall of many of them.

As for Nkomo's vehicles, which just sat gathering dust, I used to enjoy the odd respite from a hot day's interrogation at Stops Camp detention cells, by firing up his luxury, armour-plated Mercedes parked just outside the fence surrounding the facility, and sit for a while in air-conditioned, leather-seated comfort! The Mercedes had been a gift from an influential Indian businessman in Bulawayo who ran a chain of cash-and-carry and bottle stores, night clubs and the like in Bulawayo. The Indian also 'donated' vehicles to luminaries in ZANU (PF)—no doubt just to hedge his bets.

Dumiso Dabengwa had languished in Chikurubi for four years, even after a trial court had found insufficient evidence against him regarding the caching of huge amounts of war matériel near the former ZAPU assembly points in Matabeleland soon after the ceasefire and general election of 1980.

Dabengwa as ZAPU military intelligence chief, Lookout Masuku as their army commander and Joshua Nkomo as the party leader, have sworn under oath, and have denied ever giving the orders for the ZIPRA guerrillas to cache the majority of the war matériel they held in their assembly points, and only hand in old weaponry at the ceasefire.

But the CIO, Mugabe, and his former security ministers and commanders know that these orders for the arms caches, did in fact come from these three men who, if all else failed, wanted to create the federal state of Matabeleland—a coup by any other name. They knew they could not overthrow the government in Harare, as their support base was limited to western Zimbabwe, but they did have plans for a federal Matabeleland, and for that they went on trial and were detained.

The reader should understand that as a security organization, the CIO had thoroughly infiltrated Joshua Nkomo's political movement, ZAPU. We listened to his telephones, opened his mail, and monitored his movements, and that of Dabengwa and Masuku, even while they were senior members of government and the military.

We had numerous sources of our own that we dispatched to these men with 'stories' from ZIPRA guerrillas in the assembly points, giving them briefings on the progress with the huge arms caches.

And in latter years our emissaries were sent to Nkomo with briefings on the dissident activity in Matabeleland. Nkomo would often tell the 'boys' to carry on with their mission (to destablilze Zimbabwe to the extent that the people would out-vote, or even revolt and overthrow Mugabe).

The broad picture gained by the intelligence world in Zimbabwe from these initiatives, our infiltration of Nkomo's ZAPU movement, in both Zambia and Botswana, from hundreds of interrogations of ZIPRA dissidents and National Army deserters, and from our own spies in the assembly points, indicated that arms caches were planted on instructions from the ZAPU high command and further, that Nkomo was continually in touch with dissidents in Matabeland. They can and still do, deny it, but it's a fact. Pure and simple. It's a fact and was established by months of interrogations of former group leaders from the ZIPRA army who received and carried out the instructions to cache the weaponry while they were in the assembly points.

There have been stories over the years that the CIO planted the arms caches—these are totally without foundation. They were ZAPU arms caches. It would have been impossible for anyone to covertly plant the huge caches—some of them less than a hundred metres from an assembly point which was holding around 3,000 armed and very tense ZIPRA combatants. And this is what the stories say—that the caches were the work of the CIO to justify the clampdown on ZAPU of the early 1980s.

Duplicity all round.

Dabengwa was awarded the Home Affairs ministry by Mugabe as part of the Unity Accord—a position where he was the head of the police force—the same force that I served in and was in charge of a plain clothes unit in Bulawayo. It was while I was there that I discovered one of the enormous ZIPRA caches of weapons, at Filabusi, some 100 kilometres east of Bulawayo—a cache that was constructed on orders from the abovenamed ZAPU members to the ZIPRA occupants of the assembly point at Silalabuchwa.

Even though I was a policeman simply doing my duty, when I found this cache of weapons, Dabengwa took it as a personal assault upon himself, and has hated me with a passion ever since. With our positions reversed, that is, me on death row in jail, and him as the home affairs minister, he must have relished every opportunity that came his way to try make my life a little more of a misery. Even though he could make no real decision that really counted, like my release, or even a prison transfer to another facility in Harare, he would go through the motions and make a fuss about how much of a threat I was to the state (rich coming from one who had been planning a coup just a few short years earlier).

Dabengwa never forgot the travails he and ZIPRA were subjected to—which he blamed on me—and I have it on reliable authority that as far as he was concerned, "Woods can rot in prison".

What would he have expected his police force to do, while he served as minister in the unity government? Ignore the cache of military hardware? There again, these days in Zimbabwe a policeman is totally ZANU (PF)- i.e. Mugabe-orientated, and is not allowed to act upon his own judgement and do his duty, especially when the merest hint of politics comes into whatever case he may be working on.

Dabengwa had been held in the FA section of Chikurubi where, among other luxuries such as a bed to sleep on, sheets, pillows and blankets, he also had a fridge. I can show you to this day the rust marks imprinted on the concrete floor in FA where his fridge once stood. And yet ...

While I was in Chikurubi and fighting for food, clothing and medical treatment, Dabengwa labelled me in the press as having a, "superior-being attitude" and said that he would not entertain any petitions from people with an attitude such as mine. I would look at the stain from his fridge on my cell floor and think "that's fucking rich" coming from him, who squeaked and squawked every day of his internment, demanding things like fridges!

Dabengwa is thoroughly ensconced on President Mugabe's gravy train, and now, well into the year 2007, he is one of Zimbabwe's ruling elite, even though he has been dumped as cabinet minister simply because he holds no support from the people of his own tribe in Bulawayo. He remains a vociferous ZANU (PF) supporter and appparantly holds no sympathy for the thousands of his own people murdered by Fifth Brigade, preferring to ride the gravy train than to search his soul for his morals and to stand up for the persecuted people of his own nation.

This is not my own opinion either. It is the opinion of the Ndebele people, which has just been reinforced by Dabengwa's stance against an independent member of parliament. Jonathan Moyo is MP for Tsholotjo and is trying to pass a *Gukuruhundi* bill in the Zimbabwe parliament which will hopefully commission an inquiry and make recommendations for some sort of recompense for those who are the victims of *Gukuruhundi*. A noble enterprise, by any measure of thought, you would think?

Not so for Dabengwa who was in Zimbabwe's courts over a civil matter with Moyo in mid-May 2007 and refers to Jonathan Moyo's tenure as a former ZANU (PF) cabinet minister: "I was indeed surprised that he [Moyo] could spoil the opportunities that had been made available to him by the party, by doing something that went against party procedure." So, there you have it—opportunities and perks from the party are the driving force, and not right and wrong.

Mugabe vehemently denies the genocide. The furthest he has gone is to call it "a time of madness". According to his doctrine mass graves do not exist. "When you have operations you have untoward incidents," Mugabe says, "but not mass graves. Nothing like that exists in Matableland. Even to this day I don't believe it was Fifth Brigade who stands accused—if anything did in fact happen."

Yet he will not allow a full investigation and exhumation to take place. So what is he hiding? Will his successor? I doubt it, and until all who were in command and control of those insane people on the ground are dead and buried, probably all at Heroes Acre, there will never be full closure.

The impact of *Gukuruhundi* will never be erased. Tribal leaders in Matabeleland have have said that while the liberation war was acutely painful, there was a purpose to it. But the genocide is all the more difficult to understand and live with because it has never been acknowledged by the government. Mugabe rejects appeals for a commission of inquiry with comments like: "If we dig up history, then we wreck the nation, and we tear our people apart, into factions, into tribes." (*Robert Mugabe* by Martin Meredith.)

The blame for the genocide in Matabeleland lies entirely with Mugabe and his security chiefs. Mugabe was determined to create a one-party state in Zimbabwe and he provoked the civil war against ZAPU as a means to that end. Fifth Brigade was the instrument he used, and when they had completed the mission—albeit unsuccessfully as ZAPU has prevailed—the brigade was disbanded and the members absorbed into other Zimbabwean army brigades, many with new identities.

The administration files, deployment and records of service for each Fifth Brigade soldier and their commanders have long since been shredded at army headquarters in Harare, making a comprehensive commission of inquiry almost impossible, especially if any of the Fifth Brigade perpetrators are to be answerable to the commission.

Some people will wonder, and probably form all sorts of conclusions from my attempt to absolve the CIO from their perceived role as a major participant in the atrocities committed in Matabeleland. I know there were many occasions where the CIO involvement was way overboard, but I am simply telling the truth when I say they were certainly not the bloodthirsty bunch of murderous thugs that they have been portrayed to be.

As a result of overseas pressure, in September 1983, President Mugabe set up a commission of inquiry into the Fifth Brigade atrocities committed during the curfew in Matabeleland North, earlier that year. The commission was chaired by Bulawayo lawyer, Simplicius Chihambakwe. On the commission with him were a retired Rhodesian Army general Mike Shute and John Ngara, from the President's secretariat. Due to my responsibility for CIO intelligence in Matabeleland, I was tasked to carry out a listening watch, monitor and report on the activities of that went on at the commission.

CIO technical staff from Harare bugged the office where the hearings were to take place. These listening devices were placed within the light fittings and ran off the same power as the lights themselves. The radio signal from the devices was transmitted directly to running tape recorders in the CIO building about a kilometre away, in CABS building. I had a member of the photographic section in Bulawayo situated in a vacant office opposite Fife Street where everyone entering and leaving the hearings could be photographed. I had staff on the street outside the building, mingling with the public and, just to make sure, I had a voice-activated miniature tape recorder in my briefcase, in case something went wrong with the lights.

Quite a number of people pitched up to give evidence to the commission which was a surprise as Fifth Brigade were still operating in the province—it was thought that their mere presence in the rural areas, plus a few extra drive-bys of army vehicles full of their red-bereted soldiers right outside the commission, would have deterred even the strongest-hearted. The Catholic Commission for Justice and Peace gave the most extensive evidence and produced some twenty witnesses who gave harrowing testimony of the Fifth Brigade atrocities.

I can clearly recall Mike Auret, the CCJP director in Zimbabwe, arriving with a human skull. The owner of the skull, he said, had been shot at a roadblock just outside Bulawayo during the curfew by the Fifth Brigade. The skull showed a clear bullet hole. After much debate, the CID homicide section was summoned from Central police station and they took away the skull for further investigation. They were supposed to report back to the commission, but it obviously never happened.

The commission visited a few business centres in Matabeleland North and at each one I had my staff fully deployed. I couldn't just tag along without compromising my identity. Nonetheless I received full reports on the commission's hearings from Lupane, Gokwe and Nkayi.

I eventually put together a full dossier of reports on the testimony, photographs of those attending and transcribed statements from those who had given evidence. This report is probably the most detailed in existence, even more so than the one delivered to the president by Chihambakwe as I had a lot more background information as to what was really happening that the commission was unaware of. The commission finished its hearings and handed its final report to President Mugabe around July of 1984—a month or two after my report had been read by the President's Office.

In 1985, the security minister, Emmerson Mnangagwa, announced that the Chihambakwe report would never be made public.

Abduction of six foreign tourists on the Victoria Falls Road, July 1982

"You may get up before dawn, but destiny gets up before you"
Kirundi of Burundi

The Bulawayo to Victoria Falls road is a lonely stretch of tarmac, with endless, desolate kilometres of *mukwa* and *mopane* trees and wicker-dry *acacia* thorn scrub, stretching away into the distance in every direction. At most times of the year, except when it rains, which is not often, the road appears to shimmer off into the distance in a heat haze as if it's dancing on water.

It was on this isolated and seemingly endless double-lane stretch of tarmac and near the 73-kilometre peg, at the height of the dissident era, that on a mid-July afternoon in 1982, six foreign tourists were abducted by a group of Joshua Nkomo's ZIPRA-affiliated dissidents.

Theories abound about this tragic episode in Zimbabwe's history. There are stories about this abduction, which over the years have gained momentum through their repetition in pubs, in the foreign media, and wherever else 'war stories' are told.

One such version was publicized in Zimbabwe's *Moto* magazine in October 1996. According to the article, the tourists were abducted by ex-Selous Scouts who had been detailed to perform the task by a South African covert operation group. This version is as devoid of truth as most of the others. I was in charge of CIO operational intelligence for Western Zimbabwe and I know exactly what happened.

The six males comprised two British, James Greenwell and Martin Hodgson; two Australians, Tony Bajzelj and William Butler; and two Americans, Kevin Ellis and Brett Baldwin. They were part of an overland holiday tour, and were abducted from a five-ton safari vehicle by a group of dissidents who had laid a few bushes on the road as a makeshift roadblock.

Incredulously, the tourists stopped their five-tonner at the flimsy pile of leafy twigs which had been hastily thrown across the road as an improvised roadblock, when even light motor vehicles had driven right over them just before their arrival.

The dissidents, numbering eleven and led by Gilbert Sitchela Ngwenya, immediately fired an RPG-2 rocket which hit the stationary five-ton vehicle's door, failed to detonate and clattered fizzing and hissing on to the tarmac near the driver's door. Amazingly the driver still remained frozen, like a deer in the headlights, as he watched the armed men rushing toward his vehicle.

After a few moments of stunned silence, six occupants were bustled out of the rear and pushed off the road, and into the thick bush.

They then handed over a handwritten letter to the driver still sitting behind the wheel next to a female co-traveller, to be delivered to the Bulawayo Central charge office. The letter demanded the release of ZIPRA supremo Dumiso Dabengwa, a former ZIPRA intelligence commander and after independence a general in the new ZNA (later to become Mugabe's minister of home affairs in the 1987 Unity Government), and Lookout Masuku, the ZIPRA commander, and also a former general. (That's one thing Zimbabwe is not short of—generals!) At that time both were detained in Chikurubi for planning to overthrow Mugabe's government and for the possession of tons of military hardware that they had ordered cached outside the ceasefire assembly points a few years earlier.

Dissident groups in Matabeleland via the bush telegraph, knew of this abduction and over the years ransom notes for their release were frequently left at crime scenes where they had murdered farmers or executed civilians. Some of these notes found their way to the international press, but many came to nothing.

All captured dissidents were specifically interrogated for information regarding the tourists and it was not until 1985 that one of the kidnap gang was captured and the truth emerged.

A year earlier in 1984, the group's leader, Sitchela, was captured in a fluke incident where he had decided to take a few days' leave from banditry and visit a girlfriend in Bulawayo. After leaving his group with instructions, and setting up a suitable rendezvous for a few weeks' hence, he cached his AK, changed into his brothel-creepers and smart clothes and was on his way to the nearest road to catch the bus to 'bright lights', when, unarmed, he made the mistake of helping himself to a few maize cobs from a villager's field for his trip's packed lunch.

Normally any dissident took what he wanted from a village, anything from a chicken for supper to the young girls to keep the chilly weather at bay, and the local villagers could do nothing. Sitchela had been doing this for years; he just forgot that he was now unarmed, and with his glad rags on didn't look the part at all.

A group of old men and women armed with traditional walking sticks and the odd knobkerrie confronted the thief after catching him *in flagrant delicti* with the maize cobs in his hands and demanded recompense. Sitchela, being an area commander and as a self-respecting freedom fighter, declined to shell out for his loot.

Despite his protestations that he was a real bandit, with a gun and all, the villagers gave him a thorough thrashing and carried out a citizen's arrest. Thereafter they delivered a dishevelled and hugely humiliated Sitchela to the Lupane police station for theft of the mealie cob. They also dropped the bombshell at the police station that the thief claimed he was a guerrilla, armed to the teeth.

CIO was summoned and it didn't take long to establish that he was in fact Sitchela. We had quite a lot of information on the abduction gang by that time but when it came to details regarding the whereabouts of the tourists, Sitchela was an exceptionally hard nut to crack. It was a while after his capture that he started talking of the ransom note, and started demanding the release of Dabengwa and Masuku, the two ZIPRA generals who were languishing in Chikurubi on treason charges while offering the tourists release, knowing full well that he had their blood on his hands. No matter how much pressure we used in these interrogations, Sitchela would insist the tourists were alive.

Instructions for the abduction and ransom of these tourists had come from the ZAPU hierarchy with specific sanction by Joshua Nkomo. Remember that all through the dissident era Nkomo denied any affiliation with the dissidents and always vehemently rejected having any authority over them. Nkomo had addressed many rallies throughout the dissident era and always went through the motions calling for them to hand in their weapons and cease the violence, yet not one dissident obeyed this call. However, during the 1987 Unity Accord and after one Kezi rally, the dissidents heeded his call and gave themselves up. Surely this surrender by the dissidents was a clear and definite indication that he had authority over them all along?

This finding, that Nkomo had been in touch with the dissidents, just as was the finding that he, Dumiso Dabengwa and Lookout Masuku gave instructions for the arms caches at ceasefire, was not just the result of one capture. Rather, it was the result of years of intelligence-gathering, monitoring, infiltration of his closest allies and surveillance of Nkomo and his senior officials. No intelligence organization, and in this case the CIO specifically, is so naïve as to make profound judgements like this based on only a few sources of information. We would work on the culmination of years of different avenues of investigation, and intelligence-gathering from phone taps, mail surveillance, and infiltration of moles and so on.

However, Joshua Nkomo had no ties to the 'Super ZAPU' element of destabilization in southern Zimbabwe. That was entirely South Africa's baby.

His home phone was tapped and monitored by CIO twenty-four hours a day as were his lawyer's office and residential phones. CIO had irrefutable proof of Joshua Nkomo's involvement with the dissidents from many slips of the tongue by him and those who phoned, and from various other sources such as captured dissidents.

His mail was also continually opened, photocopied, resealed and delivered to him via normal post-office delivery. Whenever he had an opportunity in front of the international media, Joshua Nkomo went out of his way to condemn the dissidents and specifically so in this instance of the tourist abduction (*Bulawayo Chronicle*, 30.8.82). And in his book, *The Story of my Life*, Nkomo says, "I absolutely guarantee that neither I nor ZAPU had anything to do with that kidnapping. The diplomats of those very important countries came to my house to ask for my help in obtaining their release. I asked why they came to see me: Zimbabwe was run by Robert Mugabe. They said he had approved their visit. But I told them they were being used to divide my country, by treating me as though I ran my own little republic within it."

In this incident, Nkomo and company had originally issued instructions for a minibus-load of Rhodes Estate Preparatory School schoolboys, whom they knew were on the road that same fateful day, to be abducted and used for ransom. REPS was at that time a private school for Matableland elite's children—the obvious thought being that rich folk would have a lot more pull with Mugabe's regime than mere poor folk.

Back at the abduction scene, the dissidents subsequently made off into the bush with the tourists in tow, their hands tied behind their backs.

Meanwhile the ransom letter given to the survivors in the overland lorry had been delivered to Bulawayo Central Charge Office. Later on, the Joint Operational Command at Brady Barracks was notified and a huge follow-up deployment of troops was soon en route, helicopters et al, to the 73-kilometre peg.

The trackers used on the follow-up, most of whom were former Rhodesian-era army, were quick on the spoor, which was quite easy to follow even after sunset. For the six terrified abductees, making time over rough terrain in the fading light with their hands bound behind their backs, the going was tough and they were leaving a huge trail. Soon after last light, the dissidents realized they had the wrong fish in the net—instead of six schoolboys they had six grown men, foreigners to boot. Seriously troubled that the follow-up was close on their heels, they decided to murder the six hostages and make good their escape without any further undue hindrance.

They chose a sandy area just north of the Bembezi River, in the Nkosikasi communal land and cruelly, using strips of bark as makeshift rope, just as they bound their wrists, strangled their captives to death. They feared shooting their captives because the follow-up was so close on their heels that any shots would have given their position away. This was callous and brutal thinking; the six tourists were obviously bewildered, totally disorientated, terrified, and in near total darkness, and would never have been able to make any identification of their captors, or even what area they were in, and therefore could just as easily have been abandoned alive in the deserted African bush.

The dissidents hastily buried their victims in antbear holes and in shallow graves dug in the sandy soil of the Nkosikasi communal land. They then opened a nearby cattle kraal and quickly forced the cattle over the burial site where the beasts milled around in confusion and obliterated any signs of their gruesome deed. It must have taken all of fifteen minutes for them to murder the tourists, hastily rake over the loose soil and get the cattle to cover their tracks. Then they were off into the darkness, leaving their ghastly secrets behind which remained hidden until 1985, some three years later.

The follow-up troops who reached the kraal at first light the following morning were so furious at the obliteration of the spoor, that they shot the cattle and torched the huts. They did not go too easy on the kraal head either who, as the owner of the cattle, was suspected of being complicit in the disappearance of the tourists. Over the subsequent three years, very little intelligence was gained about the tourists and this was essentially because they were murdered so soon after their abduction—the only people who knew the truth and its grisly end were the eleven dissidents who were originally involved.

In March 1985, CIO eventually captured a member of Sitchela's group, a dissident named Pagiwa Sibanda. Under interrogation, he gave out that he was part of the group that had kidnapped the tourists. He admitted that the tourists had been killed on the same night that they had been kidnapped and said that he could identify the area where they'd been hastily buried.

As the CIO officer in charge of this investigation, it was up to me to take it to its conclusion and so a day later, with a government pathologist and supporting staff, plus the normal police CID and other hangers-on, I went with Pagiwa Sibanda to the Nkosikazi where the skeletal remains of five of the tourists were recovered. Two of the tourists had been buried in antbear holes which had been easily sealed over and three bodies were found together in a shallow grave. The enigma was the whereabouts of the sixth body.

Having indicated the graves of the five, Pagiwa obviously had nothing to gain, or lose, by concealing the whereabouts of the last body.

A haphazard dig in the general area revealed nothing. Pagiwa then volunteered the fact that on the night of the abduction and murder, Sitchela had walked off a short way from where they stood in the gloomy thick bush with one of the tourists, and had returned alone a few minutes later. No sounds of a violent struggle had been heard by the group and they assumed Sitchela had walked his captive off into the bush, for whatever reason, where he had killed him in some sort of silent manner and shoved the body down an antbear hole (which are found all over rural Zimbabwe) and then kicked dirt over it.

Sitchela had been captured a year earlier and even under vigorous interrogation, he had stubbornly denied any knowledge of the tourists. Upon the discovery of the five, I again questioned him, but he stuck to his guns, denying everything but the abduction, still insisting he would produce the tourists if the two generals were released. I showed him the skeletons of the five dead tourists and he didn't budge. Maybe he thought that he would avoid the hangman's noose by withholding the whereabouts of the last body, or by completely denying involvement? I took him to the murder area and even the threat of pushing him out of an airborne helicopter failed to loosen his tongue. We returned to Bulawayo empty-handed.

More random exhumation was fruitless and a week or so later I escorted the British and Australian high commissioners and the American ambassador to the murder scene. I gave them a brief rundown of the kidnapping, the tourists' forced march through the evening into the dark night bush, and tragically to the scene where their citizens had been so cruelly murdered.

I was under very strict orders not to mention that I'd only recovered five, not six, bodies of the tourists. A major political scoop was made about this successful investigation and its resolution. The bones of the deceased were jumbled up by CIO Harare and placed into six coffins. The excuse about the missing sixth skull was explained away as the bones having been disturbed by wild animals in the area.

The remains were handed to their respective families with the security ministers patting themselves on the back as can only happen when a government tries to blow its own trumpet and gain political mileage out of every possible situation.

President Mugabe was quick to announce that the tourists had been found, and at a press conference on 8th March 1985 he revealed that pathologists had identified the bodies of Kevin Ellis, James Greenwell and William Butler.

A comprehensive search of the murder site would probably recover the last of these poor souls, so brutally murdered, and expose the lies by Mugabe's regime about the 'successful' investigation.

જ્જજ્

During the three-year investigation many people were questioned and some were interrogated regarding the whereabouts of the tourists. One such local from Matabeleland was unfortunate to have the name Siwela (we had initial intelligence that one member of the abduction group carried that name). Siwela was detained at the Esigodini fort where he continually denied any involvement.

CIO HQ and Mugabe's office wanted results on the six tourists. Accordingly, all the brutality that HQ could muster was meted out on Siwela, who couldn't divulge anything … simply because he had nothing to tell.

As was often the situation when a high-profile case was involved, the brass got involved to polish their marbles. Siwela suffered the consequences of this enthusiasm, with orders coming direct from CIO HQ to the Bulawayo CIO head, even to the extent of bypassing my desk even though I had been tasked with the investigation. The Matabeleland CIO commander and his second-in-command got physically involved with this interrogation and on the last occasion I saw Siwela, he was lying in one of the cells at Esigodini and had been reduced to a mass of suppurating sores, broken arms and legs, most of his skin had been flayed off, and his ears severed.

I was told a few days later to send a message to CIO HQ to the effect that Siwela had been shot while trying to escape. Government went the full distance and announced this event (*Bulawayo Chronicle*, 1984). Subsequently another dissident, Austin Mpofu, was also arrested in connection with this abduction and murder. He confirmed Sitchela had taken one of the abductees off into the night and returned alone a few minutes later.

For their part in the abduction and murder of the six tourists, Mpofu and Sitchela, together with three other murderers, were hanged in 1986 at Harare Central Prison.

South African-sponsored 'Super ZAPU' dissidents

"It is those who have not died in war that start it"
Kikuyu of Kenya

South African Military Intelligence initiated a programme in late 1983 which saw them infiltrating into Matabeleland South, over a period of about two years, a number of their own trained and equipped terrorists.

The operation fell under the South African destabilization programme in Zimbabwe and was code-named Operation *Drama*. It was funded by Military Intelligence. On the ground its administration, control, training and logistical operations were the responsibility of Colonel Mac, a former CIO officer from Zimbabwe, who was later gazetted by the Zimbabwean government and awarded the dubious distinction of being declared 'an enemy of the state', as was Gray Branfield, who was attached to another department of Military Intelligence in South Africa.

Colonel Mac was assisted by a number of subordinates who were at that time attached to Military Intelligence and who resided in Louis Trichardt where they gave the impression that they were freelance insurance brokers. This was wonderful cover which required no knowledge of the insurance field and was therefore an easy pretence to maintain as they needed no special facilities, staff, or even an office.

In reality, there were never more than about sixty Super ZAPU dissidents who were eventually trained at Entabeni camp, near Messina in South Africa, and subsequently operating in Matabeleland. This suggested that this operation, although highly funded by the South African government's Military Intelligence branch, was not considered a major factor in the destabilization of Zimbabwe. In contrast, the Renamo movement in Mozambique at its zenith had anything between 2,500 to 3,000 trained and equipped combatants deployed inside that country, or in training in the Eastern Transvaal (now Mpumalanga).

South Africa's policy of simultaneously destabilizing Zimbabwe by covert military means, while at the same time blaming ZAPU whenever possible for the activity of their own dissidents, went a long way in causing the irrevocable breakdown between Mugabe and Nkomo. This made it easy for Mugabe's government to retain a state of emergency throughout the 1980s during which all means of destroying Nkomo's ZAPU were employed, under the guise of anti-dissident operations.

The military and political violence in the 1980s caused unbelievable grief for the rural people of Matabeleland. And because the rural areas were so bludgeoned and stupefied, the few cities and towns in Matabeleland that relied on labour from the rural areas barely muddled along.

Enormous losses in property, economic development and human life in the affected areas can be largely attributed to the ZAPU dissidents, Super ZAPU, and to government forces like Fifth Brigade, all of whom committed deeds of horrifying cruelty against their fellow Zimbabweans. The Fifth Brigade, with their curfews in the rural areas and blockades of the high-density suburbs in Bulawayo where the economic labour force lived and without whom factories and businesses couldn't operate, most certainly contributed to the collapse of many businesses in Matabeleland.

The majority of the Super ZAPU terrorists were recruited by South Africa's Military Intelligence from Dukwe refugee camp in Botswana. Some other recruits came from among the normal flow of border-jumpers from Zimbabwe who, due to the economic collapse in that country which was evident even in the early years of independence in 1980, braved the crocodile-infested waters of the Limpopo day and night, desperate and in search of employment in South Africa. (The refugee influx from Zimbabwe continues to this day with an estimated three million illegal migrant workers from Zimbabwe, many being used as slave labour, living and looking for work in South Africa. Stories abound of how Zimbabweans work harder than their fellow South African labourers without complaint, for fear of being reported to immigration, and then being deported, and who are paid the barest minimum from which they send back a little cash to their starving families in Zimbabwe.)

Super ZAPU was very similar to the *Resistência Nacional Moçambicana*, (Renamo), a Mozambican terrorist group formed by the Rhodesian government in mid-1970s during the war there to operate against the Frelimo government of Samora Machel. This had the added effect of disrupting Mugabe's liberation-movement guerrillas who were operating from within Mozambique.

The administration and control of Renamo was handed over by the Rhodesians to the South African government at the time of Zimbabwe's independence. The formation of Super ZAPU was the brainchild of former Rhodesian security policemen who had originally created Renamo.

The whole concept of Super ZAPU was aimed at further destabilizing Zimbabwe as a whole, and also to cause great confusion between the different military forces on the ground in Matabeleland South. An unstable Zimbabwe would affect the ability of the ANC guerrillas in their operations across the Limpopo, was the thinking behind the idea. The more unstable Zimbabwe was the less effective the ANC guerrillas would be in spring-boarding their attacks from Zimbabwe, or so the South African Military Intelligence thought.

After establishing the existence of the South African gooks in Matabeleland, I devised a plan to infiltrate the Super ZAPU programme and destroy it from within, using my own captured and turned former dissidents from Matabeleland.

By 1984, I had established a number of confidential sources in Botswana's Dukwe refugee camp, which is situated about fifty kilometres northwest of Francistown, and also in Messina, a border town in northern South Africa where the Super ZAPU gooks were being trained.

I infiltrated into the Super ZAPU programme a number of turned former ZIPRA dissident guerrillas, who had been captured while involved in the Matabeleland dissident uprising. They were murderers, rapists and bandits and had decided, after being captured and interrogated, that working for the CIO was a better option than Mugabe's hangman's noose. Not much of a choice there really.

There was always the possibility that these turned gooks would desert once I had re-deployed them, and return to join their fellow dissidents in the Matabeleland bush, or just fade away into the townships of Bulawayo, but it was a risk worth taking when one considered the possibilities of their assistance proving fruitful. My turnees were only let off the hook for crimes committed in Zimbabwe and deployed once I was convinced, as far as possible, that they would not desert.

I had to have some sort of hold over them though. Threats of prosecution were not enough. As a bit of security to keep their hearts and minds focused I had extensive dossiers on all these turned dissidents, and they knew it would be no major exercise to locate them through their relatives and friends, should they fail to perform up to expectation or if they 'took the gap'. They were also on quite a good wicket with a regular income, new clothes and luxuries like transistor radios, bicycles and a certain amount of immunity from prosecution—while they remained under my umbrella.

Minor things like petty theft, bar fights, the odd theft of motor vehicles and so on that they committed while working for CIO, including unending violent domestic disputes, assaults and rapes of their own wives and girlfriends would be 'sorted out' and swept under the carpet with the Zimbabwe Republic Police. However, they also well knew that there were parametres they crossed at their own peril, and a few who decided they could rape, pillage and murder at liberty suffered the consequences of their ill-discipline with all bets being cancelled and them being handed over to the police for prosecution.

These deserters were few and far between—a thorough thrashing in front of their comrades would usually serve as a good enough deterrent. They knew that desertion and disobedience was extremely perilous … if one got caught.

Obviously if they were ever picked up doing stupid things in the Messina area after being deployed by me, and without divulging they worked for the CIO (which would have meant summary execution) they would be given a thorough hiding and returned to Entabeni, for more thrashing, re-education, training and re-deployment into Zimbabwe. So sometimes, for both the South Africans and me, with all this to-ing and fro-ing it became quite confusing just as to where our people were, who they actually worked for and what they were doing.

Esigodini police station (formerly Essexvale) about thirty kilometres south of Bulawayo was an old venue for 'turning terrorists'. A specially constructed high-walled fort had been built within the police camp's perimeter during the Rhodesian war for just this purpose and it proved ideal for use during the dissident era. Access to the fort was strictly controlled and limited only to CIO personnel. No one else, other than detainees entered the fort. CIO vehicle access to the fort was possible, so it was easy to clandestinely move people in and out in the back of a closed-in Land Rover as they would always be out of sight.

The niceties and civility of detention records, visits by relatives and so on, were dispensed with at the fort—much the same as the CIO fort at Goromonzi just outside Harare. (An excavation and examination of both courtyards at these forts would one day be quite interesting, I reckon.)

A few weeks in residence at the fort for any captured dissident or a potential recruit would usually be enough to ensure he was completely re-orientated.

As part of the ploy, I had many of my own recruits infiltrated into Dukwe where they would pose as refugees until recruited by Colonel Mac's people or I had them dropped over the Limpopo River near to Messina in South Africa under the guise of a Zimbabwean male looking for work. Almost every former dissident I deployed, either via Dukwe or the Limpopo River was snatched up by South African Military Intelligence and found himself press-ganged into the Super ZAPU training programme.

Recruitment of my own turnees by the South Africans frequently occurred in Dukwe where they, as new 'refugees,' had to initially go through the normal

Botswanan government refugee-programme administration. Thereafter they would be approached by South African Military Intelligence agents, who by one ruse or another had access to Dukwe, or who lived there under the guise of being refugees themselves, and were soon coerced or talked into joining the Super ZAPU.

The Botswanan route was a little slower than directly over the Limpopo River due to all the bureaucracy in the refugee camp. A number of these turnees of mine were subsequently deployed back into Matabeleland by the South African military after Super ZAPU training and equipping in Messina, and made contact with my office according to my pre-deployment instructions, or with my subordinates posted at remote police stations and business centres throughout Matabeleland.

Hence, it did not take too long to build up a full picture of Super ZAPU's operation, its bases, training, ideology, and so on. It is interesting to note that all of my own Super ZAPUs who reported back to me, were adamant that their instructions and training strictly forbade the murder of commercial farmers.

It is a fact though that some Super ZAPU terrorists were involved in many dreadful atrocities and murders of commercial farmers, but can mainly be attributed to rogue elements within their ranks doing their own thing.

The debriefings I conducted on the returned dissidents I had deployed through Botswana and the Limpopo were of great interest to CIO headquarters, and also to the South African military to which I also reported. There began quite a cat-and-mouse game, with direct deployments from Colonel Mac in Messina, across the Limpopo, or via Botswana on the one hand, and me infiltrating captures and recruits back via the same routes into the Super ZAPU's programme, with the intent of destroying it from within.

It didn't take long for my activity to create quite a stink with the Super ZAPU organizers who had quite a runaround with all their potential recruits, not knowing who had been contaminated by my office.

Even though I gave my turnees passports and other documents they rarely used them upon reaching South Africa or Botswana as they had to appear to be refugees or genuine border jumpers. Being in possession of legitimate travel documents was a dead ringer that something smelled wrong. They invariably changed their names upon reaching the South African and Botswanan camps, so that ruled out the South Africans simply looking for the names of those I supplied on their passports.

On occasions I specifically issued an alias to my recruits so the South Africans would fail to detect them, just to keep them on the hop, and also to ensure I would receive untainted intelligence when they returned. This double-handed stuff is quite common in the murky world that I lived in. We military intelligence people on both sides swapped information regularly, but it was always prudent to keep a card up your sleeve.

Super ZAPU dissidents, once trained and ready for deployment into Matabeleland, were issued with AK rifles, RPD machine guns, RPG launchers, landmines and ammunition manufactured in the former communist block, normally Bulgaria or Romania. The AK rifles, RPDs and RPG launchers they carried all had their serial numbers ground off and new numbers stamped on them by the South Africans. Their cartridge cases for their AK and RPD ammunition was date-stamped 22/1980, the year of manufacture in Romania.

In contrast to this, all former guerrillas who were remnants from the Rhodesian bush war and who were now dissidents, had ammunition manufactured in Russia, East Germany and Yugoslavia, which was date-stamped prior to 1980, and which they had recovered from arms caches they had hidden prior to Zimbabwe's independence.

Obviously it therefore didn't take much to detect which group—be it Super ZAPU with their new ammo, or the ZAPU dissidents with their old ammo—was doing what, simply by checking fired cartridge cases found at whichever atrocity or murder scene, or checking for serial numbers on the weapons they were carrying when the odd capture or kill of a dissident occurred.

On occasions Super ZAPU and the local bandits had gunfights and skirmishes with each other, which resulted in fatalities on both sides or weaponry being abandoned which caused a little confusion for my office and made the identification of groups by the date on their cartridges or serial numbers a little trickier.

In general, Super ZAPU had equipment that was in far better condition as it had come out of South African special armouries and not from liberation-war arms caches in the bush. I had my subordinates attend every single atrocity and murder in Matabeleland and the CIO built up a comprehensive database from recovered cartridge cases, clothing, photographs of fighters with their girlfriends and families, their diaries, and so on. (Guerrillas throughout history, no matter how well trained, love keeping a record of their heroics, and these always are seriously valued by the relevant intelligence-gathering organizations and security forces, whoever they are ... and they were extremely valuable to my office.)

Just why Colonel Mac would allow his Super ZAPU to deploy with diaries describing their recruitment and training in South Africa is amazing and a little ironic too, because as a Special Branch officer in Rhodesia during the war he knew well just how valuable these little histories were.

In late 1984, I was quite surprised when I started detecting from recovered cartridge cases, identical AK rifles and other weaponry being used in murders in both Matabeleland South and North. The dissident groups had always maintained strict areas of operation, dating back to the liberation war, which prevented accidental clashes between themselves. Having their own turf also helped them with their own security as unknown groups could not just enter someone else's area without being seriously suspect. This basic security also hampered infiltration of turnees and Super ZAPU gooks that were being deployed by Colonel Mac and me.

So, it was extremely uncommon to establish by ballistic comparison that the same weaponry was crossing dissident borders quite frequently. It did not take long to realize than an outsider was traversing Matabeleland and committing murder or other atrocities and probably by vehicle too, as the scenes I was picking this up from were far apart. And considering the fact that both parts of Matabeleland were tightly screwed down by the curfews it could only mean that the people doing this were above suspicion, as they were able to freely move about. Someone was acting like the dissidents, but had total freedom of movement …

It soon became patently clear that a pseudo group was operating in Matabeleland, especially when analysis of their targets revealed that not only Joshua Nkomo's people were the victims, but also some who were connected to the ruling party, who were perhaps becoming a thorn in someone's side.

I had been kept out of the loop on this one. I subsequently learned that the dissident problem was now being used to settle a few of Zimbabwe's personal and political problems.

Pseudo operations date back to the liberation war in Rhodesia and were an extremely successful method of infiltrating the terrorist movements with a view to annihilating them, and such pseudo operations could have certainly been successful in Matabeleland, were they kosher. It was a very disturbing revelation that pseudo ops were now being used to settle personal issues rather than to solve the dissident problem.

One such issue involved a land dispute between the government provincial governor, who wanted land for his cattle; the people who lived in the area who wanted to graze their cattle on the mission's land; and the New Adams Farm Mission itself, in Matabeleland South in November 1987.

The pseudo group involved in the subsequent appalling murder of the missionaries, their wives and children at the school, was led by a bandit named Gayigusu. He had been recruited, equipped, and was being deployed and moved around the province in CIO and Fifth Brigade vehicles to do the bidding of his political masters in exchange for immunity for his crimes as a dissident. He and his group were later included in the 1988 presidential amnesty which exonerated all dissidents and they never had to face justice (nor did their runners in the CIO Gwanda office), for their brutal, callous and cold-blooded crimes. Sixteen men, women and children were shot and axed to death in this murder at New Adams Farm. The mission murders was just one instance in which this group was involved. This was not an isolated atrocity and I know that the CIO have the full record of this group's activities.

During the Rhodesian war, numerous dirty tricks were used to eliminate the ZANLA and ZIPRA fighters who were operating throughout Rhodesia, but who were based in neighbouring Zambia and Mozambique.

These dirty tricks ranged from pseudo operations carried out by Rhodesian forces masquerading as ZANLA or ZIPRA fighters infiltrating the movements and thereafter calling in air strikes on bases or transit routes, to using transistor radios fitted with explosives or homing devices detectable by high-flying aircraft. Some of these radios were quite clever and would either detonate on the fifth occasion of being switched on or off by the gooks. The Rhodesian Air Force refined some lethal weapons such as Frantan, similar to the napalm used by the Americans in Vietnam, and alpha and golf bombs. In addition to these, the security forces also used poisoned clothing laced with a particularly lethal mercuric oxide.

The radios and 'doctored' clothing would be stocked at helpful 'tame' rural stores in the bush from where the gooks were known to help themselves to anything that took their fancy, without payment, in the name of the liberation struggle. On occasions they would walk off with a specially prepared radio, or some poisoned clothing, taken straight off the shop's shelves. These liberators would then have a party in the bush, or at a village, wearing their new clobber and would thereafter die a terrible death from the poison, or be blown to pieces when they switched on the booby-trapped radio, or set off a beeper that resulted in an airborne attack.

Robert Mugabe and his cronies are on record, ad nauseum, complaining of these heinous dirty tricks used by the Rhodesians, yet he himself, advised by his military and CIO commanders, authorized the use of poisoned clothes by CIO in the war against the dissidents during the 1980s.

The supply of 'treated' denim jackets and longs (denim always being a favorite of the bandits) was effected in both Matabeleland North and South operational areas. It was difficult to fully establish the efficacy of this programme. The clothing was sourced and spiked by CIO headquarters and the ZRP forensic science laboratory in Harare. Many captured dissidents in Matabeleland did reveal cases of their comrades dying of horrific and inexplicable diseases in the bush, or being carried over the border to medical facilities in Botswana or at the Super ZAPU training camps in Messina.

So it's rather hypocritical for Mugabe et al to pontificate and point that specific dirty-tricks finger at the Rhodesians only, while doing the same thing themselves against their own people post independence.

I attended nearly every commercial farmer murder in Matabeleland, and frequently mounted the security force follow-up to these murders—which due to the calibre of the ZNA forces, the majority of whom were liberation-war relics and very efficient at fleeing at the smallest hint of danger, were very seldom productive.

At every murder where weapons had been used I would collect a few cartridge cases for ballistic examination. Some of the cartridge cases were examined in Harare, and just to make sure I was not hoodwinked on this, for whatever reason, I covertly delivered cartridge cases to the South African military for ballistics. Thus I had an extensive record of which firearms were being used in Matabeleland and for what reason, as did the South Africans.

I had several shootouts with both the ZAPU dissidents and Super ZAPU groups. I can recall one specific shootout at Hove Store in the Kezi area. I had stopped to pick up a few beers before driving back to Bulawayo after inspecting the Balagwe Camp and its environs, and after a meeting at Antelope Mine with the local commanders.

As I opened the driver's door of my CIO vehicle, and while standing there in the gloom of the evening sun outside the front of the store, I removed and cocked the CZ 9mm pistol I usually carried with me just as a precaution because I was alone. Suddenly three dissidents bolted out the store front, firing at me while they ran off to one side, heading for the bush. While diving for cover and returning fire at the same time, I was fortunate to plug one of the gooks with one of the several rounds I cranked off with my pistol, as the other two galloped off into the fading sunset. The dissident I killed turned out to be a Super ZAPU graduate, complete with a folding-butt AK-47, with its serial number erased and a pile of 22/80 ammunition. I carried that AK, courtesy of the South Africans and Colonel Mac as a good-luck token for the rest of my CIO days. Many people, former friends and colleagues, with whom I fished on the Zambezi or went hunting with, or gave basic anti-terrorist training to, wondered why I always carried that specific brand-new AK with me. There you have it.

During 1984 and at the height of the South African Military Intelligence recruitment programme in Dukwe refugee camp, I learned of a CIO HQ operation that had been mounted, which involved a tamed gook named Cuba. He had been deployed from Zimbabwe into Botswana with vials of active cholera virus, which were to be placed in Dukwe's water supply. The subsequent cholera epidemic at Dukwe, so the thinking went at CIO headquarters, would stymie the Super ZAPU recruitment exercise and throw a spanner in the works for Colonel Mac and his associates. The programme was real enough, according to my headquarters' source, but whether it was ever carried out, I don't know. I suppose hygiene-related diseases are quite common in filthy, overcrowded camps and Dukwe would have been no exception, so a cholera outbreak would have been nothing out of the ordinary. However, this struck me as particularly warped thinking by evil and desperate minds.

Arms caches on
commercial farms

"The sun never sets without fresh news"
Zulu of South Africa

In early 1986, I obtained information which indicated that former, (and by then deceased) Rhodesian government (Conservative Alliance) member of parliament, Donald 'Strippy' Goddard (SG), had weapons of war cached on his Shangani farm, about 100 kilometres east of Bulawayo.

SG had served as one of the twenty Lancaster House-guaranteed seats in the Zimbabwean parliament that had been allocated to former Rhodesian Prime Minister Ian Smith's party. SG was also a former member of the Selous Scouts where he had served with distinction and was especially useful in night operations because of his 'farm boy'-acquired fluency of the Ndebele language.

I was told that SG had buried two caches of weapons on Journey's End Farm. As a former member of the Rhodesian security forces, he had access to a lot of excess guerrilla weaponry during the war there and I was led to believe that SG's brother, 'JR', had knowledge of the whereabouts of the caches.

I investigated this myself and after making enquiries as to JR's whereabouts, I discovered that he had gone into hiding when he'd heard that I wanted to talk to him. This surprised me as the information regarding these caches was certainly not confirmed. My ears pricked up at JR's obvious reluctance to be found.

Before I could really get my teeth into the task of locating him, which could have proved difficult as JR was a man of much wealth and had access to private aircraft, I was contacted by his Bulawayo lawyer who worked for one of Zimbabwe's prominent legal firms. He told me that he represented JR and knew of his whereabouts. I met with Neville the lawyer and left him with the ultimatum of doing this the easy way or the hard way. We could arrange a meeting at SG's old farm, recover the weaponry and I would give JR and the rest of his family who resided on commercial farms in the general area amnesty for possession of arms of war, or I could find JR 'the hard way' and there would be a noose, not amnesty, waiting for him at the end of it all.

Such was the authority and power that my position in the CIO held that I could make decisions like this. Bear in mind too, that this was the mid 1980s, Matabeleland's civil war was raging and there was a state of emergency in Zimbabwe, carried forward from the Rhodesian war, which gave us in the security forces even more authority.

I could very easily have had JR located and arrested. After interrogation I could have recovered the weaponry on his farm and then handed him to CID for prosecution, which in the political climate in Zimbabwe at the time, would have certainly led to a death sentence for him.

This arrest and detention, even without prosecution would have definitely resulted in mass detention under the emergency regulations of JR's extended family and friends, and the forfeiture to the state of all their farms, assets and properties.

Also, the fact that JR was a white farmer and related to the brother of one who obviously supported the Smith government during UDI period would have compounded the severity of the outlook on his case and been grist to the mill for Mugabe's political and propaganda mandarins. After reaching agreement with the lawyer to do this the easy way, one of the first things I did was check with my South African runners, just in case SG had had connections in the South African military, that this was not in fact one of their own clandestine arms caches. (Which I am led to believe are numerous in Zimbabwe to this day.) I was assured that SG was not caretaking any SA military ordnance, and was also assurred that he had no SA military intelligence connection at all, which gave me carte blanche to do as I wished with the case. Had it been a South African weapons cache I would have just killed the case there and then.

According to the agreement I reached with JR's lawyer, a day or two later I rendezvoused with JR and his lawyer at Shangani and proceeded to SG's farm. I was accompanied by a team of ZNA engineers, whom I had brought along in case their skills and equipment were required, such as mine detectors and explosives, to destroy any dodgy stuff we might find.

JR led me to a spot on SG's farm called Journey's End Cave where a twenty-litre drum of different hand grenades was unearthed. A number were in poor condition and these were destroyed on site by the ZNA engineers. We then went to a bushy area a few kilometres from the farmhouse where, after a little digging, we uplifted a 200-litre drum of assorted weaponry, such as AK rifles, RPKs, pistols, grenades, flares, ammunition and claymore mines.

This drum had been well sealed and had been buried some years before as the grass had grown over the top, completely obscuring the spot. The weaponry in the drum had been oiled when it was cached and all of it was in excellent condition, even after a few years in the ground. I stuck the whole lot into my vehicle, gave JR his promised amnesty there and then, and drove the stuff back to Bulawayo where it was added to the CIO armoury in our central offices for our own use.

❧ ❧ ❧

Strange things sometimes happen. Just as I was dealing with JR and his cache, I received information that another of SG's brothers also had weapons hidden on one of his vast farming estates. I decided to play this safe and dispatched a team from Kwekwe to pick him up. I ordered no violence be used, but I did want him in a disorientated and somewhat nervous state when he arrived in Bulawayo so that when I talked to him, I wouldn't need to interrogate him harshly at all.

My team specifically arrested SG's other brother, 'JG' in the dead of the night, as a shock tactic. They slapped some leg-irons on him and handcuffed him to a spare wheel lying in the rear of a pick-up vehicle and drove him to Bulawayo where he was detained in a filthy police cell. At no time, on my orders, did they advise JG of the reason for his arrest and detention. This is simple psychology to throw a person completely off-balance and make him realize that his fate is totally in the arresting officer's hands. JG would have been feeling extremely vulnerable by the time he was locked up.

The facility at Stops Camp where I had him detained was ideal for CIO use as there was no access to any area near the cells by the public and anyone locked up there would definitely feel very insecure. Stops Camp is a ZR Police residential area, with the normal motor workshops, administration offices, sports fields, etc., plus a heavily fenced and guarded inner sanctum, very much away from any prying eyes, and certainly out of earshot. It was ideal an environment to create serious nervous tension—for the detainee!

I had JG held incognito for a few hours, and he was certainly a soft interrogation when I eventually spoke to him. I gave him the same option as I had given his brother, easy or hard. He didn't need convincing and led me to a cache of nine AK rifles on one of their farms.

I returned him to the house of a relative in Bulawayo, placed the AKs in the CIO armoury and let him off the hook. Again, I could have used this cache by a white farmer on their own property to destroy their dynasty. It was my call, my choice, and I had the authority and power … and I chose not to do so.

Some twenty years later, and after my release from Mugabe's jail, one of the first stories I heard was that JG and some of his relatives in Perth, Australia, take every opportunity to denigrate me and apparently would have wanted nothing better than for me to have died in prison.

Why did I give them amnesty? Kindred spirits for the Rhodesian era played a part. SG and I were friends and I knew a lot of his friends. Also, the weaponry was obviously a relic from the Rhodesian era when nearly everyone who served in the different arms of the security forces kept little stashes of weapons and ammunition 'just in case'—it was not a cache that was being retained for any subversive nonsense. So it wasn't such a big deal. These people were not planning any sort of insurrection. They were normal citizens. Subsequent to my release I have been told by some former CIO colleagues who were stationed at headquarters in Harare that the way I dealt with these two farmers, especially in letting them off the hook, was seriously frowned upon by the brass, and in fact was the initial trigger that placed me on the suspicion list of not being totally committed to the Mugabe regime. So in hindsight, which as we all know is always 20/20, for my own sake I should have just handed them over for prosecution and hanging.

Arrest, detention, remand, failed escape, jail

"If you want to understand somebody,
go on a journey with him."
Abalunyia of Kenya

Sunday 17th January 1988 was not the best day of my life. It was a glorious, clear, mid-summer Sunday morning and I was suffering from a serious *babalaas* (hangover), having torn the arse out of it the previous evening with a customary braai and *dops* (drinks) at my house. I was sweating pure beer, and with a cold *regmaker chibuli* (lit. 'right-making' beer) in hand, was working on a horse-lunging ring for my wife's polo ponies in one of the paddocks on my property.

So you may wonder why, with this idyllic setting, how this could not be THE best day of my life. It's a fact that when you think you're on the pig's back, and all is going *lekker* (nicely) you should really take care. Pride before the fall, and all that.

I was thirty-five years old. It was a nice feeling—being fit, healthy, young and vibrantly alive in the prime of my life, sweating in the sun, warmth on my skin and not too much going wrong in my life to trouble my mind other than the hair of the dog in the cold bottle I gripped, and that even though the beer had hooks in it with the first few swallows, it was actually starting to taste quite good. I was contemplating phoning a couple of *skelms* (lit. rogues, i.e. friends) to pop around and light the fire and do it all again, when somewhere in my subconscious my psyche became aware of the familiar old sound of a helicopter in the distance … *whup … whup … whup.*

It's amazing how smells and sounds, music and other things can in a flash, transport you to times and places in your memory where bitter-sweet thoughts, or happy or sad times dwell, and your mind's eye has instant recall.

❧❧❧

The sound of a helicopter never fails to transport me, fleetingly, back to my Rhodesian war days—days which I know carry every conceivable emotion for so many people.

As an officer in the Rhodesian BSAP Support Unit for the last two years of the war I became quite familiar with helicopters, and their sounds and smells. Sometimes I would be on an observation post in the middle of nowhere, had spotted some Charlie Tangos (CTs, i.e. communist terrorists) in a kraal I had been watching for days and using my communication radio had called in the Rhodesian Army's killing machine, the Fireforce. Fireforce was an expensive tool developed by the Rhodesian army and air force, and it yeilded impressive results. The 'Foxtrot Foxtrot' (as it was known phonetically on the communication radio network) was led by a K-car, or 'Killer-car', an Alouette III helicopter carrying the force commander (and called 'K-Car' on the communication radio), which was mounted with a single MG-151 twenty-millimetre cannon. As the K-car was the command chopper it did not carry troops and could therefore load up to the gills with cannon shells and fuel. The K-car was normally accompanied by three or four troop-carrying Alouettes called G-cars, or gunships, usually called Yellow, Red, or Green … 1, 2, 3 or 4 and so on on depending on which Fireforce section was in action. For example, the lead G-car from Yellow Fireforce would be Yellow One. The aptly named G-cars were mounted with twin 7.62 FN or .303 Browning machine guns that had a much faster cyclic rate of fire than the 20mm cannon in the K-car. Initially built in France as an interim measure, there are few countries worldwide that have not used the Alouette in police or military roles, from Rhodesia to South Africa, Europe and Asia; they've all had them in use. And the self-same Alouettes from the Rhodesian days still form the backbone of Mugabe's helicopter force.

The troops in the G-cars, usually numbering four, would be called 'stops' (from 'stop group') as they would be deployed by the helicopters essentially to 'stop' the escaping gooks. Stop 1 would come from G-car Yellow 1 and so on. It's quite simple, really.

Either me out on the OP or one of my numerous call signs I had deployed under my command could summon the helicopters when gooks were confirmed as having been seen, or the Fireforce just passing through and stopping at my base camp to refuel, would carry with it such an unmistakable and unforgettable cacophony, with swirling dust and the pungent smell of high-revolution turbines and aviation fuel.

Just the sound of a helicopter would take me there, and associated with it in my subconscious, all the adrenaline rush, the dead gooks slung in nets underneath the choppers after the fire fights, the heartache when it was one of ours being carried back inside returning choppers, the flares, the gunfire on the ground and from the G-cars and the unmistakable *da da da* of the K-car's cannon. The dust from the chopper rotors, the shouts of fighting men, smoke flares, hand grenade flash-bangs, people running and screaming, and the killing, all lie there, just beneath your skin, and are so easily awakened by any number of triggers, in this case, the sound of a chopper.

And don't forget the ever-present, high-pitched drone of the air force's Riems Cessna 'Lynx' aircraft that accompanied the Fireforce. The Lynx, with its familiar push-pull engines, was also lethal with is its cargo of machine guns, Sneb rockets and Frantan (napalm) bombs Frantan with its bright yellow/orange flames, intense heat and black billowing smoke, the flash … *crack* … *whaa! whaa!* rockets … and firing machine guns, all added up to an impressive killing machine.

It was a an intense experience to be directly involved in a Fireforce contact with the Charlie Tangos or just to listen in to the full fire fight on the communication radio. After the Fireforce had located old 'Charlie' it would go something like this … imagine the helicopters circling a remote rural village. The choppers orbit at fifty metres above ground, a height that they have zeroed their machine guns at. The choppers are carrying four-man stop groups, each armed to the teeth. The village consists of a few mud-walled huts with thatched roofs. There is a brown muddy, meandering stream near the village and one of the huts near the stream is larger than the others, probably a kitchen hut. The huts are in a clearing which is simply swept earth, there are a few chickens scratching in the dust, some women sit near the kitchen hut and are now gaping at the sky where the helicopters are making a racket, a few skinny nondescript dogs hang around and some washing, maybe, is draped out to dry over some rocks next to the stream …

"Yellow Three, K-car."

"K-car, Yellow Three."

"Roger, Yellow Three, drop your call sign [stop group] just next to that small bend in the river near the large round hut, copied?"

"K-car, Yellow Three, copied."

The drop takes about thirty seconds, the chopper just touches the ground and the four soldiers hit the ground running.

"K-car, Stop Three."

"Go ahead Stop Three."

"Roger K-car, the gooks are gapping it north across that large maize field toward that tree line and that *gomo* [hill] about 300 metres out of the kraal line, over."

"Roger copied Stop Three."

A short few seconds later, the K-car spots the gooks, running hell for leather toward a small outcrop near the village.

"I have them visual! K-car firing!"

Da da da da ...

These memories that come in a flash and carry so many images and sounds and smells with them that you have to pinch yourself to escape the reverie.

And just get a bunch of mates who had been there and done that, in similar fire fights all over Rhodesia and also in its neighbouring countries, where the Rhodesian forces would mount external raids on guerrilla camps, transit facilities or supply lines, around a braai fire or in a pub, and after a few beers, the Fireforce stories are enough to drive the women with you to distraction. But we never tire of them and the number of gooks killed in each contact always increases with the telling, as do the empty beer cans in the bin.

ولولولو

And all this in a flash of memory brought on by the sound of a chopper. There were probably only a few privately owned helicopters in Zimbabwe at that time, and the occasional noise of a military one was not really out of the ordinary, so on this occasion, as with most other times, it was just a sound carrying flash-back memories stored somewhere in the back of my mind, as I contemplated the hole my horse boys had just dug for the next lunging ring pole.

Suddenly the chopper was overhead, and at a low height it started circling my house! I stood there, squinting up at it, a bit stupidly I suppose, as one would do when jarred out of a drawn-out reverie, by the sudden appearance of a helicopter hovering directly overhead.

The Charlie Tangos in the Rhodesian war days must have felt a bit like that too, because the Fireforce didn't fly high and in easy line of sight when on their way to a possible gook presence in the bush. Stealth was the order of the day for the Fireforce, because the gooks would take cover at the mere sound of the choppers, so they would fly, balls out, just above treetop level, ducking left and right around hills, outcrops and other obstacles on the ground—so low in fact that a large tree, such as a baobab, would be an obstacle to quickly dodge. And whenever practical, the Fireforce would approach the gook area from downwind, and so fly ahead of their sound, to further maintain the element of surprise, until suddenly, bad luck for old Charlie Tango—the 'flying death' is right over you and you make the Fireforce's day.

My first gut reaction at this noisy apparition above me was fear (probably the same as old Charlie Tango in the bush), but I quickly rationalized that it was probably just a mate from the air force giving me an early-morning buzz, or something equally innocuous. It couldn't be anything serious, surely?

Squinting into the sunlight, and through the reflection of the chopper's bubble-glass window, I made out the black-skinned wrists and neck of the pilot behind the Perspex. Before I could really digest that anomaly (I didn't know any pilots who were not white, and even though they wear flight suits, helmets, goggles and gloves, you can still see who the jockey is if you look closely enough), I glimpsed out the corner of my eye and heard the arrival of numerous police, army and civilian-type vehicles off to my left, at the main gate to my property. This arrival was heralded by clouds of dust from braking tyres and furiously parking cars, together with the clanging of armoured vehicle doors, and soldiers debussing into the dust and confusion. Accompanying them were scores of blue-uniformed riot police, all carrying rifles with bandoliers of ammunition hanging over their shoulders, combat helmets and all, who were leaping over my front wall and starting to skirmish through the garden toward me.

This was, something out of a *Terminator* set! After gaining a little composure, I approached a group of these guys with their feverish imagination and who were running riot. They were obviously seriously agitated, pointing their cocked AKs and Uzis all over the place, taking cover behind the braai, whistles blowing, radios squawking, leopard-crawling and so on. Fucking hell! Remember the footage on TV of the Yanks arriving on Somali beaches to liberate that country in the 1980s while a few Somali women were going about their business with their kids on the same beach? Well, same thing at my possie (Rhodesian slang for 'position').

And there I was in a pair of shorts and vellies (*veldskoene* i.e. bush shoes), no shirt, catching a bronzie (tan) in the garden. These guys were going crazy, and I have huge experience that when a poorly trained security person has a hair up his ass and is seriously agitated or frightened and, more importantly, totally out of his depth, you must tread very carefully—no quick movements. You daren't scratch your head lest the shit hits the fan with blood and guts all over the place. You just stand there and look as innocent and non-dangerous as possible!

To my horror, I then saw my wife and two daughters, aged nine and four, being herded onto the patio near my swimming pool by a few of these zombies, and all the while the chopper was clattering and screaming overhead in a low orbit. Ja … this was not an auspicious start to my Sunday afternoon.

The helicopter, seeing all was in hand on the ground and that I hadn't done a Sly Stallone on the invaders, moved off to a higher orbit, allowing everyone to settle down a bit without the enormous roar overhead. Everyone seemed to calm down a little, thereby permitting some sort of logical thought.

There is nothing like 'leading from the front' for the brass in Zimbabwe's security forces. They rather let the cannon fodder face the danger. I was obviously thought to be an extremely dangerous person, suggested by the complete overkill going on around me.

After giving their armed goons time to clear the area and ensure that I hadn't gone beserk and was placid enough to approach, a couple of vehicles arrived with the heavies, obvious by their suits, their fat guts hanging over their trousers, their swagger and the deference paid to them by the soldiers and cops who had led the assault and who were still in different positions of skirmish and cover around my garden, hiding behind the roses, lying prone in the lilies with rifles aimed in all directions and so on … you get the picture?

With utter chaos going on around me and with pure, sheer dread in my heart, because of my wife and daughters being held captive on the patio by these frantic palookas, I approached the fattest and apparantly most senior individual among the newly arrived suits, and asked what was going on.

I had no doubt that the shit had hit the fan, and in a big way too. This sort of reaction involving choppers, army, Support Unit and plain clothes people all armed to the teeth and all crapping themselves, is reserved for serious shit only.

I have complete knowledge of Zimbabwean security force methods of operation and how these people act when a major or serious profile case is being investigated or reacted to and especially when someone as senior as I in the CIO, is involved, and where there may be a little danger. As I've said before, it does not take much for these *okes* to totally overreact.

Simultaneously galloping through my brain, and while trying to look confused and as innocent as I could, was my trip into the city centre earlier that morning to hide some cash in a toilet cistern at a petrol station for another operative, Philip Conjwayo, who was soon to be my co-accused for twenty years. That morning, I had been told by Grumpy (my former runner in SA) that Philip was in Bulawayo and was taking cover ducking a rumour that the cops were after him, and that he needed some getaway cash. I had never met him but was aware from discussions with Ronnie that Conjwayo had been used to purchase a Renault R5 motor vehicle the week before, which Ronnie and Smith had used as a car bomb to destroy a local guerrilla safe house and transit facility in Bulawayo a couple of days ago. I had my guts turning to water with the thought that maybe, somehow, this assault on my home was related to that bombing or the cash for Conjwayo. Both one and the same I mean … the bombing and the cash!

ی ی ی

I had been a South Africa government double agent for some years, as part of their Operation *Barnacle,* which consisted of four of us ex-army and -police *okes* in Zimbabwe. Essentially our brief was to attack ANC guerrilla targets in Zimbabwe on intelligence that I supplied, and to make it difficult for them to operate across the Limpopo River into South Africa.

The South African apartheid government had me on their books for many years as a covert agent for South African Military Intelligence. I was quite a valuable asset for the South Africans because of the position I held in Mugabe's CIO, which gave me accesss to any state document I wanted, regardless of its security classification.

I was recruited as a double agent by Grumpy and Gray Branfield. They approached me in 1982 soon after I joined the CIO. I had known them for many years in the BSAP and they were now working for SA Military Intelligence. They needed information on the activities of the Umkhonto we Sizwe in Zimbabwe and due to my senior position in the CIO, I had access to that information. It was easy enough for them to request my assistance, because we had been friends for such a long time. It started out as little snippets of information here and there, and quickly evolved into them developing my position to that of a full double agent. They had other sources in the CIO I am sure, but none in Matabeleland, so I was their man there.

Double-lined and bright-red-marked TOP SECRET documents were completely accessible to me. I was senior enough in the CIO to be included in most security operational briefings and plans, and in fact on many occasions, personally brief Mugabe and his coterie on the intelligence situation in Matabeleland.

I am perceived a traitor. I could debate this with anyone and maybe no definite conclusion would be achieved. Often he who takes action against what he believes to be immoral or wrong goes down in history as a traitor. Yet he who can take action and does not, will be a traitor to his conscience. If I didn't do what I was in a position to do, would I have been able to look myself in the mirror, and more importantly, could I ever look the war widows and orphans in the eye? I convinced myself that there was a higher imperative than my oath to a leader whom I knew was evil and at the risk of being perceived a traitor in some men's eyes, I betrayed that oath. However wrong my extremist action might be perceived, I did it, I hope, from the best possible personal conviction.

And I paid for it, right or wrong, with nearly twenty years of my life.

Of particular interest to the South African government was my access to document intelligence, and my involvement with the ANC and the CIO desk that dealt with them in Bulawayo.

There are things relevant to that era that few people will understand. For example, you had the South African apartheid government on one hand, the ANC liberation movement trying to overthrow that government by violent means on the other, and Zimbabwe actively supporting ANC guerrillas who would cross into South Africa, carry out violent military missions, and then return to safety in Zimbabwe on yet another.

In the CIO and working with me daily, we had CIO operatives who liaised with and frequently attended to, the communication and other needs of ANC guerrillas in Zimbabwe.

I will make a point here and explain that ANC refugees, once assessed, qualified, quantified and established as refugees, did not fall within the CIO gambit, although a watchful eye was kept on them. ANC fighters, however (who often posed as refugees), were another matter altogether and were watched closely by the CIO and therefore by South African Military Intelligence—through me.

Mugabe well knew that he would afford ANC fighters refuge at his peril. The Frontline States were hammered, time and again, by the South African Defence Force for their policy of supporting the liberation movements who were intent on overthrowing the white apartheid government in South Africa.

So we in the CIO kept a close eye on the ANC guerrillas and I told South African Military Intelligence all about it. In early 1982, President Mugabe ordered tough surveillance and a general tightening-up on ANC guerrillas in Zimbabwe. This was done by him to avoid reprisals by the South African military.

As a result, a few ANC fighters were picked up by us in the CIO in Bulawayo and under light questioning revealed a few substantial arms caches that they had hidden in the Beitbridge area. These ANC guerrillas would normally travel to Beitbridge using civilian transport and there they would recover what weapons they needed, cross into South Africa, carry out an operation, return to deposit whatever they had not left behind in the cache and return to Bulawayo.

These caches, consisting mainly of AK rifles and ammunition, TMH anti-tank landmines and blocks of TNT explosives were recovered by us and seized, and the fighters returned to Zambia by dropping them off across the Zambezi using CIO motor launches that we had moored at Victoria Falls and Kariba. This decision to openly frustrate the ANC was, however, just a smokescreen by President Mugabe, as his covert support continued right up to majority rule in South Africa in 1994. Unfortunately for the Zimbabwean regime at that time, I exposed this façade to the South Africans of clamping down on the ANC.

I did not betray Mugabe or Zimbabwe in the true sense of the word. Okay, there is a fine line here—maybe I did, maybe I didn't—it's a moot point. The fact is that I did not betray Zimbabwe, but rather, I fought against the ANC which the Zimbabwe government was harbouring—there is a difference and not just semantics, I reckon. Okay, it was President Mugabe's policy to support the armed wing of the ANC and I was employed by him, and didn't adhere to his policy. As a senior official in President Mugabe's office I had access to every top-secret piece of intelligence about Zimbabwe's economy and its industrial and commercial assets—including things like the electricity grids, generation plants, major supply-dam walls, railways, railway wagons and locomotives, bridges and power lines, Wankie colliery operations and its heavy equipment, airlines, airports and their security, vehicle-manufacturing plants, the air force and army establishments throughout Zimbabwe, their strategic plans, safe houses, and so on. You name it; I had access to it, including President Mugabe's whereabouts, his plans and his security organization, day by day. I could, with my access to Zimbabwe's central nervous system, and with all the weapons of war we had cached in Bulawayo and available to us, have destroyed the complete infrastructure of the country and have brought it to its knees.

I could have assassinated any of Zimbabwe's leaders, including Mugabe himself. Many times. On the occasions, each year, that President Mugabe opened the Zimbabwe International Trade Fair, I was personally placed in charge of his overall security. He would arrive in Bulawayo, as per normal, with his close security boys, who would then be joined by more of the same security palookas from the Bulawayo CIO close-security office. Thereafter the entire presidential convoy and entourage would come under my personal authority, command and control until after the visit and the president's departure to Harare, or wherever. Even when Mugabe did not stop in Bulawayo, or was on a visit to Victoria Falls, say, for a SADC meeting, I was given command of the security.

Only after President Mugabe and his entourage eventually departed the province would I then report to the Provincial CIO (CIO Officer Commanding Zimbabwe Internal Operations,) who was based in Bulawayo, and give him the rundown on how things had gone. Such was the trust that the CIO had in me that at no time in the preparation and execution of my security plans was I ever second-guessed.

So much reliance and authority was vested in me that I had no requirement to give the then CIO Director of Operations, as his position was known, a full briefing prior to Mugabe's arrival. I was given the task of making sure he was safe, and just got on with it.

Prior to one of President Mugabe's visits to the Trade Fair in 1984, I was asked by 'KD' (Major Gray Branfield, South African Military Intelligence chief in charge of Operation *Barnacle*—killed in Iraq in 2006), to draw up a plan for Mugabe's assassination. I declined ... pure and simple. Maybe KD was making preparation for an operation he had coming up on his own initiative, or perhaps he had been given the directive by his bosses, I just don't know.

It was common procedure to have plans made for operations which were then held in abeyance; just in case a new requirement arose (maybe an operation waiting on the shelf would suddenly dovetail with something new). It would be simple enough to implement it, if it had been planned and rehearsed in preparation.

But in all reality, the assassination of President Mugabe would have been easy. I directed the affairs surrounding his personal security when he was in Matabeleland. Be it a visit to the Trade Fair, or an SADC meeting at Victoria Falls, whatever and whenever, I was there, just behind the curtains, running the show. If it was the Trade Fair he would normally tour a few show stands and all the while he and his entourage would follow a pre-determined route that I had already worked out, done a reconnaissance on beforehand, checked, timed and planned. His entourage would adhere to the exact timing I had set as they waltzed around the fair, apparently oblivious to a pre-determined route.

I would always follow him and his herd of handlers, hangers-on, arse-creepers, the works, as they made their way along the prescribed and formerly planned route. It would have been a piece of cake to direct him past a roadside bomb, in a dustbin for instance. I would sort of drop back a few metres, detonate the bomb at the critical moment then rush forward to help out and protect the president!

Because of my seniority I would then automatically take charge of the bomb scene and the immediate reaction and investigation. So it would have been beautiful cover, being there at the blast and sending the operatives off on all sorts of false trails. Especially because after something like an attempt on the president, all the troglodytes that followed him everywhere would have gone crazy, and immediately overreacted, mainly to cover their own asses. So simple!

How much suffering could I have avoided (not only mine) by that one simple act? But I declined. I was completely willing to pass intelligence to the South Africans and help in their operations against the ANC guerrillas, but to kill Mugabe was too much. However, many were the times sitting on death row waiting for Mugabe to hang me, that I regretted that decision—warped or misplaced sense of loyalty perhaps?

The South Africans were really pissed off about me declining to get involved in the assassination of President Mugabe. However, as I was their most valued agent in place, I could call the shots regarding just what I wanted to do or not, to a certain extent. I'm told they went ahead anyhow and made plans for President Mugabe's 1984 Trade Fair visit. These plans covered a similar scenario I've described above, but also a wet job at Bulawayo State House itself involving some of his close security officers whom they had recruited.

To cut a long story short, P. W. Botha himself, so I was later told by SADF General Kat Liebenberg at a military intelligence braai at their Magaliesberg farm, had flatly refused any operation or initiative to kill President Mugabe. (On this issue and in his submission to the Truth and Reconciliation Commission, Pik Botha, the former South African foreign minister said: "I can assure you that what happened there was, I think, either Dr. Neil Barnard or one of the security personnel reported that elements in Rhodesia were endeavouring to kill Mr. Mugabe. And what we then reacted to was, we said look, tell those people they are playing with fire; it's in no one's interest and if they carry on like this and succeed in killing him. He will then become a hero and a martyr. That is, I can assure you, what happened that day in that discussion.")

This policy was apparently evident in the lead-up to the independence elections in Zimbabwe, and was carried forward, post-1980 with the continuous destablization programmes in Zimbabwe, that did not involve the elimination of President Mugabe.

Why didn't they assassinate Mugabe? I don't know. Maybe presidents, whoever they are, have some sort of gentleman's agreement, where they promise not to knock each other off. Who knows? All I can say, with some authority, is that P. W. Botha refused to ventilate Mugabe. And the old crocodile certainly knew what Mugabe was up to in Zimbabwe, with all his repression of his own people and his policy of support for the ANC.

೭ ೭ ೭

You may recall, after South Africa's bombings in Gaborone, Lusaka and Harare, P. W. waggling his trademark finger at the international press, and telling the Frontline States, in relation to the raids on their capitals, "We have delivered our first installment."

After these co-ordinated military raids, known in South African military circles as Operation *Leo*, on ANC guerrilla facilities in Harare, Lusaka and Gaborone, the South African Defence Force chief, General Kat Liebenberg, claimed at an international press briefing that they were in response to the recent ANC guerrilla attacks on the oil-from-coal facility in South Africa at Sasol 2, near Secunda in the Eastern Transvaal. He said the targets had been an operational transit facility in Gaborone, an ANC office and house in Harare, and ANC targets just outside Lusaka, all of which were bombed by the South African Air Force.

In these strikes there were no South African casualties. One Botswanan national, a South West African and a Zambian national had been killed and approximately twenty people injured ...

General Liebenberg argued that, "The forces had acted with extreme caution to prevent citizens of our neighbouring states being injured or suffering damage. Neighbouring states cannot plead ignorance regarding the presence of terrorists in their countries."

Defence minister, Magnus Malan, made South Africa's policy regarding cross-border raids very clear when he addressed parliament on 4th February 1986: "The security forces will hammer them. What I am saying is the policy of the government. We will not sit here with hands folded, waiting for them to cross the borders. We will settle the hash of these terrorists, their fellow travellers and those who help them before they enter our territory."

ممم

Coincidentally, among the Harare facilities attacked was a residence in Ashdown Park where the ANC chief representative for Zimbabwe, Joe Gqabi, had been assassinated in 1981 by a South African Military Intelligence special operations team, led by KD.

I recall some pub talk, between us crazy people from these shadowy sections of the forces, where KD complained about the 9mm Uzi sub-machine gun he had been issued with to shoot Joe Gqabi. His whinge was that the bullets had been reduced to such a slow speed that they barely penetrated the driver's window, never mind killing the target.

After surviving an attempted car bomb some six months earlier when an explosive charge was placed under his car but failed to detonate as he reversed over the triggering device, Joe Gqabi was killed in the driveway of the Ashdown Park home on the evening of Friday 31st July 1981, just as he arrived in his Zimbabwean-registered vehicle. Police said later that they had recovered nineteen spent 9mm cartridge cases and that the deceased had been hit several times.

Three teams from South African Military Intelligence had been deployed to Harare to carry out the assassination, and they were assisted by sources in CIO Harare, with the intelligence on the Joe Gqabi's movements, his vehicles' registration numbers and the different places he slept at night.

Us agents would often discuss our respective missions, successes and failures, fuck-ups, and bad and good drills worth remembering. We would meet in a quiet corner of a pub somewhere, on a boat while fishing, at one of the *oke's* houses, or anywhere really.

The South Africans had obviously gathered their intelligence for the Gqabi assassination from other sources in Harare. I was the only intelligence operative on the ground that the South Africans had outside the capital, and I only came on-stream a couple of months after the Gqabi operation.

෴

Despite this acknowledgement regarding the cross-border raids by his boss, the South African president and his peers, in almost predictable fashion similar to other former South African politicians who suffer from selective amnesia, Pik Botha, the former foreign minister, related to the Truth Commission his views on our 1986 cross-border raids. On one hand Botha, in his experienced political double-speak and under oath told the Truth Commission that, "The raids on Harare, Gaborone and Lusaka on 19th May 1986 were not discussed at any State Security Council meeting where I was present. In the light of the importance that the Department of Foreign Affairs and I attached to the relationship with our neighbours and the Commonwealth Emminent Persons' Group, and the tremendous amount of work we invested in this effort, we would certainly have opposed these raids most strongly."

While on the other hand on 27th May 1995, and as minister of energy in the new South African government, Pik wrote to me saying, "It is a source of great regret that you should have to bear this pain and suffering on account of official activities launched for official reasons." This letter was written to me, while I sat jailed in Zimbabwe, despite his denials while minister of foreign affairs that he knew anything about me or my activities on behalf of his government.

Never mind this complete *volte face* by Pik Botha, he still pleaded ignorance to the Truth Commission. In an attempt to pass the buck for our extra-territorial activity to the minister of defence, he went on to refer to guidelines for cross-border activities that had previously been approved of by the State Security Council in 1985 where Foreign Affairs was supposed to be involved with Defence, by insisting that these were only guidelines.

Mr. Botha continued to the Truth and Reconciliation Commission, "May I also point out that it was clearly stated that the responsibility for the military implementation of operations vested exclusively in the Chief of the Defence Force. The security forces considered this as essential to prevent ANC activists from initiating and pursuing armed incursions into the country. They claimed that they had reliable and confirmed information that operatives could be staging murderous activities from places which were attacked by the security forces. The security forces believed that they were acting within the framework of the Defence Act and other relevant legislation mandating them to take the action which they took. From a legal and technical point of view, my department and I could not assail or ward off the argument on the basis of illegal activities. The Department of Foreign Affairs and I, in principle, assessed a given cross-border action in the light of the predictable international consequences. In these matters, Mr. Chairperson, a clear and consistent divergence of views existed between the security forces and Foreign Affairs.

"The security establishment saw it as their prime objective to trace and stop dangerous operatives from pursuing sabotage and violence in the country. Foreign Affairs, although in principle opposed to violent pursuits by the ANC, the PAC [Pan Africanist Congress] and others, weighed the consequences of reprisals or pre-emptive strikes against the international consequences for the government.

"In the few instances where Foreign Affairs acquiesced in cross-border raids it did so on the strength of convincing evidence produced by the security establishment to the effect that a pre-emptive strike was essential to save the lives of innocent South African citizens.

"Cross-border activities against terrorists, who cut the throats of elderly couples on farms, or who set off a bomb like the Pretoria bomb [in Church Street], were generally supported by the vast majority of white voters including opposition parties and the media, but this support was limited to activities against proven targets. In some cases facts or circumstances surfaced which contradicted the claims made by the South African security forces."

I suppose with hindsight, and now with more information on the whole débâcle, I can be a little more charitable toward Pik Botha, especially as his denials were somewhat corroborated by former South African defence minister, Magnus Malan, who told the Truth and Reconciliation Commission that the Operation *Leo* cross-border raids had not been discussed at cabinet or State Security Council level. According to Mr. Malan, the SADF had wished to mount the attacks on the neighbouring capitals in late April 1986: "They approached me. I approached the State President, P. W. Botha. I explained and he gave his approval. The State President told me to keep quiet about this as it was very sensitive."

The raids were postponed to May, for one reason or another, at the time when Magnus Malan said he had again obtained permission from P. W. Botha. With the centralization of power around former president Botha, there is credence that can be given to this, so I apologize to Pik Botha for being so free with my condemnation of him and his head-in-the-sand attitude, as I perceived it, from behind those cold, grey concrete walls of Chikurubi Maximum Prison in Harare.

Can you blame me for losing faith in the South African government that I had sacrificed everything, nearly even my life for? All those years I sat in prison and all the time, especially when F. W. de Klerk was running the show, I sat and prayed and hoped for some action, some reassurance … anything from them. While I sat wasting my life away in Chikurubi Maximum Prison, the architects of apartheid whom I served enjoyed *die lekker lewe* (the good life) in South Africa. I know that F. W. and Pik tried a little to resolve our plight, but I also know that they could have done more.

In November of 1995, Pik Botha, on behalf of the National Party in South Africa where he was also a junior minister in the coalition government, demanded the release of all political prisoners in Nigeria. This was at the time that Ken Saro Wiwa and his colleagues were in jail (and who were subsequently hanged by the Sani Abacha regime). I sat there in Chikurubi, hoping against hope that Pik would at least demand our release too, seeing as he was already up on his soapbox.

Zilch.

Many years later, on 14th May 1997 when F. W. de Klerk stood in front of the Truth and Reconciliation Commission, he told them that in his capacity as head of the former government and leader of the National Party that neither he nor his colleagues in cabinet and on the State Security Council had authorized or instructed any unlawful acts. So you tell me please, where we, as a group here in Zimbabwe obtained South African Air Force helicopters for our 1986 raid on ANC facilities in the Zimbabwe capital? And remember that the Lusaka and Gaborone ANC facilities were attacked simultaneously.

Anyhow, the TRC told Mr. de Klerk just what they thought of him and his denials, inter alia: "The Commission finds that former State President F. W. de Klerk displayed a lack of candour in that he omitted to take the Commission into his confidence and/or to inform the Commission of what he knew.

"The Commission finds that Mr. de Klerk failed to make a full disclosure of gross violations of human rights committed by senior members of government and senior members of the SAP, despite being given the opportunity to do so.

"The Commission finds that his failure to do so constitutes material non-disclosure, rendering him an accessory to the commission of gross violations of human rights.

"The Commission finds Mr. de Klerk morally accountable for concealing this from the country when, as executive head of government, he was under obligation to disclose the truth as known to him."

Is it any wonder I felt totally abandoned?

ور ور ور

Okay, so now I've tried to explain the motivation and morals of my spy life and my duplicity as much as my own moral blameworthiness counts. I could have done serious damage to Zimbabwe, but I didn't. I had access to ANC guerrilla activity with which I could have done serious damage to them, and I did. I could never accept the ANC policy of taking the liberation war to the streets of South Africa. We were effective in limiting the ANC's effectiveness. I have read in Connie Braam's book *Operation Vula* that Ronnie Kasrils, the previous South African minister of intelligence, told her in the early '80s that it was becoming hard for them as MK to operate from inside the Frontline States.

Why blow up innocent people, of all races, mind you in the name of liberation? A bomb is indiscriminate— it kills all who are near it, not just whites.

The Church Street bombing, the Christmas 1985 bombing of the Amanzimtoti shopping centre, the murders of worshippers at St. James Church in Cape Town and the car bomb at Magoo's Bar in Durban spring to mind (the bomber, Robert McBride was until recently a senior Gauteng police chief!) when alternative military, commercial and industrial targets were available throughout the country and which could have easily brought the South African regime to its knees.

That's my moral perception anyhow. I felt it was indefensible for the ANC to be indiscriminate with its bombing campaign and I was in a position to do something about it. There were others in the CIO who were also in a position to do something about it. They were there in Bulawayo and in Harare but they chose to do nothing. It was their call, and it's their conscience ...

Consider also please that the Truth and Reconciliation Commission in South Africa in the late 1990s examined some of the ANC activities. The TRC found, inter alia: "While it was ANC policy that the loss of civilian life should be avoided, there were instances where members of their armed wing, MK, perpetrated gross violations of human rights in that the distinction between civilian and military targets was blurred in certain instances, such as the 1983 Church Street bombing of the South African Air Force headquarters in Pretoria, resulting in gross violations of human rights through civilian injury and loss of life [nineteen South African civilians of all races were killed in this bombing]."

The report continues: "In the course of the armed struggle there were instances where members of MK conducted unplanned military operations using their own discretion, and without adequate control and supervision at operational level, determined targets for attack which were outside official policy guidelines. While recognizing that such operations were frequently in retaliation to raids by the former South African government into neighbouring countries, such operations nonetheless often resulted in civilian injury and loss of life, amounting to gross human rights violations. The 1985 Amanzimtoti Shopping Centre bombing is regarded by the Commission in this light. Other operations though intended for military or security-force targets sometimes went awry for a variety of reasons, including poor intelligence and reconnaissance. The consequence of these cases, such as the Magoo's Bar and Durban Esplanade bombings was gross violations of human rights."

The commission also found, "while it acknowledged the ANC's submission that the former South African government had itself by the mid-1980s blurred the distinction between military and 'soft' targets by declaring border areas 'military zones' where farmers were trained and equipped to operate as an extension of military structures, it finds that the ANC's landmine campaign in the period 1985-1987 in the rural areas of the Northern Transvaal cannot be condoned, in that it resulted in gross violations of the human rights of civilians, including farm labourers and children who were killed or injured. The ANC is held accountable for such gross violations of human rights."

So where does my moral justification stand, in the light of the Truth and Reconciliation Commission's findings?

Many people can just carry on with life, look the other way and remove these mind debates from their psyche; they can sweep them under the carpet with one of many platitudes such as, "It wasn't my duty or my problem. I could do nothing that would have helped, so I carried on with my own life [and walked on by, on the other side of the road]."

✍ ✍ ✍

As I write this, there is quite a furore in South Africa regarding name changes. The ANC government wants the names of certain places changed, "to reflect the new dispensation and its history", which is fair enough. The victor, as I've said, always re-writes the history.

But in Amanzimtoti specifically, there is a fuss because the local government intends renaming the main thoroughfare after the ANC guerrilla who carried out the 1985 Christmas Eve shopping-centre bombing in that tourist resort. The bombing resulted in five people dead, including three small children. The courier of the bomb, Andrew Zondo, who had the hugely dangerous task of dropping a parcel bomb in a refuse bin at the mall and walking away, was subsequently captured, tried, sentenced to death and hanged. He was nineteen years old when he carried out his mission and was probably a fresh recruit out on his first mission, which his handlers were reluctant to do themselves, preferring to direct the operation from someplace else. The people who lost loved ones in this explosion, or whose lives were destroyed as a result of injury and disfigurement from the bomb, believe that the re-naming of the main road to 'Andrew Zondo Road' is excessively insensitive to their feelings. They say they have feelings of great heartache which are now rekindled.

There again, where does one draw the line? How many of South Africa's luminaries, from both sides of the political spectrum, some of whom are greatly respected, have blood on their hands? And have all sorts of places, here in South Africa and elsewhere, named after them?

The debate gets rather passionate too. I have heard people asking the rhetorical question: What would the people of Soweto do if their main street was named 'Barend Strydom Drive'? Barend Strydom, you may recall, is a white man who shot six black people on the streets of Pretoria during the dying days of apartheid simply because they were black. He was sentenced to death, but found himself a free man and back out on the street as part of the South African negotiations (CODESA) for a new constitution before a 1994 democratic South Africa.

In the traditional Afrikaner city of Potchefstroom numerous newly named streets have had their name plates vandalized, sprayed over, or even completely changed. In a recent case 'Nelson Mandela Drive' was altered to read 'De La Rey Drive' after the old Boer general. Of course this action plays right into the hands of those who want to paint all whites with the same brush. For some, all whites now carry the handle of 'racists' and 'anarchists' simply because of the actions of a few people. Or maybe there are more sinister forces at play with the name signs being doctored or damaged by the very people who want to poing fingers at the 'racists'. It really is unnecessary, when you think of it. Your pub or the school your child attends is still in the same place, so what does it matter if the road is called something else? Some level-headed thinking and a little less shooting from the hip is needed, all round.

The official opposition in South Africa, the Democratic Alliance is currently initiating a court action against the government about this name-changing. It's not the policy they appear pissed off about, but rather the arbitrary manner some urban councils are going about it. One district for instance has over 100 street and building changes to implement —all decided by one government official.

Anyway, I suppose I could live by convincing myself that I was working for the greater good, and that the end justified the means. I just had to accept that the politicians and the senior military people in charge of my runners knew exactly what they were doing. There again, in hindsight, it all might just as well have been part of some hidden agenda or the result of some crazy political dogma, a fuck-up, or just too much unbridled power in the the hands of the generals.

ৰ ৰ ৰ

Believe you me, operations such as mine, my job in CIO, the hidden intelligence world, the military operations, the whole caboodle, was directed by the South African Defence Force's generals, who, so I genuinely believed, obtained clearance for any military activity outside of South African borders from their political masters in South Africa's powerful State Security Council. The SSC was chaired by the president of the country. The State Security Council comprised the president's most trusted and most powerful allies in his cabinet, which included the minister of foreign affairs.

The same generals who directed affairs involving me and the other operatives in Zimbabwe also, on occasions, attended these State Security Council meetings when a special briefing was required from them. At the end of the day I suppose it all comes down to looking at yourself in the mirror. I was in place, could act and did, and was consequently labelled a traitor by Mugabe, caught, sentenced to death, and jailed for twenty years.

It was an expensive moral decision. It cost me twenty of my fifty years. Included in that twenty years is the suffering inflicted upon my wife and kids because of my probably misdirected beliefs and morals, and I have serious doubts that I should rather have taken the safer option of the middle line, like so many others.

ৰ ৰ ৰ

One thing I did realize, very early in my CIO days was that Mugabe is manifestily evil, and that his security minister, Emmerson Mnangagwa, was running a close second in that dubious distinction. One little gratification I have concerning Mnangagwa, is him walking around the CIO headquarters in Harare crying his eyes out after being fired as security minister (*the* plum job in any administration with all its perks) by Mugabe in 1988, because he hadn't detected the South African spy in his organization (moi!), despite his innumerable assurances to President Mugabe that his portfolio was squeaky clean.

And all the time there I was, a senior *oke*, undetected!

The security minister's job in Zimbabwe, as it is I suppose in most countries, is the most sought-after position in cabinet, what with its un-audited finances, safe houses (which were supposed to be used for clandestine visits but were often turned into free accommodation for the minister's women of which there were and probably still are, many), the prestige of the position as security minister and the power you wield over everyone, not necessarily excluding President Mugabe himself. No wonder Mnangagwa was shattered at the loss he'd incurred because of me, and no wonder he hates me with a vengeance to this day—a hate that he manifested to the fullest degree as the Zimbabwean justice minister under whom the Correctional Service Department fell in later years, where he had absolute control over me as a mere prisoner. In that cabinet position Mnangagwa enjoyed making my existence as miserable as he possibly could—and in return I clung onto that vision of him bawling his eyes out.

But President Mugabe takes the cake. If you combine his undoubted intellect with his evil nature, it is a mixture made in hell.

Peter Godwin has recently written a book about a crocodile eating the sun. A beautiful metaphor of Mugabe anyway you look at it. Robert Mugabe culled the Ndebele to stay in power, destroyed Zimbabwe's economy to stay in power, and now, metaphorically, by destroying their livelihood and humanity, eats his own people to stay in power.

We are all capable of evil, every last one of us. To quote Max Frenkel as written by Dr. Alex Borraine in his Truth and Reconciliation book, *A country unmasked*: "Is there a beast in each of us waiting to be unleashed by extraordinary fear, greed or fury?"

President Robert Gabriel Mugabe's place in the hall of tyrants is secure, that's for sure.

Let's cut to the chase … from another perspective, I betrayed my oath of allegiance to President Mugabe and suffered the consequences. You betray Mugabe and he will never, ever forget—that is a fact. Forget it at your peril!

His once-upon-a-time security minister, administration hot-shot, personal banker and henchman, Emmerson Mnangagwa, among many others (Edgar Tekere, Enos Nkala and so on) have tested those waters too, and despite the showmanship of loyalty and love between them, those who have crossed Mugabe lie dead, literally and figuratively. The difference is that I paid twenty years of my life for it. Mnangagwa's turn is yet to come, mark my words. Take Tongogara as an earlier example …

Mnangagwa was Mugabe's security minister during the Matabeleland genocide. He knows Mugabe's secrets about that episode in Zimbabwe's history, and Mnangagwa has dossiers, that he has quietly stashed away, which detail all Mugabe's shenanigans. Mugabe is obviously terrified of exposure by Mnangagwa, and that's why he keeps him close enough to keep an eye on him, but no longer that close where he can add to the dossier! Mnanagwa dared to challenge the right to occupy Mugabe's presidential throne a few years back when he challenged the appointment of Joyce Mujuru as vice-president instead of himself at a meeting in Tsholotsho. As a result and in comparison to the severe discipline handed to others who had the same temerity to go near the palace, Mnangagwa was disciplined but not dumped altogether as others were and was made a government minister in charge of huts in the bush where he remains to this day. Out of Mugabe's inner sanctum but close enough to watch that he does not upset any plans, especially succession manoeuvres, that Mugabe has in mind. And there Mnangagwa will stay. He will never be forgotten or forgiven.

As I write this some junior Zimbabwean army officers have been arrested in Harare for planning a coup with the intention of installing Mnangagwa. He denies it, saying, "This idea is stupid. You should ask the guys in intelligence. I know nothing about it. I am the minister for rural housing. This is a stupid thing!"

Is this all just ZANU (PF) normal smoke and mirrors? You can rest assured that President Mugabe will have this aspect of Mnangagwa's possible involvement thoroughly investigated. But even if implicated, I doubt Mnangagwa will be arrested. He simply knows too many of President Mugabe's secrets. Just watch this space.

Mugabe also loves flattery. Make a speech, grovel and worship him or call him a god or the closest thing the world has to God—and soon you're a government cabinet or provincial resident minister of traffic signs, or rivers and streams, even rural houses, or whatever.

So, back at my house in Bulawayo, that fateful Sunday morning of my arrest, with panic running around in my head and with my guts churning, I watched my wife and two daughters being led to armoured security-force vehicles; each of my family was being steered by a hand on the back of the neck. I desperately tried to think of what the fuck had gone wrong. My goose was cooked—no doubt about that. This whole security operation going on around me was clear as day that I was in the shit. Big Shit.

On many occasions, while a member of the CIO, I'd chat with other senior officers in the CIO building about ANC activity in Zimbabwe and the operations the ANC guerrillas had been carrying out inside South Africa. I knew where the ANC guerrillas stayed when in Bulawayo and quite frequently I had prior knowledge of their upcoming plans. All this information went straight to my handlers in Military Intelligence south of the Limpopo.

Every once in a while I would take a drive with the ANC desk officer in charge into an ANC guerrilla safe house in Bulawayo, be introduced to the gooks, have a beer, of which there was always plenty, supplied by the CIO—thanks to the un-audited CIO secret money float—and have a general chat with the ANC fighters. I have often wondered just how many of them are still alive, well and kicking here who will remember the white *oke* with the large black beard with whom they drank and joked with at their Bulawayo safe house in Zimbabwe.

Sitting in their safe house with me they would brag of past heroics and those to come and so on and all the while I imagined them taking serious strain from a military operation that would wipe them out and was probably being planned right then in South Africa, while I stood there socializing with them. And they did take serious strain, eventually.

One such safe house was just outside Bulawayo in the quiet and leafy suburb of Trenance, on the main road to Victoria Falls. Using my intelligence reports a military attack was planned, authorized and subsequently carried out in the dead of night on 11th January 1988.

Philip Conjwayo was a new addition to our group of four. We had previously carried out a couple of other operations in Zimbabwe and hadn't been compromised. Suddenly there was this new addition to our group, in the form of Conjwayo, and everything went pear-shaped. 'Don't change a good thing' would be an appropriate cliché. To be completely honest, as you will see, we all made our own cock-ups, which all cumulatively resulted in the subsequent compromise in this specific operation.

Philip's only task in the attack on Trenance had been to purchase a small Renault R5 sedan motor vehicle, which was converted, by adding about 100 kilograms of high explosive to its boot, into a mobile 'house flattener'.

Thereafter an unqualified SNAFU (Situation Normal. All Fucked Up!) developed, made up in equal parts by tragedy and farce and certainly coupled with some complacency on all our parts.

During my days in the CIO—as part of my normal duty and also to keep a watchful eye in case one of our operations was close to compromise—I would monitor many bombings in Zimbabwe. Due to my senior rank it was possible for me to get really involved with the investigating officer from the ZR Police on each respective case.

I would later report to my South African handlers, especially after Military Intelligence operations, where they had done well or where they had nearly slipped up. On this occasion with the bombing in Trenence, I had no CIO cover to advise whether the trail was hot or cold.

So, there we are—the R5 is primed with explosives and ready to go, the radio-controlled detonator fitted and just waiting for the press of a toggle switch that was tuned to the same frequency. Philip had hired a driver for the R5 and I had had a set of false number plates made up.

The farce began with Philip being known by the people he bought the car from! Next came the *okes* sending the driver off to deliver the mobile bomb without fitting the false number plates. They let it ride with the original plates. Good grief!

"We didn't have a number ten spanner to change the number plates!" I was subsequently told by Mike Smith, who as a farmer and qualified diesel mechanic, (one would think!) could have improvised or easily have just used a pair of pliers, or just ripped the old plates off. It's not as though the vehicle was making a long trip after all.

While sitting in my death row cell, for five years, do you know how many times I mentally tormented myself with this explanation? No spanner, for fuck's sake!

I also contributed to the farce by not listening to my inner voice. "Drop some cash at a garage in the city centre and vamoose." That's what Grumpy had asked me to do—place a roll of cash inside the toilet water cistern at Mactec Garage in Bulawayo … a garage where I was known! "Madness!" screamed my sixth sense. "Just don't do this Woodsie, check it out first." Over and over I told myself this as I rolled the bank notes into a waterproof plastic sachet.

It is important to note that none of us was completely in a *dwaal* (zombie-like state); some serious checking had been done on the South African side and huge assurances had been given to me that Philip had not been arrested but only needed cash for his getaway.

Had any of us the slightest inkling that he had been lifted the whole story and our reaction would have been entirely different.

The fact is that Philip Conjwayo made the phone calls to his South African runner, Mary Bekker, I think he called her, from the Police CID offices in Bulawayo where he was taken after his arrest in Harare. Philip had been arrested on 14th January 1988, Thursday night following the bombing in Bulawayo on Sunday night 11th January. He was questioned in Harare, admitted complicity in the bombing and driven to Bulawayo on the Friday night, 15th January. Saturday and Sunday morning was spent in telephone calls between him and his handlers in South Africa making arrangements for the garage drop of money from me. He was never tortured physically. There just wasn't time for a serious and protracted interrogation in that period.

Mere threats were enough to convince him to co-operate as he, being an ex-cop, was now in the hands of some of the people that, a few years before while a sergeant in the police Special Branch, he had tutored in the art of extracting confessions. Conjwayo did try complain about being tortured when he eventually had his day in court, but as he had no physical injuries, be they from handcuffs or leg-irons or whatever, the court didn't give his spiel much credence.

The court said it also took into account the short time it took, from him being arrested until he was in Bulawayo setting up the trap for me, to be too short to have included the horrendous, lengthy torture session he related in court.

On that fateful night in Trenance the Zambian driver, Obert Mwanza, who Conjwayo had hired from job-seekers on the Bulawayo street corners, drove the vehicle to the ANC target house. Despite the ZR Police story to our subsequent court trial that there were roadblocks at the house, he drove unhindered, straight up to the front of the premises, where he stopped and sounded the horn.

This was a signal that the vehicle had arrived, to Smith and Ronnie who waited nearby within earshot, but out of sight of the target. The driver had been given instructions to sound the horn and then to get out of the car and walk home. Incongruously and tragically, he remained behind the wheel of the stationary vehicle bomb. After a few minutes the two operatives hit the button and the vehicle with its grisly cargo was vaporized, taking along with it a few ANC operatives who had come out of the house to enquire after the hooting car.

So Jimmy (that's me in this regard!) goes and drops off the cash at Mactec Garage in Bulawayo's central business district. On arrival at the garage I told the attendant to fill up and slipped into the public toilet and hid the small waterproof roll of notes into the toilet cistern and buggered off. It was enough …

The garage owner, Stompie, knew a little too much about us and it did not take a Sherlock Holmes to pick up the trail from the garage to my house. Sunday 17th January 1988—not my best day, remember?

I will also add, that compounding my consternation and disbelief at all going on around me was the fact that I did not receive a 'take cover' phone call from South Africa. I just couldn't believe it! I had been speaking to a few of my former and current runners that morning by phone from my house and all was apparently cool. No warning! Yet I had always been assured and convinced into staying up there on the knife edge, with the promise that I would never, ever be arrested. Can't happen, I was told by the generals, and by Pik Botha's right-hand man standing around a braai at the Kop, while Pik sat right there … among the ladies.

As it always went at these South African braais, the men gathered on one side of the fire in one group, beers and Klippies and Coke in hand, where they planned all sorts of shit, told war stories and so on while the wives and girlfriends sat together, gins and tonic or whiskies in hand and talked whatever women talk. Old Pik the womanizer would always be there among the *punda* (tarts), but he would occasionally join the *manne* (men) and it was then that he continually gave assurances that I was the main man and that the brass would make sure I was secure when in Zimbabwe and well looked after when in South Africa. I am willing to bet that Pik has a memory failure about those braais. What does it matter anyhow?

Time and again, KD had very clearly told me that they had senior sources in CIO headquarters in Harare and that they would always know if I was in the shit, or even if I was under suspicion. A plan of escape for me, two plans in fact, both involving jumping in my Benz with my wife and children and heading for an isolated airstrip, one north, or one south of Bulawayo from where we would be uplifted, were signed, sealed and delivered. All it would have taken was the warning phone call. I would put the girls in the car and would have been off like a dirty shirt in a flash.

These plans for the safety of my family and me kept me there on the frontline. There is no way I'd have continued with my family at such huge risk, without an extraction plan to safety. I just would not have done it. Since my release many people have shaken their heads at my stupidity and have pooh-poohed this claim of mine about the cover I was assured of, but those on the inside track reading this, will know it's a fact—not so KD (bless you brother, wherever you are—killed in Iraq in 2006) Grumpy, Rat and others too? We all know.

However, maybe I can explain why I think they didn't know I was in the shit. It was a Sunday, CIO headquarters in Harare was off duty, other than a few functionaries there to man the radios and so on, and this was mainly a CID, i.e. a police-force arrest. The CIO were not involved in the initial developments of the case so it was probably only a few hours after I had been arrested that the South African sources in Harare would have been made aware and hit the panic button south of the Limpopo. But maybe that is just me being generous. The fact is, once Conjwayo was supposedly on the run, the South Africans should have had all their red flags up and running, *just in case!*

৶ ৶ ৶

I've been in many tight situations in my life but in every other case I'd had an element of control over the situation. In a gun fight for instance, you can shoot back, run or whatever. But when you get into a situation like this, especially with your wife and two girls being handcuffed and led off by the neck and you're leg-ironed and handcuffed and utterly helpless, you suddenly find yourself with no control.

Think of it—you want to run over there and rip the chains off your family and make sure they are safe. Yet you have completely lost control. You want to hug your wife and kids and tell them everything will be okay, when in reality, deep inside your soul you're dead, and there's absolutely nothing you can do. That's what I emphasize as being a fundamental of life—Maintaining Control.

So there I was, with total panic in my heart and mayhem all around me, as my wife and little girls were led off in chains to vehicles. I was then chained up like a rabid dog and thrown into the back of an unmarked police vehicle, where I sat shivering with adrenaline pumping in my veins while still trying to keep up the confused, indignant, innocent and baffled façade while we were driven off in different directions.

That was the last time I saw my girls as children, then aged nine and four. The next time I met them they had grown up into beautiful young women, twenty-seven and twenty-three years old. A bit of a bummer that, losing out on my kids growing up, for me and for them, and for my son who was eleven at the time and who I had just taken back to school in South Africa. I did not see him either for nineteen and a half years.

৵ ৵ ৵

Espionage is an important facet of any state. Intelligence gained from special operations such as the one involving me was greatly valued by the South Africans. It is vital that governments are kept well informed of the political plans of their neighbours thus enabling them to factor their own foreign and internal political and military plans accordingly.

The South Africans had Zimbabwe quite well covered. As for Zimbabwe it was not much of a secret what the apartheid government thought of states that supported those whom they perceived as terrorists, and who where trying to cause chaos in South Africa.

Over the years, and as part of my cover, I was supplied a limited amount of information by South Africa. This information, which I would channel to CIO headquarters, kept me in the good books with my CIO bosses and was sometimes important enough to the maintenance of Zimbabwe's security that it resulted in my promotion, ahead of other whites in the organization who had been there longer than me—which was obviously the plan; to get me as high up the food chain in the CIO as possible, where I would have more and more authority, and access to more and more information that the South Africans were interested in.

It was a fine line I walked, trying to maintain the position of trust and authority

I held in Zimbabwe, a position where I was in control of President Mugabe's personal security when he was in the province and where I would brief him face to face at the Matabeleland Joint Operational Command headquarters. At the same time I had to keep the South African military and their operations, especially as far as western Zimbabwe was concerned, on the boil.

୧୧୧

Meanwhile back at my house, and just to add to the general confusion, the CIO had arrived and a domestic dispute ensued between them and the CID regarding who was in control and under whose jurisdiction. It was quite ironic actually, watching this circus. I was subsequently taken away and detained in a filthy, lice-infested cell at one of Bulawayo's oldest police stations wearing not one, but two sets of leg-irons, one clamped on by the CID and one by the CIO while they bickered about who was king of the castle! Just for good measure they left the handcuffs on, (only one pair, thankfully). It took forty-eight hours for the security forces to eventually decide just who had jurisdiction—CID or CIO, I don't know and someone arrived and took off one pair of leg-irons.

Luveve police station is situated west of the city centre in the middle of one of Bulawayo's high-density suburbs (which means the city's predominantly black folk lived there cheek by jowl). Bulawayo in its infancy in the early 1900s had been divided into suburbs which were clearly defined by race. Blacks to the west, coloureds to the south in Barham Green, and mostly whites, Indians, and the odd affluent blacks and coloureds to the north and east.

Sitting that first night in Luveve police stocks, very alone and with two sets of leg-irons and one set of steel handcuffs on—my stomach started to churn and to to my utter dismay I suddenly needed to take a shit. This is probably a normal reaction to the fear and worry that I had experienced over the preceeding hours. In most jails in Zimbabwe the toilet is a round hole in the corner of the cell. Just try undo your trousers with your hands tightly fastened in front of you. That's the easy part. Then get them down below your knees, followed by your underpants, and then the fun starts. The hole in the floor is bucket-sized so you can't just spread your feet on either edge, not with one pair of leg-irons you can't—try it with two. The hole is too wide when you've got chains painfully holding your ankles at a distance of about twenty centimetres apart. All the while your guts are churning and it's another story to hold in hot, runny shit, even when you're not backed into a corner and trying not to slip into a filthy crap hole.

Okay, so you eventually wedge your back into the corner behind the hole in a sort of half-squat and while trying to hold your longs out of the way, you let fly. Of course your shit does not stream straight down, but rather off your inner ankle, then onto the floor, then into the hole. That does not take long. Toilet paper. There's none. Ja; catching your first crap in those circumstances results in a serious sense-of-humour failure. You do get quite good at it after a while though. Practice makes perfect, and all that.

Under those circumstances you would think that sleep was impossible. But even with just a foul-smelling blanket and lying on bare concrete, I managed it that night. Fitfully and only a little but maybe one's body just closes down after so much panic? I was exhausted from all the adreneline which was still running around in my system. Feeling utterly psychologically and emotionally terrified for my wife and daughters and quite scared and drained for myself, I dozed.

I had no doubt that things had gone pear-shaped and, to a large extent from the South Africans' perspective, were totally out of control. My mates were desperately trying to find out what was happening and the politicians were equally desperately putting up their umbrellas to keep themselves out of the shit.

I also knew that as the following days progressed and I continued with my idiot-baffled stare and protestations of innocence, that the CIO and CID—with their insinuations of bombs and murders, serious stuff after all—would soon get very pissed off and use my wife and girls as a lever to gain my full co-operation.

Police and other security people in Zimbabwe have absolutely no qualms in this regard. They will beat the living shit out of you and are not faint-hearted when it comes to abusing women and children who are in their custody, to get their way. I was fully aware of this and knew they would eventually torture my wife and girls if I held out too long. It was all about reading the tenor of my interrogations correctly and assessing just when to capitulate. I had to hold my tongue for a few days, that was for sure, so that the *okes* in South Africa could get their act together, but somehow I had to balance it very delicately.

I also had my own inner clock ticking. It had been agreed between our group in Zimbabwe that if ever one of us were arrested, for whatever reason, he would do his best not to start squealing for forty-eight hours. I say for 'whatever reason' simply because it's easy enough to be arrested for smuggling, say, which all of us were involved in (e.g. smuggling car spares and so on for sale in Zimbabwe and smuggling gold and currency back to South Africa, all for our personal gain and at our own risk) and while under interrogation for that minor crime you accidentally drop a clanger which results in all kinds of things being let out of the bag, i.e. sabotage, murder, possession of arms of war etc. So the deal we had was try to hold your tongue for two days in order to let the *manne* establish what was going on, especially as our runners had ways to do that via other sources in Harare. Then, after about two days and before serious interrogation commences and you have your head shoved into a bucket of water, you co-operate, knowing full well that whatever you reveal will fall back on you alone, while the other guys in your gang have bomb-shelled.

Its pure logic. Ask any cop. You pick up one member of a car-hijack gang for example, and you have got to be quite swift in order to catch the rest of the *skelms* from his gang because they are all going to hightail it. Any delay in follow-up and they're gone. When in the custody of the Zimbabwean security police there is no point in trying to play it tough when it comes to interrogation because they *will* break you, no matter what it takes. They will do anything. However, I knew full well that most of the time, the heavy-handed stuff only started after two or three days, especially when a high-profile case such as mine was involved. Hence we set our benchmark at forty-eight hours.

And this was a high-profile case, very much so! While locked in the stocks at Luveve, every thirty minutes or so my cell door would clang open while the cops came to check on me to see if I was still there, or just out of interest to have a dekko at this enigma. It was quite an occasion for them to have a white man in the cells and especially one who wore two pairs of leg-irons.

My home was reasonably sterile so I didn't worry myself too much when the CID arrived the next morning to take me to search the house. Stashed at my property I had some hand grenades and South African Defence Force communication radios down the well. I had a fake SA passport taped behind a rafter in the ceiling and a Textell 1000 telephone encryption device used for sending secret messages by phone in a built-in cupboard. I also had a large suitcase (left behind by Ronnie after a clandestine South African Air Force drop on a secluded farm in Matabeleland North a year or so earlier) containing about twenty large battery-operated, red flashing lights which we had used for guiding in clandestine aircraft and parachute drops by the South African military in the Zimbabwean bush at night.

The grenades and radio were not an immediate fuss. The well was about twenty metres deep with a little water in the bottom and I knew they would not rush to dive in there. (During my days as a serving policeman in Rhodesia and Zimbabwe, I had been an active member of the Police sub-aqua section and had dived and recovered many drowned people and police exhibits from wells throughout Matabeleland. I knew that diving down a well into pitch-black water was a very unpleasant task, one that the cops would only carry out as a last resort and only if they had good reason to do so.) The passport was well hidden, and is probably still taped to the rafter in that roof. The Textell was sort of a problem. But I felt I would be able to bullshit my way around that, as in appearance, it was much like a minature typewriter, similar to cell phones with a small keyboard that you could use for 'emails', and I would tell them that it was just a toy.

The flashing lights? Ja, well, no fine. I'd tell them that I used them on my fishing safaris to illuminate my floating platform boat on the Zambezi River! Wishy washy! I know. Who would believe that nonsense? But these were decisions I was making in anticipation, and were spur-of-the-moment, ducking-and-diving thoughts from a totally exhausted and very panic-stricken brain!

On arrival at my house with a huge convoy of cops and CIO in tow, and still in two pairs of leg-irons, and handcuffed, I was seriously dismayed to find the place literally crawling with police paramilitary guards armed to the teeth, bandoliers, the works! My wife was sitting handcuffed to my wrought-iron furniture; my kids were nowhere to be seen. I was not allowed to talk to her and even eye contact was impossible as we were kept too far apart. I desperately wanted to know where my daughters were. However, my anguished queries regarding them were rebuffed by the CID and CIO with comments like, "Let's see how you behave and we will tell you how they are," or "Don't worry about your children, worry about yourself," and such like, which only served to make me more anxious and frantic about them.

So they searched and searched, and turned the place upside down, and tossed the Textell aside on my assertion that it was just a toy. The Textell was in fact advanced technology for that era, maybe not in the USA, but certainly in backward Zimbabwe and was totally alien to these guys. So not understanding it, they never gave it a second thought.

True to form they never went near my well but there was a huge inquisition about the flashing lights. I tried to lie my way around them, but the detectives were having none of it and the lights were seized as evidence. Of what? I asked.

"We will let you know when we find out," was probably going through their minds.

I was yet to find out and they were yet to establish! I make light of this now, but at the time it was very serious.

They popped their heads into the ceiling which was obviously too hot and dusty and left it as is, false passport and all. Phew! My handguns, shotgun and rifles were seized as 'evidence', as well as their legitimate licences, my Zimbabwean passport, other documents, and such like. These always seem to be of great interest in cases like this, although their relevance in my experience has always been minimal. However, having been a cop most of my adult life I could relate to this activity of theirs. It was always the same—collect the travel documents, the guns, even if it was not a firearm case, and anything else you even remotely think as relevant—seize it!

I was chucked back into the Luveve police cells by a rather disillusioned bunch of cops who had obviously expected to come up with all sorts of spy and espionage goodies, such as guns, bombs and other paraphernalia. I can tell you I hadn't overlooked the fact that Stompie had also been arrested, just before me, and was obviously squealing, especially as he was not one of us 'forty-eight-hour' *okes*. And he did know a little about our activity, which was a numbing thought.

Later that day, while sitting on my own in the stocks, still wearing handcuffs and two leg-irons, my fears were realized when two people from CIO arrived carrying the Textell. "Why didnt you tell us about this, this morning, Kevin?" asked Nigel Kudzurunga. "Because it's just a toy?" I replied, swallowing my fear and embarrassment at being caught out in a blatant lie. "No it's not, it's for sending secret messages over the telephone," said Kudzurungu. "Rory has told us all about it."

Ja well, no fine, I thought. Fucked again!

Stompie (Rory) had in fact smuggled the Textell into Zimbabwe a few month before as a favour to Rat who needed it. I received it post-haste and as I was not doing a trip, asked Stompie to hide it in his dashboard for me. The Textell subsequently formed an important part of the state's case against me in my murder trial. So, thanks for that Stompie. But, my bro', I forgive you. Each man for himself and God help us all. Not so?

A day or two later Nigel Kudzurunga returned to my cell. This time he was carrying my Smith and Wesson .44 revolver (aka Dirty Harry). I owned this revolver, licensed and all legal, and used to sleep with it next to my bed, just in case I needed 'to make somebody's day'. "Kevin, how do you unload your cowboy gun?" he asked. I told him and he buggered off. Years later, after I had dodged the hangman's noose, I had my lawyers recover my licensed firearms from the police so that I could sell them and get some cash to keep me going in jail. But the .44 was nowhere to be found.

Nigel was a hold-over from the Rhodesian police, the BSAP and was quite well trusted by the Mugabe regime. He had obviously been scratching around my home on his own, picking up the odd thing for himself like the revolver, maybe my missing gold cufflinks, and a few other things while my wife and I were locked away. I wonder how many car accidents, vacant murder houses and storebreakings he stole from in his illustrious police career before joining the CIO? So, well done Nigel. I hope you enjoy my revolver, and maybe if there is any justice in this world, you use the wrong bullets, and it explodes in your hand. Being ex-BSAP, Nigel knew many former cops who are now in the covert world in South Africa, and it surprises me that he was not looked at very closely after my arrest. He used to profess to be a good friend of many ex-police members south of the Limpopo, but was always one of those who, 'smiles in your face, but hisses behind your back'.

When you bring in outsiders, even if they are friends, and let them know a little of what you're up to, especially when it's murder and sabotage, then you're looking for trouble. That's another dogma of mine. Too late she cried!

Grumpy was right in his assessment of Stompie. He had always warned that Stompie knew too much. At one stage Grumpy wanted Stompie removed from the scene—permanently—because he was deemed a serious security risk. It took some fancy footwork and sweet talking on my part to have that order cancelled.

Later that Monday and after the search of my house I wanted access to a lawyer—especially for my wife and children. This 'lawyer business' is always a subject that needs to be broached diplomatically with the Zimbabwean security apparatus—especially in a matter of Zimbabwean state security. In their minds access to a lawyer means you've got something to hide and is not a basic international human right, enshrined as it is in the Zimbabwean constitution no less. Granting you access to a legal representative is a condescension they make at their own discretion. They aren't very happy at the mention of the word 'lawyer'.

I was fully aware of this attitude the police had toward lawyers, however I was seriously worried about my family and felt I had no choice. True to form the investigating officer, Detective Chief Inspector Bernard Jambawu, fell out of his tree when I asked him to phone my lawyer, and I was given a very clear warning that outside interference by the legal fraternity would result in things going very bad for my family ... "You know all about this, Woods, don't you?" being the not-so-veiled caution.

This mantra was quickly taken up by the brass from the CID and CIO who were dealing with me. "Why do you want a lawyer? You say you are innocent of everything, so why do you need a lawyer?" and so on. Of course, when I subsequently went on trial for murder some ten months later and I mentioned this denial of access to a lawyer, I was called a liar by all the police involved who insisted under oath, "So help me God" that I had never ever asked for an attorney! The judge, Mugabe's best friend at the time, Wilson Sandura the hanging judge, went along with their stories and labelled me "a professional liar" before sending me off to the gallows. (Which was probably true. All of us in the cops, Special Branch and CIO, could lie through our teeth, especially when in court and under oath, but I really did ask for legal representation for my wife.)

At my trial later that year on a charge of murder, my attorneys told the court of the "frustration they encountered when trying to gain access to Mr. Woods" after they had been retained by friends who were worried about my family and me. (*Daily Gazette*, Wednesday, 3rd February 1993.)

The constitution of Zimbabwe in section 13 (3) provides that it was *my right to obtain and instruct, <u>without delay,</u> an attorney of my choice and hold communication with him.* However, the fact that it was my right to call my lawyer was of absolutely no consequence to the security personnel. Zimbabwe is a signatory to umpteen United Nations articles and conventions, some of which like the International Covenant of Civil and Political Rights declare the right to a lawyer. But this mattered not a bit to the Zimbabwean Gestapo as we all knew.

Further to this, their methods of coercing me into making confessions, by holding my family to ransom, with threats against their lives, is barred by principle 21 of the 1989 United Nations Body of Principles for the protection of all people under any form of detention or imprisonment, of which Zimbabwe is also a signatory. This prohibits the authorities from *taking advantage of a situation and subjecting the detained person to threats that cause him to incriminate himself.* Of course this is all bullshit in Zimbabwe. When you're arrested, all your rights, other than the ones the cops selectively want to afford you, fly out the window.

Come Tuesday morning a huge contingent of CID and CIO arrived at the new holding centre where I had been moved to in the dead of the previous night. Entumbane police station is still in the high-density suburbs of west Bulawayo, but was a little more modern than Luveve, not that this mattered much to the bed-lice population—the filthy cells and broken toilets were on a par.

My forty-eight-hour inner clock was still running, full speed. Nearly two full days and as if by magic they made it immediately plain to me that my time was up. "We have had enough of your nonsense, Woods. Stompie has told us everything [which I knew was probably quite a lot]. We are sending for your wife and children—you know we will do this and we will torture them in front of you if you do not co-operate."

Of course they denied this when I got to court. There they stood and said (under oath mind you) that I just rolled over and spilled the beans freely and voluntarily, without any duress. And believe it or not some of my co-accused also believed the cops' version of these events and labelled me a coward and a sell-out. You know who you are, don't you?

At any rate, it was time up. Mike and Barry (Bawden) had had their forty-eight hours, or close to, and Ronnie was already out of the country, having left soon after the explosion the week prior by SADF helicopter, which had uplifted him at night from near Beitbridge. So there was no one left from our group in Zimbabwe who would be at peril if I started confessing—which I did. I did not know that Ronnie had involved his brother in Harare, so when he was picked up later, it was not because of me.

I only had a couple of ANC attacks that I would confess to but I had to admit to enough to satisfy them—and I knew of a weapons cache which I knew would probably be enough to keep the peace.

As soon as I mentioned Mike and Barry and supplied their addresses the chase was on. (I didn't even know Smith's exact address, just the farming area where he worked.) The cops and the CIO were quite pissed at the delay because they also well knew that fellow members of a gang *always* high-tail it when one is caught. I didn't care—I knew Mike and Barry would be long gone—yeah sure!

A couple of hours later, during interrogation, I was absolutely devastated to be told by the investigating officer Chief Inspector Bernard Jambawu that my friends had been arrested at their normal places of residence! I felt sick. I couldn't believe it, and I was distraught, almost to tears, at the news. Again I asked myself, "What the fuck has gone wrong?"

What the fuck had gone wrong? Again and again. Why didn't they bomb-shell? I was only to find out much later, when we could eventually speak to each other, that Grumpy and his crowd had been giving Mike and Barry assurances that my arrest was no big deal and that they would be warned if the shit really did hit the fan! Sounds familiar, doesn't it? But I still find it incredulous—Barry had spoken to my eldest daughter on the Sunday evening of my arrest. (Apparently, later on the day of my arrest she and my youngest daughter had been handed to a friend for looking after while my wife was detained. I of course had not been told that my kids were not in jail.) My daughter told Barry that I'd been taken away by "lots of soldiers with guns". He told Grumpy this, yet still they were not given a cautionary order—"Okay, take cover till we see what's up". So they listened to Grumpy instead of following their natural instincts which should have been screaming at them to go to ground until the full story had been established. It was a mistake that cost them dearly.

Another dogma—follow your inner voice, or your instinct, call it what you will. Just listen to it!

The days following my detention and Barry's and Mike's arrest are a blur of interrogation and written statement after written statement with video recorders going full speed to get my so-called free-and-voluntarily-made confessions onto software.

৵ ৵ ৵

A few days into my detention I took Jambawu and an enormous entourage involving CID and CIO in unmarked vehicles, army and Support Unit troops in armoured trucks and police cars with sirens and blue lights flashing, on indications to a safe house in Bulawayo where we had an enormous arms cache. There must have been twenty vehicles all racing along, like a presidential convoy, as we hurtled through red traffic lights on our way to Waterford low-density suburb just east of the Bulawayo city centre.

The house I led them to had been rented by Ronnie and consisted of the main residence, a cottage and some outbuildings around a small swimming pool. Access to the property was down a couple of hundred metres of thin dirt track. Anyhow, we screeched to a halt in the parking area near the house and cottage, in a huge cloud of billowing dust, scattering chickens that were in the way. And there, standing on the verandah of the cottage, mouth agape, eyes popping out of his head and sheer shock all over his face was a youngster, Wayne, whom Ronnie had allowed to stay at the property for free just to keep a presence there and generally look after things like feeding the chickens and throwing some chemicals in the pool now and then. I couldn't help but laugh, seeing Wayne standing there rooted to the spot, with a glowing rolled-up *dagga* (marijuana) cigarette in his fingers! He nearly shat himself, thinking this strike force had pitched up, to arrest him for having a joint!

I had forgotten about Wayne, and had therefore not forewarned the cops about him, so they immediately overreacted and he ended up with his face in the dust, guns sticking in his face and leg-irons and handcuffs on his limbs. The cops cooled down a little when I told them he was just a caretaker who knew nothing, and didn't even have keys to the main house. But this certainly cured his drug habit. He was to spend about a year in detention at Chikurubi until the police were convinced he was not involved.

We couldn't find keys to the main house and had to break into the place where the arms cache was recovered in the two spare rooms. The cache certainly impressed the cops. It consisted of twenty-kilogram gas cylinders containing high explosive, TNT landmines, AK rifles, RPG rocket launchers with rockets, PKM automatic rifles, rifle magazines, flares, Tokarev pistols, radios, thousands of rounds of ammunition, hand grenades, flares, slabs of high explosive and so on, and of course another suitcase of red flashing lights, identical to those found at my house! There were also a couple of silenced Colt .45 revolvers and some 'cardboard' which was actually Semtex explosive on which all and sundry tramped, thinking it was just old boxes, until I pointed out to them exactly what they were standing on.

On Thursday 21st January, five days after my arrest, I was allowed to speak to my lawyer. This was not a normal lawyer/client interview that you see on television where the crook gets to speak to his lawyer in private. Does not happen. I had to speak with him in the company of armed policemen, and both he and I were under strict instruction not to talk about my arrest. All he could do was give me a few bananas and see that I hadn't been physically harmed.

Now according to hanging Judge Sandura at my murder trial later that year, that interview with my lawyer, which lasted about thirty seconds, apparently amounted to privileged access.

Seventeen days later my co-accused and I were transported to Harare in marked police cars, flashing lights and all. After a few days in the cells at Harare Central police station, we were taken to court. Once in court the statements we had made to the police—before we'd even met our lawyers for that thirty seconds and while our relatives were in detention under ransom—were confirmed by the magistrate as having been made freely, voluntarily and without any duress. I suppose this process can be compared to elections in Zimbabwe, where the voting population is beaten, intimidated, starved and psychologically defeated before they even get near a polling booth, and then the state says the elections are free and fair ... and of course some foreign observers agree.

Our wives and families who had been arrested, and who had been detained simply as ransom for our co-operation, were subsequently released after we had signed our statements indicating that we were making our confessions freely, voluntarily and without any outside interference at all. Some of our other relatives who had been picked up in the frenzy that followed our arrest were held in detention for many months before being released, and without ever seeing the inside of a courtroom.

I was sentenced to death on 18th December 1988. They don't use the words, "You are sentenced to death" in Zimbabwe—the judge just said, "You are convicted of murder with constructive intent for which there is only one sentence." Then, he just stood up and walked out.

I was alone that day. My family was not with me, specifically at my request. That was all the protection I could give them during that dreadful time of my sentencing. I just could not bear having them there when I was led downstairs.

My very first reaction on being sentenced to death by the judge was to murmur under my breath, "and fuck you too". But later, when I got back to jail and was locked up naked for the first time in the death cells, my greatest fear was for my kids, my wife and my dear old mom, who was quite frail at the time (and who passed away while I was still in jail some years later). How were they going to cope with this? I had such a huge, overwhelming sense of dread for them and of how it would be when given my final visit with my wife and kids before the bastards hanged me.

So, a short while later I found myself in Chikurubi Maximum Security Prison, just outside Harare. I was to spend the next seventeen and a half years there. A prison where I, as a policeman and Central Intelligence Organization officer, had been sending criminals and political opponents to President Mugabe for many years. It's a hard transition from policeman to prisoner.

We were placed in the old punishment block at Chikurubi, where there were single cells. One of the inmates there was a former ZANLA guerrilla, Lovemore Chimoio. He had been jailed for murder in 1981—soon after independence, when, still with his hatred of white people coursing his veins, he had murdered a white commercial farmer and his family near Rusape in eastern Zimbabwe. In a particularly gruesome touch he had severed the victims' heads and left them upright on the dining-room table. He was sentenced to life imprisonment rather than the death sentence on the grounds that being straight out of the bush and the liberation struggle, he was not entirely responsible for his own actions. And he was a bit *mal* (mad) too. He and I spent some sime talking and reminiscing. I thought that helping him might result in a few brownie points for us so I drafted him a petition for clemency and smuggled it out to Vice-President Simon Muzenda. To his delight and to our total surprise, a month later he received a full presidential pardon and was released—never to be heard of by any of us again until a year later when he was arrested and imprisoned for cattle theft.

As I was led through Chikurubi's massive brass-studded doors into that cold place, I still had a flame of hope burning inside me—that I would not be abandoned by the South Africans. I still clung, very tightly, onto the assurances I had been given and had therefore expected to be looked after, especially where getting out of jail was concerned. Surely, failing all else, the South Africans would negotiate with Robert Mugabe for my release? I mean, I was not the first spy from the CIO working for the South Africans to be arrested and detained in Chikurubi.

In the early 1980s two white CIO officers, Philip Hartlebury and Colin Evans from CIO headquarters, had been arrested for spying for South Africa and after a couple of years they had both been released and deported there, as a result of some sort of political wheeling and dealing between the South Africans and Robert Mugabe, so why not me?

Sure, I'd have to bite the bullet and get through a couple of years at the most. I accepted that. There was an alternative to a negotiated release, after all. Escape! And it's not as though a jail-break was a novelty either ...

≈≈≈

In August 1982, a South African Reconnaissance Commando group infiltrated Zimbabwe. They did so to either free some former ZIPRA detainees that they wanted to integrate with others being trained in South Africa, or were on a sabotage mission to destroy some of Mugabe's diesel-electric locomotives near Mabalauta in the southeast of the country, thereby keeping him reliant upon South Africa for rail haulage and routes. The thinking behind this second option was that instead of allowing Mugabe to have his own locos that used routes through Mozambique, thus becoming more self-reliant, they wanted him totally dependent on South Africa for things like fuel and food imports. But in my mind was the former theory that they had entered Zimbabwe to free people from jail.

Unfortunately, their group was ambushed by a Zimbabwean army contingent about forty kilometres into Zimbabwe in the Sengwa Communal Lands, and three sergeants: R. T. Beech, P. D. Barry, and J. A. Wessels, were killed. The three had been accompanied by a dozen or so 'turned' former ZIPRA gooks who survived the initial ambush. The bodies of the three soldiers were recovered by the Zimbabwe National Army and flown to Harare for the normal beating of chests, crocodile tears and propaganda circus by the Zimbabwean regime.

Denials immediately started flying all over the place, especially from South Africa's Foreign Affairs and the South African military that this was not an authorized mission. (Isn't this a cliché we have all heard over the subsequent years?)

Many years later, in 1997, and in reference to this episode, Pik Botha told the Truth Commission: "This issue brought the deteriorating relations between us and Zimbabwe almost to boiling point. The Department of Foreign Affairs and I learned of the killing of the three South African troops in Zimbabwe when Mr. Mugabe made an announcement to that effect on 21st August 1982. My

Director-General obtained as much information as he could about the incident from our trade representative in Harare and then we sent a letter to the chief of the defence force in which we told him, look, we have now heard this has happened and this is going to be very bad for South Africa. We told him this incident would give renewed impetus to Mugabe's constant allegations that South Africa was responsible for the sabotage attempts in Zimbabwe.

"I told him that channels of communication with the Zimbabwean government would be made very difficult by this. I then asked the defence chief for information on this incident. To which General Constand Viljoen reacted at a press conference and admitted that the three men were troops of the South African Defence Force who were on an unauthorized mission *to free political detainees*. So I do not know what the truth is about that mission.

"The other question was about the return of the bodies of the three men, a matter that was never resolved, and I ask this matter be taken further due to the improved relations between the two governments, so that the relatives and families of the three men can come to rest with their anxiety. I had forwarded a previous request for the repatriation of their bodies to the Zimbabwean government but had received no response. And I know that some years later, the relatives of Sergeant Beech, hoping that somehow he was still alive, had requested the help of the International Committee of the Red Cross who in 1989 wrote to the Zimbabwean government and despite several follow-up letters received no response."

One would wonder why Pik would have to write to General Viljoen when they sat around the same State Security Council table every week ...

After the Zimbabwean regime had milked this propaganda-wise to the fullest extent, the bodies of the three soldiers were cremated in Harare (so the story goes) and despite numerous diplomatic overtures from South Africa their remains have never been returned.

Earlier in the 1980s I know that KD and some of his group, together with some of our lot, had carried out a spectacular jail-break in Harare. And I of course, believing in my friends in South Africa, desperately clung to the hope that a plan would be made, somewhere, somehow, for my liberation and that of my co-accused, using military force, if needs be.

In 1981, the South African military had destroyed the Zimbabwe National Army's main armoury and heavy ammunition storage facility at Inkomo Barracks just outside Harare. In the subsequent police and CIO investigation of the sabotage, a ZNA captain, and, so it seems, a South African military agent, Patrick Gericke, were arrested, tortured and detained at Harare Central police station.

A Zimbabwe Republic Police Detective Inspector Varkevisser, was the investigating officer. On instructions from his bosses in the South African Military Intelligence, KD planned an operation to free Gericke, who was languishing in the cells at Harare Central police station while the case was being investigated. In those days there was a state of emergency in Zimbabwe, carried over from the Rhodesian-war days. This allowed the police and CIO to detain a person, any person for that matter, for as long as they wanted without taking them to court, and without charging them with any crime. This was the fatal flaw the police made with Gericke. Had they taken him to court and had he been remanded to prison, as the law provides, he would have been out of reach. But acting in true form, the police abused the detention laws while they took their time to complete their investigation.

The escape operation formulated by KD involved both the South African Air Force and its military people. A few of the operatives who had infiltrated Zimbabwe, using false passports via Harare International Airport and Beitbridge border post, approached Varkevisser one dark night as he emerged from his favourite watering hole. At the barrel of a gun they equipped him with a special belt that was fitted with a clasp that would explode should he try to remove it without its key, which they told him he would only receive if he totally co-operated. He was then ordered to go and book Gericke out of the police cells. This was not uncommon. Each prisoner could be taken out of the police cells, without suspicion, by his respective investigating officer, at any time, day or night. As added incentive, as if he needed one with an explosive belt around his waist, Varkevisser's wife and children had earlier that evening been kidnapped from his home and taken to a private landing strip outside Harare, where a fixed-wing South African Air Force plane was waiting, propellers turning. He really didn't have a choice—piece of cake.

Gericke was booked out of the cells and actually protested a bit at the late hour, as he thought he was going to be taken out and shot, as does happen in Zimbabwe when political cases need a quick solution. This was in fact something Varkevisser had been threatening to do as Gericke was not too easy a prisoner to crack.

They went downstairs to the unmarked car he used and Varkervisser took Gericke to a pre-arranged rendezvous where KD and company drove them to the aircraft and off they flew to South Africa. Varkevisser was recompensed from the Military Intelligence secret account for the loss of his house and furniture, car, dogs, cats, budgies, and his police pension. Gericke took up an SADF job, a relieved and liberated man. And everybody lived happily ever after! Well nearly. Varkevisser died a few years later from cancer and, annoyingly for some white members of the Zimbabwe Republic Police who were still serving in Zimbabwe, promotions for them were frozen as a result of this perceived treachery by Varkevisser.

During my first month or so at Chikurubi it became patently obvious to me that the officer in charge of the prison had immense authority. Thinking about this and as soon as I had sussed out the situation, I smuggled a few letters to KD and Grumpy. It was my idea, considering the authority the prison boss had, that they repeat the modus operandi as per Gericke, with my colleagues and me. It would have worked like a dream. Under appropriate duress, the officer in charge could easily have given the instruction for us to be removed from our cells and handed over to whomever, outside the prison. The South Africans had fake Zimbabwean police, army, prison and air force uniforms, so it wouldn't have been that difficult to plan and carry out, especially as immediately after our detention at Chikurubi the security surrounding us was pretty lax.

I knew an external jail-break operation like this would first have to be sanctioned by the South African president, P. W. Botha and his State Security Council. However, I was confident that the old crocodile was totally honourable when it came to his men on the ground, and deep in my bones I knew that his agreement for our extraction from prison would not be a hurdle.

I had a little history to place my bets on with this as he had pulled all stops to obtain the freedom of Recce Captain Wynand du Toit, who had been captured in Angola a few years earlier during South Africa's Operation *Argon* in that country. In that case, the French government brokered to swap du Toit for 130 Angolan soldiers who were being held by Unita in the Angolan bush and two other ANC activists who were detained, one in Pretoria and the other jailed in the former South African semi-independent homeland of Ciskei.

After his release, Pik Botha was quick to jump into the limelight and personally escorted du Toit from Maputo to Cape Town on one of the presidential jets for a huge reception with President Botha.

President Botha had also negotiated for the release of the two other CIO/ South African operatives mentioned earlier, Philip Hartlebury and Colin Evans. They had been arrested in Harare a few years earlier on suspicion of involvement with the Joe Gqabi assassination and the bombing of Mugabe's headquarters in

Manica Road, Harare. As usual, their confessions had been obtained while being subjected to severe and brutal torture, so when they had their day in court, their confessions, obtained under duress, were thrown out. Undeterred as always, the government had them re-arrested immediately after acquittal and despite numerous approaches from the South African government for their release, in exchange for Russian spies and Angolan soldiers held in South Africa; it would be four years before the deal was sweet enough for Mugabe to agree to. But at least the South Africans had persevered.

Mugabe's headquarters in Harare had been blown up on 18th December 1981, in what many assessed as an attempt on his and his ruling clique's lives, as he was supposed to meet there that day with his Central Committee. Mugabe was a bit late in arriving on that day and protocol would not allow the Central Committee to preceed him into the venue, so they all dodged the bomb which killed at least six people on the street outside and in nearby shops and injured many others.

The South African government has never admitted complicity in this attack, and even after years of pub talk I could not throw any light on the perpetrators, suggesting to me that this was probably an internal factional operation because of the divisions in Mugabe's party which had already begun to surface way back then. And there were also serious squabbles going on with Joshua Nkomo and his political party, who were quite capable militarily and logistically to carry out such an attack.

In our case, it transpired that President Botha did agree to an extraction plan for us, on condition that his military commanders ensured that the operation could be completely denied and no security force members or equipment traceable to the SADF was used. (Despite P. W. Botha's authorization of the extraction Pik Botha, the then South African foreign minister, is still insistent that our anti-ANC operation in Zimbabwe was not sanctioned by the South African government—why go to all the trouble to rescue us then? Unless, of course Pik was once again out of the loop?)

అం అం అం

On 26th January 1994, South African President F. W. de Klerk and President Robert Mugabe met in Gaborone, just prior to the installation of the ANC government in South Africa. Following this meeting, which was the first ever between the two presidents, South Afria's justice minister, Kobie Coetzee, who had publicly insisted all along that we had not been involved in authorized operations, came to Harare—the first ministerial visit by a South African minister since 1980, and held wide-ranging talks with my two nemeses, Emmerson Mnangagwa and Dumiso Dabengwa.

After the meeting Mnangagwa said that our fate had been discussed (why, if we were not South African agents?) but he did infer that there would be no speedy resolution of the issue, probably because of the wishy-washy denial attitudes of these South African ministers. So, on one hand you've got the South African government using us in simultaneous raids on three Frontline State capital cities in 1986, which they claim responsibility for, then they try and spring us from jail, then later de Klerk talks to Mugabe about our release but all the while you've got some of these security ministers denying we were ever part of their team.

The operation to spring us from maximum security was accordingly approved under the code-name Operasie *Direksie* which took place a few months later, but not according to my suggestion.

Under the command of Colonel Joe Verster, KD and his people increduously went ahead and made a plan which was approved by the State Security Council without taking into cognizance the opinion of someone actually on the ground and inside the jail.

I must admit though their plan was quite good. A few months after my move to Chikurubi I started receiving messages from KD, either by coded letters which slipped past the official prison censor or in smuggled letters via the guards. In the correspondence I was told that an escape attempt was going to be made by the South African government involving him and others. All we were to do was keep as fit as possible, and make sure we were handcuffed to one another and not to a local common criminal when in transit to court for our bi-monthly remand appearance. My co-accused and I stuck to a very strict exercise regime. Press-ups, sit-ups and jogging in a small figure-eight circuit for kilometres on end—each and every day. No booze and healthy food from our relatives, which we were still allowed to receive as we were not yet convicted prisoners, added to our fitness.

The planning and the fixed date of the escape remained secret; however, from within my limited perspective I guessed 30th June 1988 was our day. I knew basically, that the prison vehicle taking us to court would be stopped and the guards persuaded to hand us over, after which we would be extracted to South Africa. But exactly how it was to go down was a mystery. As you can imagine, with total expectation of freedom the next day, there was no sleep that night of 29th June.

Thursday 30th June 1988 dawned a cold, clear and crisp mid-winter morning. With huge amounts of adrenaline pumping through my system, I'd sanitized my cell, as had the other *okes*, so that after we'd bust out, and during the huge cover-ass interrogation that was sure to follow in the jail, nothing even remotely implicating our prior knowledge of the escape would be found.

Without a hint of suspicion we were taken to the reception area of the prison and from there handcuffed together and led to the prison Grey Mariyah waiting outside. No guards fussing, no guns, all was quiet. As we were led out from the huge brass-studded, wooden entrance door to the prison (the doors that seem part of every prison), a helicopter belonging to the Zimbabwean Air Force passed overhead. This was being flown, I established later, by Flight Lieutenant Gary Kane, who had been recruited by the South Africans to 'borrow' one of Mugabe's precious Bell helicopters. This was then going to be used to uplift us from the prison Grey Mariyah, which was to be stopped en route to court, and would convey us to a rural landing strip west of Harare where a South African Air Force Dakota was on stand-by, engines turning over, to convey us and Kane to South Africa.

I've subsequently established that P. W. Botha had also authorized a flight of South African Air Force Mirage jets, which were at that time high over Zimbabwe, concentrated around Thornhill air base in Gweru where Mugabe's Hawk fighter jets were stationed, to prevent any of them taking to the sky.

A couple of hundred metres above us, Flight Lieutenant Kane was watching us get into the back of the prison truck. The door was slammed shut and a small padlock attached to the hasp and staple and we were off. The Bell helicopter followed us in the paddy wagon and followed it … and followed it … All the while he was fully aware that the air traffic controllers at New Sarum and Harare International Airport, on the other side of Harare were watching him on their radar. He also knew that he was in a chopper that was getting hotter by the minute, as his unauthorized 'borrowing' of the helicopter would very soon become evident to the operations room at Harare's Zimbabwean Air Force base, New Sarum.

To his complete credit, Kane stuck with us right until we entered the built-up areas of Harare when he finally realized that our rescue mission had gone balls-up. He dropped to the ground close to the prison we had just left and picked up a few of the other team members, with whom he had no radio communication, but could see hanging around their allotted positions. They were still in the dark and didn't know that things had gone wrong because the vehicle with their communication radios had not pitched up. Finally throwing in the towel, Kane then flew to Chegutu where a South African military plane painted in civilian colours was waiting. (He could not just fly back to New Sarum and say, "Here is your chopper, thanks for letting me take it for a spin.")

After landing the Bell Agusta helicopter some of the guys, in a totally unnecessary and irresponsible action, gave the chopper a quick squirt with 9mm bullets, just to give Robert Mugabe the finger. Their version, which I suppose carried some credibility, is that they wanted to disable the chopper to prevent any follow-up as they took off into the sunset in their South African Dakota. Quite a few bullets hit the helicopter and totally wrecked it, but horrifyingly one 9mm round from this little coup de grâce ricocheted about a kilometre away and hit a little girl, injuring her badly. Immediately Mugabe's propaganda machine went into overdrive about the, "callous shooting of this little girl".

Meanwhile back at Chikurubi, as we were being driven out and sitting in the rear of the paddy wagon, we saw a white sedan parked near the prison gate with a bulky, bearded white *oke*, surrepticiously checking under the bonnet. My heart was a thumping roller coaster. As we drove past I caught sight of him nonchalantly closing the bonnet, getting back inside and falling in behind our vehicle.

All we needed now was for someone to stop the prison truck. And it had to happen along this short, desolate stretch of tarmac as one immediately leaves the prison, rather than on the busier roads leading into Harare. So all had come together! It was happening. Rock 'n' roll time! We drove and drove, reached the main Arcturus Road into town, turned into it, and there, my soul fell.

There was no way that the front ambush party would be here on the main double highway. Something had gone wrong. We drove into Harare, right through the central business district and reached the court. We were unshackled and locked into the court cells where we sat, hopelessly looking at one another and wondering what had gone wrong. Had the operation been cancelled at the last moment? Or was it something else? What? No, it had to have been a last-minute cancellation. Still, the *manne* would do it on the next run to court in fourteen days. Suddenly that little bubble was burst as scores of Support Unit paramilitary and army troops, all agitated and armed to the teeth, stormed into the court premises, with many of them positioning themselves right outside the cell door where we were held. We could hear shouting and the drumming of running boots as they crawled all over the court building, totally surrounding the place.

We were finished, that's all I knew. The vehicle or the *okes* that formed the front ambush had not arrived. As the day wore on, all other prisoners were removed from the court premises leaving us five for last, and then under heavy air, military and police escort we were returned to Chikurubi Maximum, split up and locked up.

ஜ ஜ ஜ

All this happened in Harare while there was another parallel drama unfolding in Botswana. The CCB (South Africa's innocuously named Civil Co-operation Bureau) people who had made the decisions regarding this operation (Joe and his merry *okes*), had, in their wisdom, recruited a dozen mercenaries to execute the escape. I have recently learned that a budget of around seven million rand was made available for our escape.

Numerous former Rhodesian police and army personnel who knew all or some of us had volunteered to help with our extraction, for free—for friendship and 'old times' sake'. But no—the decision to recruit mercenaries was final—and by the time KD took over the operation with Grumpy, they found the recruitment complete and only the planning outstanding.

The day before in Botswana, two mercenaries, Sam and Jim, were carrying the communication radios, which were needed for communication on the ground and with the helicopter during our escape, hidden in their vehicle. They were pressed for time to get across Botwana, through Kazungula border post, into Zimbabwe and up to Harare to deliver their cargo for the mission. They initially had two days for the trip, and there are several versions as to why it had become a race across that vast southern African country. According to some versions they were on a pub-crawl across Botswana and fell behind with their schedule after having one too many at Nata Lodge instead of getting to Harare, while others have said it was simply logistics, all botched up. The simple fact is, that they had the radios but didn't get to Harare.

Sam, one of the mercs, was to join us in Chikurubi, and I spoke to him in detail some years later after I was off death row—his version is a mixture of both. I don't really think they would have gotten paralytic; they are both experienced soldiers and knew it was quite a dangerous mission that they had signed up for. But the fact remains …

Sam told me they arrived at the Botswanan-Zambian-Zimbabwean border junction late in the afternoon and accidently boarded the river ferry over the Zambezi to Zambia! Once across they realized that they had made a balls-up and had gone to the wrong country. They promptly re-boarded the ferry and returned to Botswana, obviously thereby raising a few eyebrows.

Back in Botswana they found the short road to the Kazungulu (Botswanan-Zimbabwean side) entry post, arriving a few minutes after 1800 hours, which was just after closing time. Whereupon, while pleading with the border officials and emphasizing that they had to get to Harare that night, they created a little too much fuss to be let into Zimbabwe, obviously chucking in a few lame excuses for the urgency that couldn't wait until the morning.

Patently curious and a little suspicious of their intent, the Zimbabwean immigration authorities allowed them to enter but then promptly summoned the customs and CIO officials at Kazungula to come and have a look.

The vehicle that Sam and Jim were using had been specially purchased for the operation and contained quite a lot of camping gear, as decoy material, but also contained some concealed panels in the door compartment which held the military communication radios sealed in foam. These were well disguised although a thorough search would probably have eventually resulted in their discovery.

Most of the other equipment (other weapons, vehicles hired for the purpose, fake police and army uniforms and so on) needed for the escape was already in Harare with the other operatives who were taking part in the operation but the radios were a crucial part of the operation.

Their vehicle was taken into the police compound where it was driven onto a service pit for an underneath inspection. Sam and Jim could probably have brazened it out and we would have been free, but their nerves failed them when the customs people started tapping the inside of the doors and going through the motions of attempting to open them. This mercenary life is not for the faint-hearted, but I suppose in that position, nearly everyone would have taken to their heels … which they did.

The two bolted for the Zambezi River some 100 metres away, and with the immigration, customs and CIO in hot pursuit, they plunged into the darkening, crocodile-infested waters and swam across to Zambia.

With no Mark Spitz among the pursuers, a short while later, they again braved the dark and fast-flowing river, this time heading upstream into Botswana.

They made it! They crawled out onto the Botswanan bank and hid out among the reeds while trying to check out if there was any pursuit still in the offing. Sensing no real danger they hid out in the sticks for the night and then walked the short distance to the small town of Kasane where they managed to hire a light aircraft to carry them back across the country to the capital of Gaborone in the south.

Why they didn't contact KD and arrange a secure extraction from the Kasane area is anybody's guess—at least it would have given the Bell Agusta's helicopter pilot, Kane, in Harare, time to stand down his own part of the operation and not check out the helicopter, (as he did have authority for his own flights), in the hope of a re-run later. Kasane, in northern Botswana, is just a river-width from The Caprivi Strip, which in those years was part of South Africa and crawling with South African troops. A helicopter was literally a stone's throw away.

At Gaborone International the two bought air tickets and phoned through to their handlers in Jo'burg. It was decided that catching the flight would be too risky, so they were told to wait out the day and after dark walk along the main power lines, a short stroll of some twenty kilometres, back into South Africa. There was a permanent Botswanan Defence Force roadblock on the main road between Gaborone and the border, so they were told to stick to the power lines, which run parallel to the road.

Later that evening the two intrepid mercs got their act together and off they went, following instructions and walking along the electricity grid. Unfortunately Sam was taking a little strain. He had a marked limp from an old war wound which had been compounded by all the exertion of the past few days—dodging hippos and crocodiles through the thick reeds along the Zambezi River hadn't helped his condition at all. He chose the easier route of walking along the side of the main road, while Jim stuck to the rougher terrain along the power lines. Soon enough Sam's luck ran out and he walked into the Botswanan Defence Force roadblock and was arrested. Jim walked the rest of the way along the power lines and crossed into South African territory near Kopfontein.

The night of 29th June was not too pleasant for Sam who was brutally tortured. He revealed the details of our escape operation to the Botswanan authorities who then drove him to the Zimbabwean border post at Plumtree the next morning and handed him over to the Zimbabwean Central Intelligence Organization.

Sam underwent a short but very cruel interrogation in Plumtree and just as quickly the shit hit the fan in Harare where we were sitting absolutely dejected at the Harare court building, having been driven there with our hearts in our mouths in the completely unguarded prison Grey Mariyah a few hours earlier.

And it all fell apart because some *okes* either went on the piss instead of doing the job they were paid to do or because the logistics hadn't been planned well enough and therefore there were no communications for the operatives in Harare. Why there hadn't been a duplication of radio communication devices, by a secondary route in Harare, is again a question that remains unanswered.

The huge lesson here in my rather subjective opinion, (I say 'subjective', simply because that fuck-up cost me twenty years of my life) is that when you have a difficult job to perform and it's one that requires a little determination and dedication, use people who have their hearts in the right place. Money alone does not always deliver the best results. And make sure the timing of everything is correct too. Because, as we all know, even out here in the hustle and bustle of normal life, when you're in a hurry to get somewhere there are going to be delays—lost keys, traffic jams, whatever. Isn't it amazing they only happen when you're late? Plan correctly, leave a bit earlier and then everything is as smooth as a baby's ass.

కో కో కో

Back at Chikurubi that night, you could have heard a pin drop among our cells as we all sat alone and contemplated our fate. I knew that it was now all over … at least for some considerable time. There was no way another escape would be planned, certainly not with the enormous security blanket now enveloping us. I also knew that a murder trial now awaited me, sure as night follows day.

Over the next few weeks Chikurubi saw some serious transformation as, after the horse had tried to bolt, the security surrounding us was turned up, considerably. Extra perimeter fences with kilometres of razor wire were installed around the prison; closed-circuit TV cameras that had been broken for years were repaired; army bunkers were quickly dug and sandbagged and 12.7mm DSKA and 37mm single-barrelled AAA anti-air guns were placed around the perimeter. In addition to this, permanent police, army and CIO personnel were stationed among the prison guards. And this tight security was to stay in effect for the rest of my incarceration, some nineteen years-plus. Even after the new dispensation in South Africa, the frenetic security blanket was enforced despite the basic logic that with Nelson Mandela now as president of South Africa there would be no more escape high jinks.

It was quite ridiculous really. I mean, who was going to rescue me, after the old South African government that I served was gone? Ten, even fifteen years after death row, and South Africa with Nelson Mandela as president and then Thabo Mbeki, the Zimbabwean authorities still carried on as if there might be an imminent invasion to spring me from jail. Every time I set foot outside of the prison walls, be it to go for a tooth filling or a heart check, I'd be taken in an armoured vehicle, bristling with guns. Quite often with air cover too! And the premises I'd be taken to, be it a dental surgery or doctor's rooms, would have been physically searched and cordoned off, just in case there was a detachment of commandos hiding in the alleyway, ready to spirit me away.

To illustrate this attitude, I will relate how in 2003 I managed to get a court application into the Zimbabwean Supreme Court seeking heart treatment in South Africa. The Zimbabwean minister of justice, Patrick Chinamasa (who notoriously, a few years later was shoved in parliament by MDC member Roy Bennett, causing him to slip and fall on the floor, after he had called Bennett and his ancestors thieves for stealing all the productive farm land from the black people of Zimbabwe a hundred years before), told the Supreme Court in answer to my application that I was more of a risk to Zimbabwe in 2003 than I had originally been when I was a double agent and saboteur some fifteen years prior during the days of the former South African apartheid era!

Not satisfied with that, he went on to insinuate that my South African citizenship was not legitimate (yet amazingly, on the date of my release, I suddenly became a South African citizen and was immediately deported) and, in reference to another part of my application, that I had never been held in Chikurubi in solitary confinement. (As you will see in a separate chapter, I was locked up naked in Chikurubi's death row for five years, alone and in a cell measuring 1.2 metres x 4 metres for about twenty-three hours of every day. From my cell I could not see if it was day or night, and had no form of communication with the outside world except for the occasional fifteen-minute visit from my wife—if that is not solitary confinement, tell me what is!)

Continuing with this wisdom, Chinamasa rambled on to the judges of the Zimbabwean Supreme Court that the stress which caused my heart attack was self-inflicted, that public interest demanded I remain in prison for life, that it must not be forgotten I was a murderer and that I should be grateful that the death sentence had not been carried out on me, pronouncing also in his opinion (as a heart specialist I suppose) that in fact I had no heart problem and my release from prison was unthinkable. If it were not so serious it would be funny.

They see ghosts behind every bush. No matter how short-staffed the prisons were, and no matter how short of vehicles, every time one guard would have sufficed, I had twenty or more escorting me to hospital or to the dentist, with red flashing lights and sirens blaring. And every time I left the confines of the prison I'd be handcuffed, leg-ironed and shackled to a guard.

Who was going to try and rescue me? After the end of the apartheid government I'd worked for? Who? And if I made my own plan to escape where would I go? If I ever managed to run away I would have stuck out like a sore thumb as the suburbs surrounding Chikurubi are all high-density areas occupied by the black population of Harare. A white man, dressed in white canvas prison garb, high-tailing it through there would have been rather easy to spot.

The security they had in place for my nineteen and a half years years must have cost an arm and a leg, which the impoverished prison service couldn't afford, when you think of it, which I do. You have hundreds of prisoners dying monthly of Aids, TB and other diseases, many of whom who would have survived if the prison's financial resources had been put to better use, be it for anti-retroviral drugs, other drugs, or just better nutrition. Instead, they wasted a fortune with ill-founded and excessive security measures … for me!

Chikurubi was built by the Rhodesian government in the late 1970s, and by its physical structure is quite impenetrable and extremely difficult to escape from. There are scores of doors—you cannot walk from one side of the prison to the other without going through numerous solid wooden doors, all of which have to be opened by a single officer sitting either side of the door. Electronically opening doors do not exist in Chikurubi or in any other correctional facility in Zimbabwe.

There is no electronic central control room which controls the doors. Each and every door has its own key and its own guard on the one side, with a little peephole drilled into the centre to check through. It is totally medieval, but highly effective. It is impossible to run from section to section of the prison because of this simple routine.

South African correctional services with all their mod cons and control rooms overseeing all doors and the movement of prisoners would do well to go back to these basics. There are scores of jailbreaks in South Africa each year and all that's needed to prevent these most of the time, is an extra locked door barring the way, to which another person holds the key.

This is not to say it is impossible to escape from Chikurubi. Now that I am no longer there, the anti-aircraft guns have been removed, but the fences and razor wire and cameras (when they have power) remain. Anyone with the resources to get an armoured helicopter to uplift you from the exercise yard near the large halls could do it. The authorities had foreseen this while I was there and the exercise yard where I was held was covered with an enormous steel-bar overhead structure. But the other exercise yards remain open to the sky, so does the centre court, a large area that all prisoners have access to. Many times a week those same prisoners will walk around the centre court, open to the sky. A little planning and timing and off you go … so long as you have a helicopter. Which I didn't.

There was a prison break at Chikurubi in 1998. It was everything out of the movies too—daring and deadly. A group of former Zimbabwean soldiers, who had been jailed for a string of armed robberies and murders under the leadership of Stephen Chidumo, did the unthinkable. They were held on the second floor of F Hall, adjacent to where I was held in FA Hall. They had smuggled in a piece of heavy-duty hacksaw blade which had been hidden inside a large tube of toothpaste (after this escape large toothpaste tubes were banned … the stable-door syndrome).

The authorities at the prison were constantly fixated with the security surrounding my colleagues and me that they allowed security to lapse in other sections of the prison. In one such instance they had jailed Chidumo and his gang members together in the same cell. Over a period of a few days one of Chiduno's gang remained hidden upstairs in F Hall during unlock (0700 to 1500 hours), simply by stripping naked and hiding in the ablution area where most of the lights were out of order. No prisoners are allowed back in their cells during unlock and that's why he had to conceal himself in the dark until the rest of the prisoners had been let out into the exercise yard where they would remain until lock-up at 1500 each day.

Over the next few days, for six hours each day he patiently and laboriously cut through the steel bars and mesh of the cell where he and Chidumo slept. Once he had sawn through the mesh and bars, he secured the loose piece in place with a few small pieces of string and then hung a towel over the whole section. A lot of the prisoners would have washing on the mesh fence of the cell each day so this specific towel aroused no suspicion.

The difficult part was then to saw through a single bar on the inner centre-court side of the passage opposite the cell he and Chidumo occupied. This was a little tricky as, being on the inside, that part of the hall is exposed to the centre court and should someone walking there look up at the right time they would see him sawing away. So he had to leopard-crawl down to the end of the passage that was partially obscured from most of the prison and there, lying on his side and naked to keep camouflaged in the gloom of the passageway, he did his deed.

Through sheer determination and a lot of luck he did it, making only one cut and leaving the 25mm bar in place, needing only to be bent upwards to leave a gap sufficient for one thin man to get through. And most prisoners in the Zimbabwean prisons are thin.

Time was now of the essence for Chidumo and his group. These cuts in the metal would have been detected during a cell search by the officers or by one of the sell-out prisoners who spend their whole lives snooping around the jail, trying to catch people up to nonsense in order to gain brownie points with the guards.

Chidumo and his three co-escapees chose the dead of night a day or so later to break out. Three o'clock in the morning is the best time to try anything like this—the guards change over at 0200 hours and guaranteed are dead to the world by three. There was only one guard on duty in Chidumo's hall, but a full complement of guards in my adjacent hall (because of the security fixation the new officer in charge had toward me instead of placing this extra manpower to watch over the gangs of murderers, car-jackers and robbers that he had all over the prison).

That dark night the guard decided to position himself on the upper floor where

Chidumo and company were held, and promptly and true to form (especially because the jail-break had been planned a day or two after pay day when it was guaranteed that the guard would be drunk), he fell soundly asleep.

Chidumo and his bunch, naked but carrying a few brown prison-issue clothes, slipped out the hole in the front fence of the cell, tiptoed past the sentry post in the corridor and reached their sawn-through bar at the end of the passage. And all through this the other prisoners on that floor, in the gloomy light, slept soundly. The prisoners bent the single bar inwards and slipped through, managing to scale the outside bars of the inner part of the prison with its convenient cross-members (welded at perfect intervals by the original builders of the prison) and then climbed onto the prison roof. From there they scooted across to the outside catwalk, which the officers normally use while patrolling the outer perimeter of the prison building. Each cell has a single solid glass window through which the officers on the catwalk can peep.

Once on the catwalk they galloped around the prison toward the western perimeter where there were no houses or other buildings outside the fence—just bush. During this circumnavigation of the prison building they bumped into a sleepy guard who was actually doing his job and walking around, instead of hiding away in some warm corner.

A mad free-for-all ensued during which the guard managed to get out a few panicked screams. This awoke a few other guards dozing in various nooks and crannies, and the shit hit the fan. The siren went off and the four escapees, now also panicking, were subsequently picked up, still running around in circles on the catwalk.

From there it was a quick trip for all four of them to the then unoccupied condemned section, which us *okes* had vacated some years earlier. Here they were thrashed to within an inch of their lives, stripped naked, shackled, handcuffed and locked up in the solitary confinement cells.

You would have thought that was that? Not with these former soldiers who, now with an extra ten years for attempted escape added onto their original sentences of more than a hundred years each, were even more determined to wash the Chikurubi dust from their heels.

The condemned section had had a security upgrade while I was there with the addition of a massive steel overhead structure to prevent any escape by helicopter. However, with their blind faith in the overhead steel cover, the authorities had omitted to burglar-bar a window which gave access to one of the lower catwalks from under the steel anti-air structure.

This window was clearly visible but as it was about two and a half metres off the ground, it was of no consequence to the guards and no use to me when I was there as I was only ever allowed into the exercise yard on my own.

Not so for Chidumo and his gang. About a year later, security gradually eased and the four of them were frequently allowed into the exercise yard together again. They soon made their plans and one day, while the guards were having morning tea found themselves alone in the exercise yard. It was simple for the four to give each other a leg-up through the window (which had no glass!) and onto the lower walkway around the prison.

Once on the catwalk the four of them repeated their original steps—but this time knew where they were going, having been there before. On their way back to the western perimeter of the complex, they deprived a catwalk guard of his FN rifle during yet another frantic free-for-all (which later sealed their fate and set up a meeting with the Grim Reaper). By then their disappearance from the death section had been detected and the sirens throughout the complex were wailing like banshees. This got the adrenaline going and the four got desperate, lost their heads and panicked … again.

Suddenly a gun fight broke out between the four musketeers with their single FN rifle and prison officers in the satellite guard tower, six of which surround the prison building. One prison officer was shot and died on the spot as the four galloped toward the western-perimeter satellite tower, and freedom. The satellite towers are all about five metres high, so it was quite a leap to the ground as all four squirmed out of a small window in the tower. One escapee broke a leg and lay there as the other three dashed, under sporadic and inaccurate gunfire, the fifty metres or so toward the fence.

The tower guards usually have only ten rounds of ammo each and by that time those who could see the action from their tower had already expended their ten bullets. The three, diving into a water drain that had been dug under the perimeter fence, were under the fence in a flash. The heavy steel fence with its coils of razor wire erected to prevent a second escape attempt by me had been overlooked by the helpful plumber who had installed the drain. Obviously some guard, possibly the same one who had brought them the hacksaw blade, had told them of this water pipe without which they would have battled to scale that final barrier to their freedom.

Off into the thick bush they went, while on the inside we were hurriedly being locked back up in our cells by some seriously frantic guards who realized that there was some bad shit going down. And there we stayed for the rest of the day. As the hours passed, helicopters came and went; the bush to the west was set alight in an effort to flush them out and dog teams could be heard going crazy outside, creating an atmosphere of general pandemonium all around the jail.

The day would eventually end with the officer in charge of the prison checking for the umpteenth time that I was still in my cell. Grey and ashen-faced, he knew he was in deep trouble because of the escape of these criminals. He also knew full well that were it I, Mugabe's personal prisoner, who had escaped, he would be the one occupying my cell that night.

Broken Leg was to die a few hours later in his cell in the condemned section where he had been thrown. Despite his broken leg, he was beaten and kicked to death. In their search, one escapee, Chauke, was arrested, kicked, beaten and thrown into a cell on his own. Another accomplice was shot and Chidumo disappeared into thin air.

A couple of months later the Zimbabwean police, on a tip-off from their Mozambican counterparts, found Chudumo at his girlfriend's house in Maputo where they arrested him. After handcuffing and placing him in leg-irons, they shot him through the thigh just for good measure and to stop any more slippery nonsense from him.

In Zimbabwe they have a law called 'Common Purpose' which basically says that if you are involved in gang activities, you are responsible for everything that happens while that gang is up to its unlawful activity—no matter what part you play—there is no proportional responsibility, you all get the same punishment. So the remaining two, Chidumo and Chauke, who swore blind they were not the wielders of the stolen FN rifle which had killed the prison guard, were hanged for murder on the first Friday of June 2000.

For me, the determination displayed by Chidumo and his accomplices to escape prison at such high risk and small chance of success is more of an indictment against the inhuman conditions in Mugabe's prisons than an extension of their criminal nature.

Back to my story. After the botched attempt to spring me from jail I sat on my own, locked up in Chikurubi and I have never, ever been so dejected and close to suicide. Over the subsequent years, especially those on death row, I was to contemplate taking my own life many, many times, so desperate was my depression. But that escape night was probably the worst. I suppose it was because I had trained and hyped myself up so much for the escape.

Boy oh boy, was I down. It took a lot of willpower not to go the easy route and hang myself there and then. I had to convince myself that I could take whatever the future held. Others had taken worse. There was no second place in the race that lay ahead—only winning and losing—and I knew there were no ribbons or trophies here. I just had to hang in there and be tough, and tell the Grim Reaper who, as always, was there sitting on my shoulder egging me on to make a noose and end it all, to "Go get fucked".

Somewhere from my Sunday-school youth I recalled something along the lines that said, "When God sends you down stony paths, he gives you tough shoes".

And I knew my road ahead was going to be a rough one. I was terrified for my wife, who knew nothing of the planned escape, but who was still in Zimbabwe, unlike most of the other wives who were now living in South Africa. She would obviously be grilled about this whole fiasco. I was worried about the other families too, all of whom would be caught up in the fall-out that was surely to start very soon … which it did.

Before light, huge numbers of army and Support Unit troops, using mobile generators and spotlights, had dug in around the prison, amidst enormous noise and chaos. One thing I had taught myself that night was that *a closed mouth gathers no feet* and I would absolutely deny any knowledge of the escape. I was already up shit creek with one murder charge hanging over me. I did not need to compound that. I would have to survive on my acumen and wits and would never again set myself up for a fall … no way!

I knew I'd be wasting a lot of my days in the shadows of my mistakes and over the next few days I became determined not to allow my mind too much flexibility with regards to my immediate future by wallowing in my own self-pity. I also tried hard not to inundate my brain with all the 'if onlies' in the world. You let in a few 'if onlies' and they don't ever stop. Over and over it's there … if only … if only … if only …

Get through today, I told myself. And for the first time in my whole adult life, I prayed. Prayed that our Heavenly Father would protect and help the people I loved and the families of the *okes* in there with me, through whatever was to come. "Get through today, Woodsie," I told myself, which became a sort of 'Hail Mary' for me that I'd repeat over and over, together with my other prayers, everyday for the next nineteen and half years.

As expected, there was a huge security fuss in Chikurubi over the next few days. We were shuffled around from section to section within the prison as if they didn't really know what to do with us or where we would be secure. I was finally placed in the small condemned section with a few of the other guys. Other men from our group found themselves scattered throughout the rest of the prison.

Above left: Burning huts in the Mount Darwin area, 1974.

Above: A ZANU (PF) victim—this one a white farm manager brutally beaten by 'war veterans' during the notorious farm invasions.

Left: More ZANU (PF) victims—this time black locals in the Ruwa area.

Bottom: Chikurubi Maximum Security Prison.

Key
A. Prison centre court, out of bounds to prisoners other than on inner catwalk.
B. Prison building, hexagonal in shape, comprising six large cells divided into different sections with their own exercise yards.
C. Prison hospital outside main external wall.
D. Seven-metre-high concrete perimeter wall, six-sided and topped with razor wire.
E. One of sic satellite guard towers, connected to main complex via overhead walkway.
H. Road to Harare. It was at this point that the back-stop vehicle was seen by Woods and his co-accused as they left for court on 30 June 1988, the day of the botched escape. Gary Kane was in his stolen helicopter, circling the prison at the time.
I. Prison kitchen.
J. Small 10m x 10m concrete exercise yard for condemned prisoners, divided from all other sections by a seven-metre-high wall and overhead steel mesh and overlooked by a guard tower in the northeastern corner.
K. Exercise yards for normal prisoners.

Aerial photo courtesy of Google Earth

Harare Central Prison

Key
A. Centre court.
B. Condemned section block with 80 single cells, 70 of which each held a condemned man while Woods was incarcerated there.
C. Prison hospital.
D. At the back of the hospital block is the execution chamber with the gallows.
E. Concrete football field
F. Old condemned section cell block where Woods occupied one of the single cells.
G. Prison kitchen.
H. Small 10m x 8m concrete exercise yard for condemned prisoners, separated entirely from the rest of the prison by concrete wall with razor wire on top.
I. Six-metre-high external concrete wall topped with razor wire.
J. Prison mortuary.
K. Remand prison for awaiting-trial prisoners.

Aerial photo courtesy of Google Earth

Happy Christmas sunset camel thorn.

Bird of paradise.

Buffalo.

During the latter years of his incarceration,
Woods taught himself to draw and paint. Above,
opposite and overleaf are examples of his work
in prison.
Top left: Kalahari cheetah.
Top right: Flame lily.
Centre left: Sunbirds.
Centre right: Broad-tailed whydah.
Above: Love birds.
Right: Monkey having a *dop*.

"MUKUMBURA EXPRESS"
By Kevin Woods

"SONOP"

Above left: Caricature of a rural donkey cart with drunk in the rear, tailing kraal dog, dung beetle rolling his cargo and empty beer cans.

Above right: Baobab sunrise in the Zambezi valley.

Left: Zebra.

By Kevin Woods

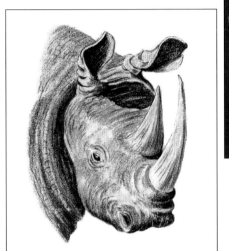

WHALE TALE

SABI STAR

HELLO!

FOREST TREE FROG

Top left: Rhino.

Top right: Moonlight serenade.

Left: Tree frog.

Above right: Sabi star/impala lily.

The author, 2007.
Photo: Joyrene Kramer of Rapport
© copyright 2007, Joyrene Kramer/
Rapport

Opposite: Oil painting by Craig
Bone.

Above: Tie a yellow ribbon … July 2006. *Photo: Ken Swanepoel*
Below: Six-metre steel cargo container the author painted soon after his release and which is used as a business storeroom at an accountant's office in Durban.

Among the detainees now held with me down in the condemned section was a South African agent, Leslie Lesiye. He was an excellent chess player and we spent many days trying to outwit each other at that lovely old game, mostly with me being the loser. Leslie was a South African Military Intelligence covert agent and had for some years been infiltrating the ANC. Some of his operations were quite hairy, including, as ordered from time to time, poisoning the odd ANC militant, using crates of doctored beer or pills that he was supplied with.

By the time I first met Leslie he had been in Chikurubi for a year or so and had initially been severely tortured by the CIO. He had been arrested in connection with a booby-trapped TV that had exploded in Harare in 1987. He had been given the TV by his South African handlers with instructions to deliver it to the ANC's chief representative in Maputo. Once delivered and the target confirmed as being at home, the handlers would detonate the explosive device therein.

Lesiye, with his impish nature, was not the most effective and disciplined of operatives around, and also had a bit of a police record for minor theft, housebreaking and drugs. However, he seemed to have been doing okay of late so was entrusted with this operation which was quite sensitive as it involved a senior ANC member on foreign soil.

Once in Maputo he decided that the TV would instead make rather a nice present for Peter Mhlope, a friend of his. So after opening up the set and neutralizing the explosive, he handed it over to his hombre and they went and celebrated their friendship at a nearby bar.

Mhlope already had a TV so once Lesiye had left to make his way back to South Africa he gave it to a friend called Frank who took it to Harare and gave it to his wife. She connected it up to the electricity point resulting in a huge explosion which tragically killed her. So much for Leslie's capability regarding the handling, and especially the de-activation, of explosive devices.

The police followed the trail back to Maputo and picked up Lesiye before he managed to travel back to South Africa. He was then driven across the border to Zimbabwe, together with his South African-registered motor vehicle, and soon his pistol was discovered in a hidden compartment in his vehicle. He was then tortured and thrown into Chikurubi. The evidence against him was tenuous to say the least, and he had been brought into Zimbabwe from Mozambique without any extradition procedures being followed, so in a dilemma, the police threw the jail keys away, content to leave him in Chikurubi and shut off from the world for as long as they could.

I told our lawyers, who on occasions met with the South African trade consulate in Harare, about Lesiye, and a little while later he subsequently appeared on someone's military intelligence radar in South Africa. It didn't help him much, as he was still in Chikurubi without any detention order or warrant, until Mugabe lifted the state of emergency in 1990. He was then deported to South Africa along with a few other South Africans. Until the expiration of the state of emergency (inherited from the Rhodesian era ten years prior) the police and CIO had the legal authority (legal in Zimbabwe only, that is!) to hold in detention and without trial anyone they chose to, and for as long as they wanted.

South African Special Force agent Odile Harrington was also jailed at Chikurubi. She was held in the ladies' condemned section, two floors up from where I sat. Like Lesiye, she was also released and deported after approaches from South Africa upon the expiry of the state of emergency. She had been arrested for, "trying to infiltrate the ANC in Zimbabwe" (what kind of a criminal offence is that?) and had been horribly tortured and sexually assaulted by her interrogators and ultimately sentenced to twenty-five years imprisonment.

Despite her torture, the judge who handled her case, Wilson Sandura (him again), said twenty-five years, the maximum he could hand down for her specific crime, was too lenient and had "wished he could have her tied to a stake to be shot". (That was back in the old days when Sandura was Mugabe's pet hanging judge—they fell out in later years after Sandura displayed some independent thinking on the bench that was not in line with Mugabe's thinking.)

Ronnie's brother 'GT', who had been detained the same time as us, was also deported in 1999 when the state of emergency lapsed. He hadn't been an official member of our group but Ronnie had used him a few times without telling us, mostly when operating in Harare. On his release and when back in South Africa, GT was full of stories of torture by the Zimbabwean security, which he said had ruptured his bladder. Subsequent tests revealed a growth in his bladder which caused a little blood in his urine and which was treated with minor surgery. He mounted all sorts of challenges in the South African courts against the South African minister of defence for pain and suffering, and loss of property. He was eventually paid, mainly to keep him quiet, as his continual complaining to the press was not helping us in jail, and about whom he didn't give a shit. At one time he publicly referred to us as 'the convicts'. Nice one, especially considering one of 'us' was his brother.

He had originally been accused of complicity in the bombing in Harare of Soviet-trained ANC guerrilla, Jeremy Brickhill, but the state had not yet got around to prosecuting him, considering him a nonentity, and thus he was just sitting in Chikurubi on indefinite remand.

Brickhill had done some of the intelligence work for the Church Street bombing in Pretoria in May 1983 where many civilians of all races had been killed and injured. The South African State Security Council, so we were told, had authorized his elimination in Harare. Ronnie and GT obtained a Citroën in Harare which they fitted with explosives. Surveillance on Brickhill took a while until it was decided to eliminate him in the Avondale shopping centre carpark, in Harare.

On 13th October 1987, they watched him park his car in the parking lot and walk off to a coffee shop owned by his brother, which he frequented most days. Upon his return and using a remote-control initiator they detonated the bomb in the Citroën, which they had placed next to his own vehicle. Brickhill went up in the proverbial cloud of smoke. He was not killed but he was seriously injured, which put an end to his ANC guerrilla activity till well past the end of the liberation war.

While I was in Chikurubi, Brickhill, together with Channel 4, produced a documentary about South Africa's hit squad and dirty tricks department, called *The Hidden Hand*. I was locked down in death row without any knowledge of this at the time and it was quite cruel the way the situation developed for us. Brickhill and his crew were only allowed access to the prison at 8 o'clock at night and so, around that time one night, we were removed from our death cells to do an interview with him and the press. I had known all along that any release of me and my co-accused would be publicized, so when I was called up to the prison administration for an interview well after dark, I just knew, with every bone in my body, that this was it—home time!

"Be nice to the press, don't ruffle any feathers and you are out of there," was the message we got from the authorities as we were led from the condemned section to the administration offices. And could you blame me for getting my hopes up? The minister of justice himself, my former Central Intelligence Organization boss, Emmerson Mnangagwa was there in person! So was the director of prisons, with the press, video cameras—the works. What else could it be? I thought to myself.

In the excitement of the moment I'd forgotten the callous deviousness of Mnangagwa and his unbridled power under the authority of Mugabe. It took about twenty minutes in front of bright camera lights and being interviewed by Brickhill for me to realize that this was simply a propaganda stunt. What an awful anti-cliamax.

I terminated the interview and was taken back to my death cell, seriously pissed off and depressed. Next morning, by pure chance, my lawyer visited and I gave him the rundown on the previous night's fiasco. He subsequently obtained a court injunction against Brickhill and his cohorts, prohibiting them from airing the footage of me and my colleagues in prison, as we owned copyright of what had been recorded through pure deception.

However, in flagrant disregard of the court order and every year to date, *The Hidden Hand* is screened on national TV in Zimbabwe—Independence Day, Heroes and Ancestors days, and just about every national hero's funeral when you will see Woods and company paraded around the screens of the nation.

The Zimbabwean regime blows up independent newspapers and radio stations, even when their own courts have given the independents authority to broadcast and print newspapers under Zimbabwe's own laws. They kill their own people, they arrest and torture opposition members into making murder confessions, simply to justify their excesses and their extreme oppression of the Zimbabwean people. Would they listen to a mere court order not to air my *Hidden Hand* interview?

I feel I must highlight some of the above paragraph because at first glance any reader would think I'm really slinging it now ... and for some readers this would be justified in thinking that in this day and age. No government would behave like this, surely?

Well, the *Daily News* used to be one of Zimbabwe's most successful publications, by far outselling the government-owned papers. Unfortunately for themselves, the *Daily News* produced a newspaper in Zimbabwe which was critical of the government, simply by writing the truth.

During the 2000 general election campaign, Mugabe's war veterans prevented the sale of the *Daily News* in the rural areas, confiscating, destroying and burning any copies they found while the police looked on, arms folded. Anyone caught carrying a copy would also receive a thorough beating, and still the police would do nothing.

After the *Daily News* published photographs of government officials delivering bags of maize to people who had invaded commercial farms, and thus exposing Mugabe's lie that the invasions were a spontaneous reaction by the people, and thus not sanctioned, the leader of the war vets, Chenjerai (aka Hitler) Hunzvi warned the editors that, "they would be dealt with, sooner or later".

Soon thereafter, on 22nd April 2000, the ground floor of the *Daily News* building in central Harare was bombed. That had the government press crowing that the opposition MDC had carried out the attack, *to try and make the government look bad.*

Needless to say no one was ever convicted for the attack. Thereafter the *Daily News* and the government were, farcically, in and out of court with the latter continually ordering the police to prevent publication while spurious court orders were sought by the government, to portray some sort of legality behind their desire to close down the *Daily News* once and for all.

Eventually, after numerous court orders giving the *Daily News* authority to publish their stories and with the editors and journalists in and out of jail without charge, and after even more threats from Hunzvi, the company's printing press was bombed and totally destroyed on the night of 28th January 2001. Essentially, although trying to hire other presses, this was the end *of* the *Daily News*. No one has ever been arrested and convicted of the bombing.

Cain Nkala was a war veteran, staunch ZANU (PF) supporter and chairman of the Bulawayo War Veterans' Association. The theory goes that he was involved in a ZANU (PF)-ordered murder of an opposition political party member in Bulawayo and was going to spill the beans about who gave the order. A few days later on 5th November 2001, and in broad daylight, Nkala was kidnapped from in front of his home in Bulawayo's high-density suburb of Nketa. The government immediately started blaming the MDC. Before Nkala's fate was even known, Vice-President Msika accused the MDC of killing him. Unbelievably, the vice-president actually had no way of knowing yet from the police investigation that Nkala was already dead. Surely he must have had inside information?

There followed numerous arrests and the recovery of the body of Cain Nkala from some bushes outside Bulawayo. Nkala had been strangled with his shoe laces, the state media said. They went on to remind everyone that this was a notorious way of killing people, as perfected by the Rhodesian-era Selous Scouts, who then were insinuated to be training the MDC in fighting and assassination tactics.

Cain Nkala was declared a national hero, an honour in Zimbabwe that has to have the express sanction of President Mugabe himself. Mugabe used this platform at Heroes Acre on 18th November 2001 to remind the nation that Zimbabwe would not tolerate terrorism on its soil and blamed the MDC and white farmers for, "trying to reverse our sovereignty". The opportunity was too good to miss and ZANU (PF) war vets went on the rampage in Bulawayo, destroying the MDC offices by setting them alight, while the police stood by and actually stopped the fire brigade from gaining access to the flaming building. Despite years of detention for some of the MDC people arrested and tortured for this crime, no one was ever charged and convicted.

165

Please allow me a few more lines on this theme. In 2000, the government published legislation banning anyone from owning radio-broadcasting equipment. The regulations required that anyone operating a radio station was to be licensed by a board selected by the information minister, and also went on to set licence fees far beyond the means of most people. Independent stations would also have to broadcast government propaganda, whenever required, for free. Short Wave Radio Africa, an independent broadcaster with a court order giving them authority to broadcast, was hounded out of Zimbabwe after having their equipment seized in the early 2000s. They now keep the candle burning, on short wave, from a broadcasting station in the United Kingdom.

Radio Voice of the People used to produce tapes at their recording studio in Harare which were then broadcast by Radio Netherlands. They had their office and recording studio bombed and totally destroyed on the night of 29th August 2002. Of course, no one was ever brought to book for this attack either. Harassed into exile in Johannesburg, they still broadcast nightly for three hours into Zimbabwe and worldwide via short wave, determined as ever and a lot safer too.

Another radio station which cannot broadcast from within Zimbabwe is Studio 7, which broadcasts nightly from Washington DC in the USA. Incredible that all these stations have to do their work from outside the country.

It does not take much to see right through these cases and so many others, that all reveal the desperate measures the Zimbabwean government will go to, in order to maintain its grip on the people's hearts and minds. Free press, freedom of speech and independent radio are anathema to the Zimbabwean regime.

❧ ❧ ❧

And there are always pardons and amnesties dished out for Mugabe's drones, just in case something goes wrong and an over-zealous policeman might want to do his duty, like arresting a ZANU (PF) functionary.

Mugabe has the presidential power of pardon, but also issues blanket amnesties. In 1982, he decreed that people caught acting for or on behalf of the state in good faith, be they army, police or civil servants could not be held responsible for their conduct, be it civil or criminal. This specific decree was issued during the massacres in western Zimbabwe and displays his customary total disregard for the rule of law when it suits him and his government.

President Mugabe influences every aspect of Zimbabwean life. He runs the parliament and the courts and everything else on a system of patronage. He makes laws about anything and everything no matter how irreverent. In the early days his ZANU (PF) party obtained most of its funding from abroad. Now that he has fallen off the wall and the funding has dried up, he has made it illegal for any other political party (including his, because they get nothing anymore) to receive funds from abroad!

In Zimbabwe it is now illegal to make any gesture toward his armoured presidential convoy as it goes speeding past—simply because people were giving him the finger or the more extravagant 'brown eye'! You can't even wave with an open hand at his gleaming six-wheeled armoured Mercedes because the main opposition party in Zimbabwe, the MDC, has an open-faced hand as its party slogan.

The laws abound and cover every aspect of life. Look at the president or one of his ministers, that happen to be flying past at the time, who then may misinterpret your look as an insult and you're apt to end up in the slammer, after a thorough kicking. It's in the law books—just as it is illegal for churches and non-governmental organizations to conduct voter education in the uneducated and rural areas of the country. Even to this day many Zimbabweans fear the voting booth because of government's frequent violent reprisals against people it thinks have voted against it, and this makes the rural population even more vulnerable. They need to be educated that their vote is secret and of course that's the last thing the government wants them to know.

It is illegal to "engender hostility toward the president", which means that opposition parties cannot expose his shortcomings to their constituencies. Criticism of the army or the police is also outlawed. Okay? I think you get my drift.

❧ ❧ ❧

Back to Chikurubi. It's probably true to say that no physical ailment can have as devastating an effect upon a person as does worry, sadness, fear, or any other form of heartache, but one thing, almost as an extension to Murphy's Law, even if you expect the worst, it will still surprise you when it comes, and I had some serious time ahead of me. I was absolutely helpless and without hope. There were so many times when I would be totally overwhelmed by the prospect of yet another soul-destroying, wasted day in jail.

Over the next few months, as a direct result of our botched escape, the police went into overdrive to get our criminal prosecutions settled in court. It became obvious that the whole idea was to pin me down, because I was perceived as the main threat to the president among us all, resulting from my knowledge gained while a senior officer in his CIO. With so many of his secrets inside my head, the worry for him was that I would cause serious problems for him if I ever wanted to exact revenge. I was therefore treated like a common criminal, instead of a political prisoner, with its limited privileges. There was also a concern for him of behind-the-scenes negotiations and my possible release—resulting from political wheeling and dealing, which I naïvely kept solidly in my sights as a future hope to get out of jail.

Later in 1988, and obviously acting on political orders, the cops, in their sheer determination to convict me of as much as possible, served me with two indictments—both for offences committed under the Law and Order Maintenance Act. Ironically this was legislation specifically implemented to counter political crimes that the Zimbabwean government had inherited from the Rhodesian government, and one which I, as a policeman in the 1970s had used to send many offenders to jail, and indeed some to the gallows.

One of the indictments was for the 1988 Trenance bombing in Bulawayo in which the driver of the car-bombed motor vehicle and some unacknowledged ANC guerrillas from the safe house that we attacked were killed. The Zimbabwean government never admitted that some ANC guerrillas were in fact killed in this car bomb, because in so doing they would have had to admit complicity to aiding them, and that confirmation would have given us justification, from South Africa's perspective, for the attack. So they stuck to that one death—that of the innocent driver. The second indictment was for the 1986 bombing of the ANC headquarters in Harare, including the bombing of the ANC house in Ashdown Park (where Joe Gqabi was assassinated a few years earlier) and for possession of weapons of war found in Bulawayo, including the red flashing torch lights from my house.

ﻉ ﻉ ﻉ

Later that year I was in the dock and on trial in the high court, Harare, charged under Zimbabwe's political laws, together with Mike Smith and Philip Conjwayo for the Bulawayo murder. After the trial during which our enshrined human rights, such as access to a lawyer, freedom from mental torture and so on were thrown out the window we were, in November 1988, convicted of murder with constructive intent (which means we all played an equal part in constructing the bomb and exploded it with the intention of killing the ANC guerrillas, but also with disregard for the possibility of killing the innocent driver too), and sentenced to death by Mugabe's hanging judge, Wilson Sandura.

Sandura convicted us on the basis of acting in common purpose, even though the parts that we played were hugely different. For instance, Conjwayo's role was limited to purchasing the car used as the bomb, and dropping it off at an isolated pick-up point in Bulawayo. He had no knowledge that the vehicle was to be used to blow up the ANC house. I did the intelligence work on the operation and helped out with the explosives and the false number plates and so on. However, on the night of the explosion I was in South Africa and this absence from Zimbabwe at the crucial moment was accepted by the prosecution. In his statement to the court, Smith admitted to being in a command vehicle with Ronnie in Trenance the night the bomb went off—yet we all received identical sentences.

This same common-purpose law was applied six months later when I appeared back in the same dock, with Barry Bawden and Mike Smith. This time, The judge, Justice Ebrahim, was a little more level-headed and only sentenced us to seventy-five years with hard labour—forty years for the ANC office attack, twenty years for the house in Ashdown Park and fifteen years for the weapons cache. We subsequently appealed this sentence and the Supreme Court reduced it to twenty-five years—which for Smith and me was neither here nor there, as we were already in the cooler awaiting the noose.

સ્વ સ્વ સ્વ

A few months later Sam Beahan was sentenced to life imprisonment for his involvement in our botched escape. This was after a deal had been made between the attorney general and our attorneys. The attorney general was initially going to push for the death sentence but it was agreed that he would ask for a life sentence only if Beahan did not prevail with exposing his Botswanan and CIO torture experiences. He was sentenced to life with hard labour, but this was reduced to twenty years upon appeal to the Supreme Court. After being sentenced, Bawden and Beahan were locked up together with the other prisoners in the general population.

We three, 'The Harare Three' as we became known, had a rather tougher time ahead of us.

Death row

The condemned section at Chikurubi is one of the most depressing places on Earth. With only eleven solitary confinement cells, each measuring 1.2 metres wide by about 4 long, it was never meant for the normal criminal murderer. Chikurubi Maximum Security Prison was built by the Rhodesian government, with the condemned section designed especially as a holding centre for politically motivated prisoners.

The inner and outer walls of the prison, the floors, and the doorways are all reinforced concrete grey. This must be one of the most dismal colours—grey. Try spending five years in solitary confinement in that grey world and you will find all mental activity hard to come by, let alone thoughts of a political nature.

In each cell there is a concrete slab, supposedly your bed, raised about half a metre off the floor. Level with that is a round hole in the concrete which is your toilet. A very short piece of pull-string is attached to a cistern above the hole. A light burns in each cell twenty-four hours a day, every day. Water to drink is kept in a plastic bucket in each cell. There are no taps in those cells. There are no windows open to the outside world in the condenmed section. There is one cold-water pipe, protruding from the wall in a shower 'area'.

The day I was locked up in the condemned section I was shaved bald and had to strip naked. I remained in that little cell, naked, for nearly three years of my five years on death row, with only a couple of coarse grey blankets and a hard felt mat—I remember finding it ironic that I was sleeping on a mat manufactured in South Africa with an SABS stamp on it.

There is an exercise area which leads off the condemned section down a small passage. Sunlight does not enter the condemned section. If you manage to get out of your cell (which is a very infrequent event) and stand in the right place, you can see down the exercise yard and sometimes you can make out if it is day or night by guessing the position of the shadows on the concrete. From most of the cells though you cannot see anywhere near that passage to the outside, sunlit, concrete exercise yard, so you remain in your brightly lit cell without knowing whether it is day or night, morning or afternoon, what day or month or even year it is.

The three of us were locked up alone in the condemned section. Over the next five years we occasionally had one or two other prisoners thrown into one of the other empty cells, but mostly it was just us three. It is possible to converse in the condemned section with one's fellow prisoners, but you can only do so in a raised voice. The three of us were not exactly the best of buddies, so we didn't really bother talking to each other. Each day we were allowed out of our cells, to have a cold shower or to sweep our cells—one at a time, for thirty minutes in the morning, and again in the afternoon for thirty minutes. Not thirty-one minutes mind! They were very strict about that one extra minute. The rest of the time we were locked up, in our small, tomblike cells. We were allowed a Bible but nothing else. There were no radios, no televisions, and no newspapers—nothing.

After about two years an old transistor radio was found somewhere and we were allowed to have that playing for a few hours a day in the condemned section. And goodness me, what a lifesaver that little radio was! Even though it could only be tuned to FM and therefore the government-sanitized radio stations, it was an absolute joy to hear some music, any music, in that dead place.

๛ ๛ ๛

Before I was sentenced to death I had been allowed to receive and write letters, as many as I wanted, and my wife was allowed twice-weekly visits for thirty minutes. This changed dramatically once I was sentenced. Visits were reduced to fifteen minutes once a month and only during working hours. And I was suddenly only permitted to receive one letter from the outside world a month, to which I could respond with only a single page.

It was most distressing as once a month the guards would arrive at my cell door with a handful of letters and I had to peer into the pile and choose just one. The rest were thrown away. I'd always try to pick out a letter from my wife so that I could get an update on her and our children. At one stage I asked her to use brightly coloured envelopes so that her letters were easily distinguished from others, after making the odd error and choosing the wrong letter.

The agony of another month without news of my family or from loved ones the world over, was very palpable. After a few years of this interference with my correspondence I managed to retain a human rights lawyer who obtained a court order allowing me to communicate by mail, without hindrance. In 1994, the court found in my favour that it was a basic and fundamental human right for me to correspond. This successful court challenge opened the way for all sentenced prisoners in Zimbabwe to be allowed the right to correspond—as long as we supplied our own envelopes and stamps! This Supreme Court ruling was case number 124 of 94, and over the following years I communicated with people worldwide. I had to smuggle most of my letters, both out and into the prison, because many contained a lot of politics and requests for intercession by people like Mandela. I felt the ruling started some sort of revolution as every other prisoner soon started communicating with friends and families, as long as their visitors dropped them off some stamps and envelopes.

৵৵৵

The wheels of justice turn very slowly in Zimbabwe. I had to go through five years of solitary confinement on death row, before I managed to obtain that court order to communicate with my loved ones. There you sit, condemned to death, and as if that wasn't enough, the prison system does everything possible to destroy any unity and togetherness you may have had with your family.

As I said, upon being sentenced I was locked up naked for twenty-three hours a day. I was not allowed into the sunlight in the vacant exercise yard attached to the death section, which was nothing more than a twenty-metre-square concrete box with a huge steel-mesh covering the top anyway. No sunlight. That was tough. During my condemned-section exercise time of thirty minutes outside my cell each morning and afternoon, I would stand and gaze down the corridor leading to the exercise yard with such a profound longing to feel the sun's warmth on my naked body that sometimes I'd think my heart would just squeeze itself shut with heartache. It got so bad that I would eventually avoid looking at the gate that led to the exercise yard and warmth. Out of sight, out of mind! Rather than torment myself with thoughts of the impossible, I stayed at the other end of the corridor and away from that self-punishing temptation to go take a peek.

It was interesting at that time to hear of a medical specialist from Bethseda University Hospital in the United States proffer the opinion that my living conditions even violated the laws governing laboratory-research animals under existing United States and Commonwealth legislation.

Three years later I was to obtain yet another court decision in my favour. This deprivation of sunshine resulted in the Supreme Court ordering the prisons to allow all prisoners on death row to have an hour in the sun twice a day. What a thing that was, after nearly three years without any sunlight to suddenly feel the its warmth again, albeit somewhat diluted through the steel mesh covering the exercise yard. Just to stand and tilt my head back and feel the sun on my face was such a wonderful delight.

This court decision specifically applied to *all prisoners on death row*, and not just us three, yet, some fifteen years later, when I was transferred from Chikurubi Maximum Prison to Harare Central, I was astounded and dismayed at the prison's ability to flout court orders—here I found prisoners on death row that were not benefiting from the court ruling as they were still only out of their cells for thirty minutes twice daily. The condemned cells at Central do have a window which allows a little fresh air in, but it is just a hole in the wall covered by three layers of steel mesh, so not much light can penetrate in at all.

The inmates' problem at Harare Central is that very few of them have any legal representation. Compounding their fear is that they watch other inmates being taken away to be hanged—every year on the first Friday of June a number are hanged, so those who have missed the hangman's noose that time don't rock the boat with court challenges lest the Mugabe regime will bump them up the hanging list a bit!

�� �� ��

The routine on death row is enough to drive you mad with boredom. Each day at about 8.00 a.m. you get a cup of runny maize meal for breakfast. 10.30 a.m. is lunch time which is always stiff maize meal porridge (*sadza*), and a little bit of overcooked leafy vegetable in the water used to boil it, or if they're feeling flush, you get a plain boiled potato for lunch. Supper is at 1.30 p.m. and is either a repeat of lunch or instead of the leaves you get a quarter cup of boiled beans. All things being even, once a week or so you receive a piece of boiled meat, beef or pork, about the size of your thumb (if you have a small thumb) instead of the beans. And that's it. No coffee, usually no tea, no sugar, etc.

You fantasize about food a lot in prison, more so on death row where it is impossible to smuggle the odd tidbit from outside. It is almost physical, your longing for the most basic of dishes like a fried-egg-and-bacon breakfast, or a piece of fresh bread—just basic stuff like that, never mind things like roast beef, or *wors* (sausage) on a braai.

You can go crazy thinking about food. I prayed a lot about this longing for food and it was only after many years that I found the inner strength to push thoughts of food out of my mind.

Thank you God for that.

Three times a year your family can deliver some food to the prison which has to be to be consumed that same day. As a prisoner who is not on death row, you can usually keep your goodie parcel for maybe a week or two before the guards come and destroy what meagre bits and pieces of biltong (jerky), sweets and so on you have saved, and then it's back to the swill from the kitchen.

ৡ ৡ ৡ

There is nothing to do on death row, but to think—and that can drive you to madness and beyond. The thinking I mean. I spent years pacing slowly up and down my little tomb, wrapped in a blanket, three and a half steps up, three and a half back. I'd walk with my eyes tightly shut in a vain attempt to mentally transport myself from that dismal place. I relived my life; month by month, day by day, as far back as I could go. I relived good times, which were amazingly few, and all the bad, which were plenty. It's quite hard to remember good times when you are in a place like that.

I owned a mobile discotheque in the early '70s. You know, one of those wooden cabinets with two turntables, a couple of crates of 7-single records and some coloured flashing lights. I even graduated to a spinning-glass mirror ball suspended from the dance floor roof on which I shone a few strobe lights … remember those things? My brother-in-law, Guy, and I would hire ourselves out for weddings, twenty-first birthday parties, New Year's Eve and generally any piss-up occasion where the people wanted to shake it down. As the DJ, I got to know a lot of songs, the words and the tunes, and I'd compete with myself on death row trying to remember each song and its lyrics exactly, as I walked slowly up and down, back and forth for hours and hours each and every day. Many songs in my head have their own memory attached. You know how it is? A particular song will immediately take you to a particular event, person, lover or time and place. Every time you hear it you're immediately transported to that place again. I've got so many songs like that, many bitter-sweet, many sad, and a few happy, and I'd find myself singing softly to myself and allowing the songs to take me out of that place, often with my heart breaking and tears running down my face.

It sounds pathetic and I suppose it was, but it kept me going. Somehow I had to get through. I owed it to my kids whom, as a free man, I had taken so much for granted. Now removed from them and with a very hopeless future, all I wanted to do was be with them, kiss them, tell them I loved them, but couldn't.

Being so utterly helpless and hopeless is mind-destroying. It's a huge lesson in life, being sent to death row. Never ever take a blessing like your kids or your wife and family and friends, for granted. That is so important … never take life for granted.

Tell your kids you love them. Don't just show them your love by doing the normal parenting thing like sending them to school, caring for them when they are sick, buying them stuff, feeding and clothing them etc. Tell them you love them. Every single day, say the words 'I love you' lest something, whatever it may be, happens and you regret, maybe for the rest of your life, or theirs, that they didn't hear those words from you. So if you take nothing from this book other than this, you will all be more the richer in your soul and so will your family. Go and tell the people you love that you love them, not later when you put this book down, for tomorrow may be too late … before you even read on, do it now!

People on death row pray a lot. I did. When you've nothing, absolutely nothing to hang onto, God makes it so easy for you to lean on him. You don't feel God's help—but you have to lean somewhere, and why not God? Hope is a wonderful thing. Hopelessness will destroy you. Often I would manufacture hope, just to get me through each agonizingly long day, when there was actually nothing to hope for …

Many were the times I was swathed in blankets, kneeling on the floor of my cell, utterly devoid of hope and the willingness to carry on and all I had was a five-word prayer: "God, please give me hope!" It must have worked, that same short prayer time after time, wearing my knees bald from kneeling on the rough concrete … because I did it … I got through.

I'd have imaginary hat pegs on my wall and I'd hang my *hats of hope* there, right there where I would see them. There's my Nelson Mandela hat, for instance. He was released from prison on 11th February 1990 and that was a *huge hat of hope*— my lawyer paid us his monthly visit and told us Nelson Mandela was pursuing the release of all South African agents held in Frontline State jails. I just knew that Mugabe would not refuse Nelson Mandela, surely not? Nelson Mandela became South Africa's first democratically elected president in 1994 and the first foreign president invited to South Africa on a state visit was President Mugabe. There was much pomp and ceremony attached to that and the Zimbabwean propaganda machine went bananas.

So did we all because it was all over the world and in the Zimbabwean and South African press on 29th August 1994, that President Mugabe, while on his state visit, had this to say: "We will soon review the cases of Military Intelligence agents working for the old South Africa who bombed an ANC house in Bulawayo seven years ago. Now that South Africa and Zimbabwe are free it is possible to look more leniently on political crimes committed in the past."

Can you blame us for being over the moon when our lawyers rushed to Chikurubi to give us this news? All of us tore up all old papers and unwanted letters and were ready to go. For weeks we sat there, nerves strained to breaking point in desperate, hopeful anticipation, as they were a few months earlier when Nelson Mandela called for the release of all jailed South African agents.

Relentless as ever, that euphoria slowly but surely ebbed away with the passage of time and pretty soon we were once again sitting there dejected and with our hopes crushed.

I wrote to President Mugabe so many times and asked him about this review of our sentences that he had promised to look into while on his South African state visit. I doubt that even one of these letters got anywhere near his office, let alone into his hands. Justice Minister Chinamasa was, years later when my lawyers cornered him with my heart-treatment application in court, to say in his affidavit that the president had personally (yeah right) read every one of my letters and petitions.

He went on to say that the president had long ago reviewed my sentence and had declined any leniency. It was nice of them to have told me. Again this was all froth and bubble from Chinamasa. But one would have thought that President Mugabe would at least have had the balls to honour his statement made in South Africa.

In March of 1995, the *Pretoria News* reported that Nelson Mandela had once again requested Robert Mugabe to release us. And once again, fool that I am, I got my hopes really high. For once again, nothing.

Because Mugabe is absolutely motivated by malice, once Mandela stole his thunder by proving himself Africa's true statesmen, Mugabe's behaviour just went downhill, and now everything that is said and done in Zimbabwe has become focused on his remaining in power. Nothing more.

With this in mind a number of inane and unjust laws have been procalmied in Zimbabwe, such as prohibiting people from gesturing at Robert Mugabe's passing motorcade or forcing people to vote in their home constituency, in a situation where the man in the street cannot afford emergency travel to take a relative to hospital, or just to go to work, never mind going back home to vote, thereby limiting the number of people who can vote.

Zimbabwean human rights soon flew out the window, then came the theft of commercial farms, thereafter economic collapse was close behind. The rest, as they say, is history.

It is these policies which are meant to maintain the ruling clique's status quo that have led Zimbabwe to where it is now, with inflation according to official government statistics at approximately 3,000 per cent per annum. (A recent World Bank assessment puts Zimbabwe's inflation at 5,000 per cent per annum and a staggering 1.5 million per cent by the outgoing United Sates ambassador by the end of 2007 if the rollercoaster continues its current downward spiral.) More than 85 per cent of Zimbabweans are unemployed. And that is compounded because that figure takes into account the twelve per cent of the population who are working in the civil service. Aids deaths are at over 5,000 per week throughout the country, and those are just the reported cases. The right to education and adequate medical care are way beyond the majority of Zimbabwe's legions of the sick with the most common medical treatment now being nothing more than a wish and a prayer.

Life in Zimbabwe is marked by a struggle against illness, hunger and death. Families are selling their meagre possessions to raise money to save their ailing loved ones. HIV-positive people seeking anti-retroviral drugs are sent away empty-handed and accident victims are lucky if they get a tetanus jab. You have to take your own medicine and needles to hospital and even surgical gloves are a thing of the past. When the poor die, be it at home or in the government hospitals, as they inevitably do, the bodies are simply stacked up in the mortuaries as families cannot afford the prohibitive funeral costs.

In 1990, life expectancy in Zimbabwe was sixty, now it is thirty-four. Mugabe's answer to all this is to blame it on the West, and drought, of course. Yet when Zimbabwe has good rains, it's still the West who is the cause of all woes. Foreign media is all but banned in Zimbabwe—the BBC has to report on Zimbabwe from Johannesburg, some 600 miles away.

There are more orphans per capita than anywhere else in the world, with an estimated thirty per cent of the adult population being HIV-positive.

Despite Mugabe's and his ministers' continual insistance that no one will go without basic medical treatment and schooling, millions suffer in their poverty with often less than one meal per day and without access to the most basic of medical care schooling. The basic wage for a government employee is equivalent to ten loaves of bread per month (at time of writing). Fuel is a scarce commodity and mostly only available on the thriving black market where one US dollar is equal to 400,000 Zimbabwean dollars and rising (hourly), meaning a government employee earns three US dollars a month or less. Twenty years ago the US dollar–Zimbabwe dollar rate sat at one to one!

Electricity and water cuts are an everyday occurrence and even coal is absent throughout the country, in a situation where the coal deposits at Hwange in the west and Gokwe in the north are sufficient for Zimbabwe's needs, plus enough to export for decades to come. Zimbabwe's major export crop, tobacco, has almost dried up since the land seizures. Just a few years ago the crop earned nearly US$300 million annually—now, if luck is on their side and weather conditions are absolutely perfect, the total tobacco crop is estimated at just US$40 million.

The Zimbabwean crisis represents a total leadership failure where those in Mugabe's ivory tower have corruptly and utterly enriched themselves to levels that the man in the street can only dream of and which are considered seriously opulent in even most Western democracies. The rule of law is impossible to implement in this system where the head of the nation's police force has openly declared himself one of Mugabe's disciples and where political succession to the top job is impossible to achieve. Anarchy stares people in the face as Zimbabwe's *povo* are subjected to sorrows such as meted upon the peoples of Sudan, Democratic Republic of Congo, the old Liberia, Sierra Leone, Somalia and many other utterly failed states.

While the elite live in luxury, the poor grovel to eke out a living where selling a fire-roasted maize cob on the side of the road can earn you a through beating from the police, simply because Mugabe wants his cities to be clean and smart without flea markets and shanty towns, which have now all but been destroyed. The government called this destruction of the shanties and small businesses Operation *Murambatsvina* (Operation 'Drive out Trash' in May 2005). The United Nations Secretary-General Kofi Anan sent a special envoy to assess this operation, and its impact on Zimbabwe, during which President Mugabe's cruelty toward the poorest of his citizens was exposed. The reason for this clean-up had nothing to do with Mugabe's desire for cleaner cities, but was once again single-mindedly directed at his staying in power. Most of the opposition party, the Movement for Democratic Change, is comprised of urban dwellers, many of whom resided in these pitiful little shacks that were razed to the ground. The regime destroyed their homes and also their livelihood by trashing their hawker stands where they would sell roasted maize, and other flea-market paraphernalia, as can be seen in every city the world over. The informal sector is a major source of income for many of the poorest people but with the destruction of their shacks these people—men women and children—were left with nothing, and were left to live exposed to the harsh winter elements.

With Zimbabwe being rated as Africa's worst-performing economy in 2006, owing to heightened political and economic problems, what future is there for the man on the street?

None?

If they don't flee the country they will die—either at the hands of Mugabe's death squads or from starvation. This is yet another Rwanda in the offing ... and as usual the world watches, uncaring.

வ்வ்வ்

It is important to maintain as much control of one's life as humanly possible. I had been in many tight situations before this, but in every case I had had an element of control. Suddenly all control of my life was removed. Not only of my own life, but I also no longer had control over my children's lives and this became such a craving I'd drive myself almost insane trying to get messages to my wife about the specific direction I needed my children's lives to take. As any father does, I suppose? You take so much for granted when you're in control. You can more or less do as you please, take a walk on the grass, go for a beer, or kiss your child. Just have that control removed from you and you then realize just how much we all take for granted, every single day.

I was to go through over 7,000 days without walking barefoot on grass—and you know what a nice feeling that is, walking barefoot on grass, I mean. And the smell of the first rains? Just how glorious is that beautiful dust-in-the-air smell?

Once or twice during the five years I spent on death row the wind would be just right, and a small gust would waft into the cell area from the outside courtyard, carrying with it, a hint of that smell of the rain. I would stand there at my cell door, with my head tilted back, nostrils flared, to get every scent before it was gone, eyes streaming with tears at the beautiful smell that I once took so for granted, but also with such huge emotion at the realization that this was the precursor to yet another rainy season, and the soul-destroying fact that therefore another year had gone.

Gone for good.

It is quite sad when the only guage that you have for the passage of time is the smell of the coming season's first rains. Time is so precious, even time wasted, but when it slips through your fingers like sand in an hourglass, and takes a bit of your soul with it each day, it is probably one of the hardest things to do, to just carry on. There was a time, in the condemned section, just after our botched escape that a huge thirty-metre-tall gum tree just outside the prison wall was struck by lightning. Out of the blue, this huge bang and crack of lightning had all of us in the condemned section leap a few feet into the air with fright. I watched this huge tree wither and die from the lightning. Three years later, when I was eventually allowed into the exercise yard of the condemned section, I could just see the new leaves of the same tree's regrowth as it appeared at wall height. Eventually that same tree was once again towering above the exterior wall just before I left that prison for good.

Talk about an interminable guage of time? That tree surely was.

I don't ever remember having a *lekker* belly laugh in jail, not once for the full 7,140 days, almost twenty years. There is not much humour in jail.

The darkest time for me was when I was on death row, simply because you have to carry everything yourself. There is no one to share your load with—you have to deal with everything, mentally and physically, alone, naked and in a tiny, windowless cell.

I made up my mind, quite early into my stretch on death row that if ever the time came for these bastards to hang me, as part of my control psyche I would hang myself. I did not want to give ultimate control of killing me to the Zimbabwean government. I was as determined as a man can be to leave this world on my own terms.

It's easy enough on death row to commit suicide. You can't hoard pills or keep a razor blade or such like, as your cell is turned over by the guards a couple of times a day. But in the wee hours of the night, with the guards asleep in their chairs, it's an easy thing to make a thin, strong piece of rope out of a few strips of blanket twisted together, and just as easy to tie one end to the bars on the door or some other purchase point near the toilet cistern. I was going to do that—in all seriousness I'd promised myself that. And it was my way of convincing myself that I had ultimate control over my life.

Suicide thoughts are inspired by the devil in you, that's for sure. Demons and angels, they're all there, and you've got to keep your wits about you as all too quickly you can lose sight of where you are and suddenly they have traded places. It's a hard thing to do, but we can all rise to the better angels within even when it's all too easy to succumb to our demons.

Little did I know but when the day comes for a death sentence to be carried out, these cruel people don't give you any notice—no death warrant is ever served on a death-row prisoner. They just pitch up in the dead of the night, slap you in leg-irons and handcuffs and lead you away to the death cells.

I was cut off from the world, and I was in a time warp. There is nothing with which to gauge the passage of time on death row, no daylight, no clocks, no mirrors, but I'd catch the odd glance of myself when I was taken out the death section to see my lawyer or for some other administrative reason, and it was always horrifying to see an aged, haggad reflection staring back at me.

Every Thursday while on death row, every week of the year, the guards arrive with a bathroom scale to weigh you. The reason for this little task is that the hangman needs your weight and they do the weighing every Thursday so that you never know when you're in for the long drop. I watched my weight fall from 95 kilograms (210lbs) when I was first arrested down to 69 kilograms (150lbs). I am about 185 centimetres tall (slightly over six foot), so at 69 kilograms, as you can imagine, I was a bit *skraal* (thin). I also went bald—my hair was a bit thin on top before death row, but the added stress and no sunlight put paid to any proper regrowth.

After the death-row initiation of shaved head and beard, I began to regrow my beard, which was probably my first rejection of some of the prison's pedantic bureaucracy—that prisoners should shave. They do not allow you your own razors on death row, obviously, but expect you to use a razor blade that one of the prisoners (delegated as barber) produces. My reasoning was, "If you're going to hang me, what difference does it make whether I have a beard or not?"

It was quite distressing to watch myself decline like this, and develop a jailhouse pallor. I wasn't brown, I wasn't white, just an in-between, unhealthy, pale colour, and now being quite gaunt, I found a startled yet lost sort of look had developed somewhere in my eyes. This worried me—imagine what it did to my wife on her monthly visit when she would put on as cheery a façade as she could, at a time when she was very worried about my deteriorating health. Amazing what a difference a little sun makes and maybe some decent food once in a while—and a little serenity too. The stuff we all so often take for granted.

When you sit there, all alone for years on end, you find that every ache and pain takes on a new meaning. Your piles that won't stop bleeding, or a little more angina, dizziness, or reduced urine flow. I had all this shit wrong with me but if you sit there with nothing to do your mind goes crazy and you imagine everything worse that it actually is. Time and time again I'd have to slowly talk my way through these ailments. It's nice if you have someone to talk to, someone who can simply tell you that you look fine, don't worry. Repressed anxiety is an emotion you have to be very aware and wary of. It can sneak up on you and before you know it you're dreaming and imagining all sorts of crap.

I was never tortured, not by the cops or the guards. Not the way you think of torture. They simply locked me away in purgatory, gave me poor food and ill-managed medical aid. And I dreamed my life away. I dreamed as I wasted away and thought and thought until I thought I'd die of emotion. It was such a difficult thing to come to terms with, to know that my war was now part of history, and I was still jailed for it just as it was for the Prisoner of Chillon:

> *When day was beautiful to me, as to young eagles being free*
> *With spiders I had friendship made*
> *Oh God! It is a fearful thing to see the human soul take wing*

♤♤♤

1989 saw me back in court for the Harare bombings. And once again I was charged for political offences under Zimbabwe's colonially drafted legislation and not as a plain criminal for common-law crimes. They charged me with the same laws that were drafted in Rhodesia for specific use against politically motivated people, like Mugabe himself and many of his peers. Yet, during my nearly twenty years in prison, not once would Zimbabwe classify me as a political prisoner. Work that one out.

The security forces were now well practised with the convoy rigmarole to and from court. Three of us, Smith, Bawden and me, were each placed in a seperate Zimbabwe National Army APC (armoured personnel carrier) armed with mounted machine guns. There were also military, police and prison vehicles ahead and behind us with armed troops. A mobile 14.5mm anti-aircraft machine gun was also in the convoy.

All pretty impressive were it a visiting head of state and not just us three *skelms*. A week or so later, the palaver was over and I was back on death row with an extra seventy-five years' sentence … same old shit.

The Jeremy Brickhill mobile circus with their cameras, justice ministers and *The Hidden Hand* came and went, as did Nelson Mandela's release in 1990.

♤♤♤

There's not much to do on death row. You can sit and think, or walk up and down and think, or sing songs to yourself, as I did. Or you can just sit. Or lie down. But there's a limit to the amount of sleeping you can do—especially when it is never peaceful sleep.

Quite often I would be hugely excited to find a little jumping spider on the inside hinge of my door. This was a change of activity for me and I'd spend hours watching this little chap sit on the hinge looking for something to eat. I'd make a movement with my finger and he would immediately tense up as he focused on this possibility of graze (food). On occasions when I had a resident on the hinge I'd catch those little fishmoths that creep out of nooks and crannies and then feed my little friend his live dinner, straight from the tips of my fingers. This little *oke* would leap a few centimetres from his perch, seize the fishmoth, or mozzie (mosquito), and dash back to his hinge. Days when I caught some bait and couldn't find my little predator were real bummers. What can a man do?

During 1989, President Mugabe declared an amnesty for all security forces and gooks who were involved in the Matabeleland massacres, including anyone else who "acted in good faith" during the dissident era. About 120 dissidents came out of the bush, were pardoned and went on their merry way. Among these dissidents were a couple of the South African Super ZAPU fellows. The amnesty order specifically excluded 'foreign military agents' meaning me and the guys with me. Yet the Super ZAPU dissidents, who as I've said were trained, equipped and deployed by South Africa, were not classed as foreign military agents. That was predictable logic straight out of Mnangagwa's ministry of justice, who would have been tasked to draft the conditions of the amnesty.

If you don't use it you lose it. That's a fact. Your senses become numbed through lack of use. My once-excellent eyesight deteriorated as the years passed and I found it increasingly difficult to judge distances. My horizon for nineteen and a half years was a six-metre concrete wall, topped with razor wire that surrounded the exercise yard. I wanted so badly to see a horizon that was not made up of razor wire. On occasions while en route to the government dentist in downtown Harare, I'd be amazed and distressed that my vision was blurred and I could no longer judge distances, be it from a vehicle in front of us to houses on the side of the road.

Years later after I had been released, I didn't let on to passengers in any vehicle I drove that I had a problem judging distances. No one would have gotten in for a ride, that's for sure. However, driving a car is like riding a bicycle—you get back on and it all comes back to you. I thought I was quite hot a few weeks after my freedom when I was first allowed to drive again. I don't think that my kids, who were my first passengers, will entirely agree with this assessment though.

I missed smells more than anything. The smell of rain, of a braai, grass, a river. I missed these so much that I thought I would go fucking mad but your sense of smell eventually deserts you too. In retrospect this was probably a blessing because on the odd occasion while on death row, Christmas time say, the guards would have a braai in their camp and the wind would waft that glorious barbequed meat smell right into the condemned section where I had just eaten my boiled potato.

You do not lose your sense of touch in jail, but you crave to touch or be touched, especially by soft things. One thing I craved for was to walk barefoot on freshly cut grass, and just to feel grass under my feet, which I didn't do for twenty years. Your dog licking your hand, or giving him a scratch, or simply to hold someone's hand is impossible, and you miss that so much.

My sense of hearing has always been acute and that was a hassle for all the years of my imprisonment. It's one sense that didn't fail me—to my detriment—and I have the bags under my eyes from years of lack of sleep to prove it. A pin drops and I am awake. Doors slamming, officers and prisoners with their incessant jabber jabber, and there I'd lie in my solitary cell, or in a crowded one, wide awake, trying to relax and all the while getting more and more frustrated and angry (envious too) of people snoring and farting all around me.

A couple of my co-accused were hard of hearing and could sleep through anything—which I really wished for ... so many times. Eventually after death row I was sent some silicone earplugs—heaven! But by then the years of no sleep had taken their toll and in addition to permanent bags under my eyes I developed a heart problem.

The prison doctor was actually quite good. He was an Indian *oke*, and he diagnosed me as having had a mild heart attack while on death row, brought on by years of mental stress and anguish. He also said that I was now suffering from stress-induced angina. I was on all sorts of heart drugs by mid-1993, but not given access to a heart specialist in the city centre—no way. I was too much of a state-security risk to be taken into town to see the doctor. I had to wait until I was off death row for that. It made no matter though—every government heart specialist I was taken to, even after the tests I was subjected to proved I had heart damage, declined to put his cock on the block instead of sticking to his Hippocratic oath and diagnosing me properly.

They were all under serious intimidation to state that my angina was not a major problem, and that I certainly didn't need major heart treatment. Yet every one of them prescribed a number of heart drugs for me. I would get so incensed by this attitude. I've read a lot about revenge and hate and continually tried, even with those doctors, to restrain my thoughts of fixing them one day. Hate destroys the vessel that holds it. That is a dead certainty so I had to beware I didn't just exacerbate my daily stress—which was already overwhelming me—with fury against people who didn't count in my life.

I'd just have to hope for everything but expect nothing. Which is a bit pathetic, but there you have it.

Upon arrival in South Africa, and only after my release in July 2006 did I manage to go for proper heart tests, and the angiogram I had at Luthuli Hospital clearly showed that I needed a triple bypass.

The minister of justice knew full well that proper heart treatment was not available in Zimbabwe, and if I had been diagnosed as requiring a bypass, I would have had my human rights lawyer seek a court application for treatment outside the country. I would have accepted treatment just about anywhere it was available and not necessarily in South Africa. So to avoid that it was far simpler and cheaper for the Zimbabwean regime to have the heavies put the screws on the heart specialists.

After my release, having suffered from untreated heart disease for fifteen years, it was only through the goodwill of my sister's general practitioner and a heart-specialist friend of his that I could obtain an angiogram—the definitive test I'd been waiting for since 1993. The angiogram immediately picked up three compromised arteries. I am due for a triple bypass as I write this.

Consider that I was on a low-salt, fat-free, almost meat-and-dairy-free, booze-and-cigarette-free regimen for twenty years and here I sit needing a bypass. So, when your doctor tells you to lay off all the good stuff like the fat along the edge of your steak, or a couple of *dops* (drinks) just quote the medical example of Woods!

Incredible as this sounds, you worry about your health a lot on death row, because there is a good chance that you will be hanged of course. You sit and continually fret about your little aches and pains. Smith smoked in the cell next to me, and it would drive me scatty when his secondary smoke would seep into my cell, giving me visions of lung cancer as I frantically tried to waft the smoke away with my blanket.

Sense of taste is a huge one too, that you lose if you don't use. We all know what decent *skoff* (food) tastes like. Twenty years of boiled food sorts that one out. But it is a joy, I tell you, to be on this side of the prison wall where I can rediscover all the old and new culinary delights of life.

෴෴෴

The years on death row passed, somehow, and in late 1993 the government eventually managed to provide our lawyers with a typed transcript of our first trial. Five years down the line, and at a huge financial cost we finally got this basic right. Without a transcript one cannot lodge an appeal, which we then did, appealing that the statements we originally made to the police were extracted under ransom for our wives, families and children who were being held for that sole purpose—to ensure our total co-operation.

The Zimbabwean Supreme Court in the mid '90s still had some independently minded judges. However, they didn't last long and were chased off the bench by President Mugabe's rabid war veterans. According to the Zimbabwean constitution, Robert Mugabe does not have the power to fire a judge, especially if the judge is only making rulings he is not happy with. He can fire a judge if he turns out to be a crook or a rapist or some such, but not for doing his job. So the easiest way for the regime to get rid of a judge is to send a bunch of war veterans to give him, or her, the living shits, and to ensure they have no back-up from the cops. That usually does the trick. It's happened to a few judges who have had the temerity to think for themselves. They've been chased away.

Our death-sentence-appeal judges went ahead and accepted that our confessions were made voluntarily and reconfirmed our death sentences. Things happened quite fast after that ruling. At Chikurubi I had been held on the ground floor of the condemned section for five years. The female condemned section where South African Security Police spy, Odile Harrington, had been held and was serving twenty-five years was two flights of concrete stairs above me. The floor in the middle of us was the death chamber where there were four holding cells and the gallows.

Within a few days of losing our appeal, we heard scraping and thumping noises coming from directly above us—from the death chamber! And without even trying to fathom out the origin of the noise it was plain enough to hear that some sort of maintenance or rennovation work was going on. The gallows and its holding cells had been locked, probably since the prison was built in the late 1970s.

The Supreme Court's decision was that we three were active participants in the wilful murder of the driver of the Bulawayo car bomb and deserved what we were going to get.

Reprieve

"More things are wrought by prayer than this world dreams of"
Author unknown

Earlier in 1993, the Harare chapter of the Catholic Commission for Justice and Peace had mounted a Supreme Court challenge on behalf of thirteen prisoners at Harare Central Prison who had been on death row for many years. They sought relief for these men on the grounds that it was cruel and inhumane to hold a man in the shadow of the gallows and in suspense of being executed at any time, for years on end. The Supreme Court ruled in favour of the prisoners and altered all thirteen sentences to ones of life imprisonment. While this was a huge relief for the thirteen, in the minds of Mugabe's wicked administrators, all it meant was that they would have to hurry up and hang the rest who were sitting on death row, including us three, before the Supreme Court started to let everyone off, depriving Mugabe's hangman of a living!

So after our appeal failed, our lawyers, indominatable as always, went to the Supreme Court and filed an application asking that the same relief be applied to us, as we had been on death row for five years.

As soon as our application was filed, the shit hit the fan with the minsitry of justice lackeys, who were gleefully rubbing their hands together at the prospect of silencing Kevin Woods once and for ever. The attorney general immediately filed papers indicating the state was going to vigorously oppose any relief whatsoever for us.

Our lawyers and the attorney general's office were then advised by the Supreme Court to be prepared to argue the issue four days later on the following Tuesday.

Our lawyers slogged the whole weekend and presented themselves before the full five judges at the Supreme Court, 9.00 a.m. sharp on that appointed Tuesday morning. Typical of the Zimbabwean regime, when no political decision is to hand, they do nothing. So, no one from the attorney general's office pitched

up, despite harried court orderlies making frantic phone calls and dispatching runners up and down the court building to find someone, anyone, from the AG's office. Believe it or not, on that Tuesday morning, all the AG's law officers, AG included, were nowhere to be found.

Tuesday you see, is the day Mugabe meets with his cabinet in Harare and obviously Mnangagwa, the justice minister, hadn't told Mugabe that we were about to slip the noose, and he didn't know what to do.

Come 4.00 p.m. that Tuesday, *voila!* a law officer from the attorney general's office arrived in sack cloth and ashes, crocodile tears and all, apologizing that they had all been in an urgent conference and could the matter please be delayed to the following Tuesday.

Our lawyers smelled a rat and were furious, as was Chief Justice Anthony Gubbay (who was run out of office a few years later by war veteran, Joseph Chinotimba, who was doing the regime's dirty work, acting outside the law but obviously on instruction and with absolute impunity, like throwing commercial farmers off their land, terrorizing MDC supporters and generally playing the ZANU (PF) loose cannon). The matter was grudgingly delayed to the next Tuesday.

The state meanwhile was up to its shenanigans to circumvent the ruling but needed to change its fundamental human rights law in the constitution. In any civilized country the constitution is the fundamental law of the land and is sacrosanct. Not so in Zimbabwe where, since independence, Mugabe has continuously been amending and panel-beating it to suit his own agenda.

President Robert Mugabe is deaf to criticism from friends and foe alike. Highly intelligent as he is, he surrounds himself with idiots who give him the advice he wants to hear. Some of his amendments to the constitution and Zimbabwean law go a long way in illuminating just how fawning a bunch they are.

At the time of our appeal against the death sentence, the Zimbabwean parliament was in recess. It comprised 150 members, thirty of whom were chosen by Mugabe—and all of them, with the exception of one independent seat, were ZANU (PF) puppets. So it was no big thing for the regime to get two-thirds of them into the house, if a constitutional amendment was required. The Zimbabwean constitution had a clause which forbids cruel and inhumane treatment and provides for protection of its people from such treatment—such as holding a man for an indefinite period on death row. The problem for the justice ministry was that the parliament was in recess and Mnangagwa only had a week before the following Tuesday, with nearly every parliamentarian away, preparing for their Christmas break.

A frantic day or so later, with enough members of parliament found and recalled to work, Mugabe could now institute an urgent sitting of parliament—the reason—an urgent constitutional amendment.

All this just to make sure he could hang me when he wanted. It would have caused quite a fuss, even for him, to have gone ahead and strung me up while documents fighting my execution had been already filed with the Supreme Court. So to pretend he occasionally followed the rule of law, he had to go this route.

On the Thursday just after their no-show-Tuesday, they tabled the constitutional amendment which specifically stated that, regarding Zimbabwe's Bill of Human Rights, when it comes to prisoners on death row, any delay, no matter how long, would not be considered as cruel and inhumane treatment. The bill was read twice on the Thursday and all the members of parliament were required to return on Friday morning, where it was read for the third time, and passed by every single drone sitting there. They then all promptly went back on Christmas holidays, their duty done. All that was now required was for Robert Mugabe to sign it into law and publish it in the *Government Gazette*. (Quite why he bothers with such legalities!)

Unfortunately the government printers produced the weekly *Government Gazette* every Thursday, for consumption on the Friday. So they were not able to produce a new gazette for the same day. No sweat, a special extraordinary gazette was produced and published on the following Monday. You could almost hear the sigh of relief from the ministry of justice from inside death row, where I sat, sweating a little, I can assure you.

Come Tuesday, and all parties to this little drama were on stage in the Supreme Court—the five judges, the state's full complement (no special meeting today) and our attorneys. The state immediately argued that as the constitution of Zimbabwe had now declared that as the holding of a person on death row, ad infinitum, was neither cruel nor inhumane, my application was therefore null and void. Just like that, without even blushing.

The Supreme Court was not swayed by this tomfoolery and ruled that it would not implement the constitutional amendment retroactively even though Mugabe's drones in the state's law office had it specifically incorporated as part of the constitution that if you had been sentenced before the amendment it didn't count! So accordingly, in their judgement, which was printed a few weeks later on 18th December 1993, a full five years after I had been sentenced to death, the Supreme Court in a four-to-one decision ruled that my death sentence be set aside and replaced with one of life imprisonment.

PHEW! That was close!

Just to show you that I am not making this up, because Mugabe's government is going to try and denigrate everything I say in this book, I am going to reproduce, verbatim, the Constitution of Zimbabwe, Amendment No. 13 dated 5th November (coincidentally my birthday) 1993.

Section 15, sub-section 1, which I reproduce for clarity, is the basic law, and this has not been amended. It reads:

15. PROTECTION FROM INHUMAN TREATMENT

1. No person shall be subjected to torture or to inhuman or degrading punishment or other such treatment.

However the amendment, just a few lines down reads:

5. Delay in the execution of a sentence of death, imposed upon a person in respect of a criminal offence of which he has been convicted, shall not be held to be contravention of sub-section (1). And:

6. A person upon whom any sentence has been imposed by a competent court, whether before, on or after the date of commencement of the Constitution of Zimbabwe Amendment (No. 13) Act 1993 in respect of a criminal offence of which he has been convicted, shall not be entitled to a stay, alteration or remission of sentence on the ground that, since the sentence was imposed, there has been a contravention of subsection (1).

Our reprieve was a huge relief for us and for our families and supporters. However in Zimbabwe, life sentence is still indefinite, and you remain in jail at the whim of the president. So there was not much change; it was just going to take longer for them to kill me in prison. But at least, by not being hanged, you're still in the race and have a chance of going the distance, no matter how soul-destroying an indefinite sentence is. You're alive and kicking, and another hat peg, a huge one, was suddenly hammered into my imaginary hat rack.

The political masters, sulking at not getting their way, refused to give the order to the prison services to remove us from death row and place us with other life prisoners in the normal sections of the prison. They were obviously seriously pissed off at not being allowed to legally string me up, and were cracking their skulls trying to scheme up some other plan to circumvent the court's decision. Christmas 1993 came and went with us three still held, incommunicado, on death row.

ورورو

With the adrenaline of victory still coursing through their veins our attorneys opened the 1994 court calendar by preparing and filing an urgent court application for us to be treated equally to all other prisoners serving life sentences, of which, there were over a hundred at Chikurubi.

The case was set down for 29th January as some of the judges were obviously a bit frustrated at the state cluttering up their time with this nonsense, so we were jumped up the court waiting list. Under normal circumstances we would have had to wait months on end for a Supreme Court hearing.

On the morning of 29th January, the Commissioner of Prisons phoned our lawyers and told them there was no need to fuss with a court case as we were to be moved to the general cells that day!

Obviously everyone was thoroughly overjoyed with the new development, but as our lawyers had engaged a few advocates to prepare this court case someone had to foot the bill for their time and effort.

We demanded repayment from the prisons, whose own delay in not moving us out of the condemned section had caused this legal expense. Prisons refused to pay for the lawyers' time, so back to court we went to obtain an order to force them to cough up. The result a couple of weeks later was that Prisons had to pay for the lawyers' time wasted in preparing our case to get us out of the condemned section, and for their time spent preparing the new case to decide whether the prison was liable or not.

ورورو

I am a proponent of the death sentence!

Even after going through death row in Zimbabwe, and knowing the agony my loved ones suffered while I sat in the shadow of Robert Mugabe's gallows, I am all for capital punishment. Take the crime scene in South Africa today. These robbers and rapists have no compunction about killing their victims because, whether the rob you or murder you, they're going to spend about the same time in a cushy jail. The sentences being handed down, even the multiple life sentences are absolutely no deterrent. Telling a person he must go to jail for life, or for a hundred years is actually beyond one's reality. You notice it when you're sitting there in jail, as each day just follows the other and you're going nowhere, but while out on the street, for these career hijackers, rapists and armed robbers it is just a figure. They can't touch it.

I spent many years in prison with people sentenced for armed robbery, rape, hijacking and murder. People serving twenty-four years for drug-smuggling, child molesters, rapists and the like were my companions for all those years. I used to ask the drug smugglers, for example, why they didn't ply their trade in the Middle East where you can get huge money for drugs. "No way, Woods. Are you mad? If you get caught there they chop your head off!" they'd reply.

In Zimbabwe there are mandatory sentences for drug-smuggling. Twenty-four years for anything over ten grams of cocaine. You can get a quarter off if you pay a huge fine. In that event six years is removed and you go to jail with an eighteen-year sentence. Six further years will be removed for good behaviour. So that's twelve years you will spend in jail. And of course people would rather spend twelve years in jail, simply because they are frightened of the death sentences for the same offence in other countries. Anyone say that the death sentence is not a deterrent?

I can promise you that if a few of these bloodthirsty killers walking our streets, hijackers, armed robbers or rapists were strung up in South Africa, the crime rate for those offences would fall immediately.

The death sentence does not count for fools like me who did these crazy things for some sort of moral or political belief. The distinction has to be made in this regard, and you have to have a set of criteria for offences for which you will be killed, much like in certain parts of the States and the Middle and Far East. Murder and rape for example, should be capital offences.

I sat there on death row a few times and heard other inmates being removed in the dead of night, to be taken to the death chamber which adjoins the prison hospital. I heard their chains dragging on the floor, I heard their spine-chilling wails and screams, and I heard the deep *kalunk* of the trapdoor as they were killed. I remember so well the horror and dread in me, but I have no qualms in being very pro the death sentence.

Of course the death sentence has to be overseen by an objective panel of judges who are above political influence. That is so important. In Zimbabwe, for instance, government-sponsored murders are carried out specifically to instil fear in the political opposition. Political opposition in Zimbabwe is interpreted as almost treason by the ruling elite. So is just about anything else that may endanger their ride on the gravy train.

Killing a policeman should also be right up there with these other capital crimes. Like them or hate them, the cops are fantastic people who have a low-paid, shit job, and everything should be done to keep them out there on the street.

Considering where I had been for five years and just how close I had come to being strung up, I feel a quote by Theodore Roosevelt is quite apt:

"You've never lived until you've almost died.
For those who have had to fight for it, life truly has a flavour,
That the protected will never know"

Transfer from death row

"Almost, is not eaten"
Xhosa of South Africa

That night of 29th January 1994, having been removed from the condemned section of Chikurubi Maximum, I was locked up in an overcrowded cell with my old friend and co-accused, Barry Bawden. Together with him was Sam Beahan, the mercenary who had been part of our failed escape bid all those long years before. We had a lot to catch up on, the failed escape being a very hot topic, especially as Sam was now also squatting in jail due to his integral part in the cock-up regarding our breakout.

It was then, after I'd been removed from the condemned section, that a few friendly prison guards told me that the banging we had heard coming from the upstairs floor of the death row after we had lost our appeal, was indeed the prison security technicians getting the gallows into working order.

Around that time the South African government was engaged in the CODESA (Convention for a Democratic South Africa) negotiations and Nelson Mandela, who had been released four years previously, was soon going to be the first black president in South African history. CODESA was coming up with all sorts of sideline agreements, one of which saw a number of ANC prisoners, and some, but not all, from other liberation movements being pardoned and released from South Africa's jails. People like ANC foot soldier Robert McBride, who at one stage in the late '80s and early '90s was on death row in Pretoria for bombing Magoo's, a restaurant and pub in Durban, and right-winger Barend Strydom, who had occupied an adjacent cell to McBride for shooting dead some people on the streets of Pretoria simply because they were black, were also released as a part of the CODESA talks. It's an understatement that my hope hats were innumerable at that stage, especially when I heard that the CODESA talks involved the release of all prisoners who had been jailed for politically motivated crimes in South Africa and the Frontline States of Zimbabwe, Botswana, Angola, Mozambique and Tanzania.

Soon after Nelson Mandela became the South African president, he called upon all Frontline States, emphasizing that the liberation of South Africa, and in fact Africa as a whole, had been achieved, to release all those jailed for fighting in the South African struggle for freedom, on whichever side. Sure enough all Frontline State presidents, eager to go along with the liberation euphoria did just that; they released all the politically motivated prisoners they held... except Robert Mugabe. Mugabe, watching from the sidelines, saw his star start to fade in the ever-increasing brightness being exuded by Nelson Mandela, and he backed himself into a corner. And there he stayed for a long while. After failing to get attention in the form of the worldwide grants he was so used to, he and his cohorts started misbehaving ... worse and worse. Apparently with no depths that he would not go to to remain in the spotlight, from where his diabolical soul emerged, he has dragged Zimbabwe to where it is now.

In 1996, Bawden and Beahan, through a blunder at the ministry of justice found themselves included in a presidential amnesty that saw their sentences being reduced by five years. The amnesty also saw a couple of hundred common criminals going home. No one at the ministry had thought of excluding *sabotage and possession of arms of war* from the amnesty criteria.

Prisoners serving life sentences were specifically excluded from the amnesty. So that kicked one of my hats into touch. The ministry of justice tried to alter the wording of the gazette which had given the criteria for the amnesty, but had to relent after enormous pressure from our lawyers. Beahan and Bawden were subsequently released in 1999 and 2000 respectively, leaving us, 'The Harare Three', behind those reinforced grey walls of Chikurubi Maximun Security Prison.

An issue I had with this was that, as Beahan was convicted of possession of arms of war and attempting to jail-break and Barry was convicted of sabotage for the 1986 bombings in Harare, why then did they qualify for amnesty and us three, who were convicted of exactly the same offences (committed at a slightly different time), did not? And if it was so important, why didn't the Zimbabwean government go all out and obtain the extradition of the people we worked with and who were living and working in South Africa?

If this was such a big thing that the constitution of Zimbabwe had to be changed to make it legal to hang me, and if I was such a threat to Zimbabwe's national security, what of the people I had worked with and who were free and living just across the border in a friendly country? Who was more of a security threat? Me in jail or the *okes* in South Africa who also had access to nearly every weapon they wanted? I'm not knocking their release, just trying to make a point.

Ever since the 1994 election, the South African high commission had been conducting consular visits to us at Chikurubi. Prior to that our lawyers had a casual relationship with the South African trade commissioner in Harare who had absolutely no political clout, and who was obviously under strict orders from the de Klerk regime to stay as far away from us, in public, as he could.

I qualified for South African citizenship by descent with both my mother and father and their forebears being born in the Republic of South Africa. On my father's side my ancestors arrived on a ship from England way back in the 1820s. My South African citizenship was certified by the South African Department of Home Affairs on 4th August 1994, some six months after President Mandela took office. Mugabe was incensed by this citizenship change, insisting that I was a Zimbabwean.

The Zimbabwean *Financial Gazette* (29th May 1997), in an exclusive interview with President Mugabe, had this to say: "Mugabe rejected a request by President Mandela to free five jailed saboteurs. He said he had made it clear to Nelson Mandela that 'we will keep these people in prison until such time that we are satisfied we should release them, if at all, we will release them'. He said Zimbabwe's position would be 'hardened' as long as government gets external pressure especially from whites [ex-Rhodies]. Mandela on a state visit last week had requested him to free the five 'but he understood our position because these people are Zimbabweans and not South Africans'. Mugabe dismissed their citizenship. 'I do not know how they can become South African citizens because I don't know whether South African citizenship can be bestowed by remote control,' he said. 'President Mandela did not raise the issue of citizenship with me last week. These are Zimbabweans who violated Zimbabwean law.' He said 'they are free to apply for parole through their lawyers, and should use the existing legal channels.' [The fact of the matter is that there is no parole system in Zimbabwe and I had my lawyers write to Mugabe and ask him exactly what parole system he was talking about. I had no reply to this, or even an acknowledgement of the lawyer's letter.] Mugabe went on to say 'but they can't be released because the government is being challenged by some people in South Africa. These attempts by some group will not move us a bit,' he declared.

"Mugabe said that he was certain that after his talks last week with Mandela, the South African authorities would not raise this issue in future as it was an internal matter between the local judiciary and its nationals."

So much for my South African citizenship, which was 100 per cent kosher. Amazingly on the day that I was released some years later, I was deported to South Africa as I was deemed to be a South African citizen by the Zimbabwean immigration department, on orders from President Mugabe's office.

৵৵৵

Over the years that I was jailed I tried to maintain contact with different South African politicians. At one point in 1996 I received a letter from Alfred Nzo, South African foreign minister, informing me that President Mandela had been speaking to Mugabe about our release. In addition to Foreign Affairs I battled and wrote to Correctional Services to obtain a prison transfer, which Zimbabwe has on its law books, but not South Africa. I also tried the Truth and Reconciliation Commission, Foreign Affairs, Home Affairs and always got the basic runaround.

Mr. Tony Leon of the Democratic Alliance was an enormous supporter for my release. Obviously he did not align himself with my morals and activitiy which had dropped me in the *kak*, but I presume he could sympathize with me regarding my unwarranted, continued detention for activities on behalf of the previous South African government.

He wrote numerous letters to the presidents of South Africa and Zimbabwe, asked innumerable questions in the South African parliament and visited me in Chikurubi. Unfortunately, not much heed was given to him, especially after Nelson Mandela retired. Leon went so far as to have prisoner-transfer legislation drafted but unfortunately the ANC majority in parliament refused to pass it into law.

It was one the hardest things I've ever done to write and ask Mr. Leon to back off his campaign for my release, simply because of personality clashes between himself and members of the South African cabinet, especially with President Mbeki himself.

Anything he tried to do for me became a personal issue which resulted in exactly the opposite of what he was asking to be done. I will always be hugely indebted to Tony Leon, as I am to Mr. Marthinus van Schalkwyk, the current minister of environment and tourism. When Marthinus van Schalkwyk took over the reins of the New National Party from F. W. de Klerk, one of the first things he did was to acknowledge responsibility for me and my colleagues in Chikurubi.

Positive answers started coming from the South African parliament instead of prevaricating innuendo. Marthinus van Schalkwyk visited me in Chikurubi and it was an enormous morale boost to see him and his entourage receive the red carpet at the prison. He has access to President Mbeki and I believe his support and effort played a huge part in my eventual release.

But the main problem was Mugabe and his ego. "It's all about face," a senior member of the Zimbabwean ministry of foreign affairs who does not want to be named, told me while I was still detained. "If the president agrees to your release it will not have happened if he is asked by a president of another country, no matter the country, and especially if the request is in the press, because it will immediately appear as if he is dancing to someone else's tune and he thinks he will look silly."

Okay, so who could I get to intercede on my behalf that would not piss Mugabe off? It's amazing sometimes how the world turns—people who at one time detested me and cheered at my death sentence, eventually became proponents for my release. So many people only got to know me via correspondence while I was in jail and I believe this led to many people's perceptions of me changing, including my own.

One such lady is former Rhodesian prime minister, Sir Garfield Todd's daughter, Judith. During her life in Rhodesia she was demonized and bullied as a *kaffir boetie* (literally 'kaffir brother') simply because of her belief in equality of all people. She was haunted and harassed by the Rhodesian police, of whom I was a member, and she was an active supporter of the Rhodesian and South African liberation movements. What more unlikely friendship—Judith Todd and Kevin Woods!

My ultimate crusader and best friend, my brother Mike in Australia, who never ever ceased with his prayers and support for me in jail, had corresponded with Judith for a few years before she and I began correspondence. This ultimately led to our release from prison

≈ ≈ ≈

I actually had a serious problem with F. W. de Klerk's administration which was the successor to P. W. Botha's in South Africa. From my peephole perspective, as I saw time slipping through my fingers in jail, it was easy to condemn F. W. and his foreign minister Pik Botha for doing absolutely nothing to resolve our plight. We had laid our lives on the line for their government, after all. Never mind all the denials and fancy footwork; they know, we all know, that we were their front-line soldiers.

As 1994 and handover to the ANC loomed, and I became ever more frantic that we were totally abandoned, I smuggled a letter to F. W. de Klerk. I am told that this letter was hand-delivered by the SA defence chief, Magnus Malan. In the letter, short and sweet, I implored F. W. "not to abandon us".

Throughout our detention and especially up to 1994 when the reins were handed over to Nelson Mandela, South Africa maintained a preferential trade agreement with Zimbabwe. This had lapsed some years prior to our arrest, but was still technically in operational effect, although it had not been re-instated by the two governments. This agreement could also just as easily have been a pressure point for F. W. de Klerk to use, as most of Zimbabwe's fuel supply came by rail, through South Africa.

Most of Zimbabwe's railway wagons are hired from South Africa. P. W. withdrew them in the early 1980s to put the squeeze on Mugabe when he started reneging on his promises not to allow the ANC sanctuary from where to springboard their raids. Why not again? If there had been a will there would have been a way—that's my opinion.

F. W. and Pik will have all the excuses and political explanations ready but the fact is I am the one who lost those years of my life—not them. Subsequent to my release, I've heard that Pik and F. W. did speak to Mugabe about us just prior to 1994, in Gaborone and according to Pik, Mugabe seemed favourably disposed to our release *before Christmas that year*. But true to form he returned to Zimbabwe and did nothing. President Mugabe well knew that the 'Boer' government was on its way out so he didn't have to honour any kind of gentleman's agreement with F. W. or Pik.

There are a few educational programmes in jail—as long as you can fund yourself you can study primary and secondary schooling—obviously not while you are in the condemned section but while in the general population. Robert Mugabe and several of his current cabinet members and parliamentarians obtained numerous university degrees while in jail in Rhodesia, all funded by the then racist regime, but today a prisoner has to fund his own education. But on death row, no matter how many years you squat there, you are not allowed to study. There are qualified teachers employed by the prison service who are there to do just that—teach—but if you can't supply your own materials and most of your set books, you're lost.

You cannot survive in jail in Zimbabwe if you rely solely on the food and medicine that the prisons supply. Because of the economic collapse of the country, all rations to prisoners have declined proportionally with the money the government has at its disposal. You have to smuggle in food, medicine, letters and whatever else you need in order to survive. This smuggling business in prison is no big deal. Everyone does it to some degree or other. The prison guards receive slave wages and nearly all of them will take the chance to smuggle, both in and out, for no great recompense. It's sad to take advantage of the prison guards in this way, but everyone's got to survive, them and the prisoners.

ڡ ڡ ڡ

My sands of time continued running and the years dragged by slowly but surely. You don't follow the date in prison, especially when you've got an indefinite sentence with no end. What's the point of counting the days to nowhere? You have to try and stop thinking of wasted years, just to get through each interminably boring, useless day after another. I aged dramatically in prison, because of the unending stress, of worrying about my family, and simply trying to get myself through each day. I had to do something to pass the time instead of just sitting, or pacing up and down the exercise yard, and a man can only play so much chess. So I obtained some colour pens and pencils and taught myself how to draw. I concentrated on nature's wildlife, with birds and animals being my favourite. Many people seemed to love my drawings and everyone commented on the bright colours I used, be it a bird, or a vivid African sunset. I suppose after living in the grey world that surrounded me for so long, the bright colours I used were my way of adding a little colour to my world. My family and friends and people who supported me, who prayed for me, loved and helped me over those interminable years, seemed to enjoy receiving my pictures too.

At one stage I smuggled some drawings to a friend in the UK and he auctioned them on eBay. Some people out there actually paid for my drawings. I remember a young hippo that I drew was bought for 100 British pounds. That was enough to fund my correspondence, stamps, and aerogrammes and so on for a long time. A few friends would also send me some money from time to time, which was always very touching and very much needed.

They say that a country's attitude toward human rights can be judged by the standards applied in its prisons. The presidents of some countries don't give two hoots if others attempt to judge their standards and monitor human rights that they apply in their country. They will hide behind façades of smug righteousness, believing that their country's independence is their sole creation and no matter how they behave against their own prople, they think it is their God-given prerogative to do so, since they were the original liberator.

Robert Mugabe is one such leader.

He will not turn the other cheek. While he will ignore and brook no outside interference in the *sovereign affairs of Zimbabwe*, he quickly loses his cool when leaders of mostly western countries have adverse comment for him regarding human rights in Zimbabwe.

Any attempt by other world leaders, human rights organizations or other supporters of human rights, is slated as outside interference in the domestic affairs of Zimbabwe i.e. Robert Mugabe's personal domain. It is his sovereign right, so it seems to him, to butcher, bludgeon and steal from his citizens, a policy well favoured by all in his establishment, and who now comprise the fabulously rich in Zimbabwe, and who ride well and truly in the first-class seats of his gravy train. There is no middle class in Zimbabwe. You have the fabulously rich and the hideously poor—*chete* (only)!

Zimbabwe's prisons are very isolated from the outside world. This does not mean that there are never any visitors, but all international and local human rights visitors to Zimbabwe's correctional facilities are well screened to avoid any unfavourable commentary regarding the conditions and human rights therein.

All human rights organizations, such as Amnesty International and Zimbabwe Lawyers for Human Rights were prohibited access to me. They all had me on their records and followed my case, but there was absolutely nothing they could do for me because of Mugabe's stubborn, dogmatic attitude towards my case.

Upon admission to the Zimbabwean prison establishment, and it does not matter whether you are convicted or just on remand, you are expected to metaphorically remove your human skin and your human rights at the prison gates and then adorn the skin of some lesser mammal, a baboon perhaps, and are expected to just accept the total deprivation of some fundamental rights— without any fight or complaint. It simply does not matter that the Zimbabwean government of Mugabe's regime is the signatory to sundry United Nations and other charters regarding human rights.

What concerns Robert Mugabe with regard to every aspect of Zimbabwean life is 'Mugabe's will–Mugabe's way'—finished and *klaar*—and nothing else is of any consequence. And for many years now Mugabe's way is entirely focused on maintaining the status quo, with him in the driving seat … forever.

As soon as anyone starts exposing prisoner abuse, from whatever quarter, it's straight back to the sovereignty spiel for the government's mandarins. And of course it's always, "colonially minded whites who want to undo the gains of our revolution and re-colonize the country" or if the person or organization doing the criticizing are from Africa, or heaven forbid, the former black American Secretary of State Colin Powell, then they are "puppets of the west" who have the temerity to cast aspersions on the application of human rights in Mugabe's Zimbabwe.

Everything that is going wrong or has gone wrong in Zimbabwe is blamed on nature, other people, enemies of the state, or whomever it is convenient to blame (Blair was a popular whipping boy). Good scapegoats are droughts (even during good rainy seasons), sanctions and people (anyone) with hidden agendas. You name it—the blame lies elsewhere.

It's not only Mugabe who talks this drivel—his coterie and all others with their snouts deep in the trough sing from the same hymn sheet. Aids, for example, is blamed on Britian, who introduced the disease to Africa in an attempt to re-colonize the continent, according to Joshua Nkomo, who said this after the Unity Accord and as vice-president of Zimbabwe when he buried his son (who died of Aids) in the Kezi area of Matableland.

৶৶৶

When you are jailed in Zimbabwe you take a step back in time ... to the Middle Ages. "Incarcerated for rehabilitation of the offender" is probably the biggest oxymoron used by the prison services in this regard. You are simply *jailed* and you make it through, one way or another, depending always on your wits, craftiness, your will to survive, and most importantly, your financial status. If you've got the bucks, apart from being locked up on death row, prison is a breeze.

Prisoners with no family connections rarely survive prison in Zimbabwe. It is tragically ironic that the abject poverty we have in Zimbabwe causes the chicken thieves, the petty housebreakers, the pickpockets and so on to fill the jails. Especially when you realize that their penury is a direct result of economic mismanagement by the very government that throws them inside. Their struggle to survive is as a result of Mugabe's economic policies, which at the time of writing has 80 per cent of his people struggling beneath the poverty datum line. And of course it's the poor which make up the majority of the prison population.

The prison service administration operates on a bunch of rules and regulations that were drafted and implemented by the settler regime of Rhodesia, no less! And typical of so many ad-hoc policies and laws in Zimbabwe, in the prison service, you go from one extreme to the other while incarcerated.

For example, there is no parole system in Zimbabwe—for first offenders, second, third, fourth, or white-collar crime, and so on—no parole! "Ah yes, but we have a parole system for habitual offenders," they will exclaim in defence of their advanced 'prison system'. I will explain this: career criminals who are best behind bars, who have been in and out of jail for most of their lives, and 99 per cent of whom revert to crime as soon as they are released, benefit from an early release board—no one else.

There is no parole board to assess prisoners who may be serving a long stretch and who, by nature of their character or their remorse, will simply never, ever revert to crime again and who are only in jail due to circumstances beyond their control.

Prisoners jailed for for political offences, or for other crimes, who owe no debt to society and even prisoners serving life sentences, have absolutely no hope other than a presidential pardon. Life sentence in Zimbabwe means just the same as a death sentence—you die in jail—it just takes them longer to kill you.

Diametrically opposite to this zero-parole attitude the Zimbabwe prisons operate an open-prison system where prisoners nearing completion of their sentences can have weekend home visits: "No beer allowed to be consumed."

This system is obviously abused, as all else is in Zimbabwe where patronage and special favours are applied. Certain prisoners who have connections or a large enough bank balance are transferred to the open prison immediately upon admission and without doing any time at all.

ye ye ye

In Zimbabwean prisons the officer in charge of each facility is God. He runs the prison mostly as his own kingdom. He can make enormous carte-blanche decisions and he can be a saint or a shit.

Take an example: you need a new mat to sleep on, nothing fancy, just a felt mat about 15mm thick. No big deal huh? ... First of all a prisoner is prohibited from supplying his own bedding and clothing, regardless if you're sleeping on the cold concrete floor or walking around in rags due to the required clobber being out of stock. So here you are, sleeping on a piece of threadbare felt, which is torn and broken, full of holes and about one millimetre thick. You can either ask a junior guard, who hopefully shares your daily *sadza* ration with you, or whose wage packet you can supplement (with a quick visit to your relatives out there in the world he can always collect a bonus). In that event he will just swan across to the prison stores and requisition a mat.

If he is not your friend or not on your personal gravy train, then you have to go up the food chain a little and try your luck with the prison guard in charge of the stores. Simple, if he has the inclination to give you a mat— however, if he has a problem with that, then it's off to the officer in charge you go—he can then give the order and *voila!* you have a new mat. But if the officer in charge declines, which he does quite often to avoid repercssions (in my case, simply because the other prisoners including one of my co-accused 'Mhlati' was too lazy to make a request of his own), he would normally create a huge fuss as to why was the *murungu* (white man—me) was being given preferential treatment.

Quite often this *murungu* spiel would result in the prisoner who was complaining being given a thorough thrashing by the guards (except for Mhlati as he was one of us political prisoners) who would emphasize their beating with the words: "He gets the mat because he is not a fucking thief like you!" But mostly we were simply told there were no mats.

Anyhow, if the boss says no, that's it. You can throw a tantrum, summon your human rights lawyer, scream and shout, even go to court and you will get diddly squat. His word stands and even the commissioner of prisons will support him.

You could always just get a few cigarettes smuggled in and buy a mat from one of the other prisoners.

Cigarettes are enormous currency in prison where everything imaginable, except probably your liberty, is for sale—from an extra ration in the kitchen to medicine from the hospital. A few smokes can get you a twist of *dagga* (marijuana) from a friendly guard, or a 'short time' with one of the youngsters, if you are so inclined—a 'short time' being just that, a few minutes of homosexual sex in the toilets while a few of the 'pimps' stand outside to keep watch. A full night of debauchery goes for maybe a pack of twenty, and a 'marriage' for a carton of 200 cigarrettes. (A couple of cartons if the 'bride' is pretty and a virgin.)

There is so much sex going on in jail. Maybe it's boredom? It's certainly not because most inmates have homosexual genes, that's for sure. The prison officers generally turn a blind eye, but on occasions they vent their spleens on those caught playing 'snooker', with blood-on-the-wall types of thrashings, during which the 'female' of the pair is forced to wail like a banshee, as she is supposed to do, according to the macho status in prison, and the male has to show his *conjones* and take the beating in silence, like a man! Sometimes it's quite amusing, but most often the antics of these jail-time-only homosexuals is just sad.

I would always insist that the people in my communal cell were prohibited from pomping each other, because it always involved a lot of bickering between the 'girls' and the boys. I suffered from a serious lack of sleep for the twenty years I was in prison so I used to become incensed if there was a domestic during the night in my cell that woke me up. I would leap out of my bed, kick the shit out people making a noise in my cell and in the morning I would complain to the guards who would give the offenders a serious hiding and move them to other cells. Homosexuality was still rife in my cell but eventually they kept it as quiet as possible. Before the jail-break involving Steven Chidumo in 1998, the lights in the cells were dimmed at 8 o'clock at night so that you could hardly see from one side of the cell to the other—the 'snooker' players really enjoyed that. But after Steven Chidumo, all lights were left on full, which put a bit of a damper on their antics. As for me, I was a bit of a womanizer before I went into jail so to not have sex for twenty years was a huge mental problem for me. I was horny, but never for okes. I suppose it was just in my genes or something, that I could never contemplate homosexuality. I was never threatened with rape or any *kak* like that either.

On occasions the authorities would do the Aids routine—speeches and posters—which were totally ignored by nearly all the prisoners. Aids posters would be stuck up on the walls and the prison chaplain would do his best to preach the fact that giving your china a 'shot up the *gat* (hole)' is a death sentence … all to no avail.

On a few publicity occasions, the prison luminaries, who apparently hadn't even enough finance for proper food, clothing, medicine and amenities, would tell the press that prisoners were being supplied with condoms. Good grief, there's old Woodsie, locked up in jail for nearly twenty years and these jokers are talking of condoms.

On one of these condom 'occasions' I smuggled a letter out to the *Independent* newspaper. The letter was published and in it I basically intimated that instead of condoms I'd prefer a proper ration of food, or warmer clothes in winter. My oh my! Did that letter cause a fuss with the prison brass. Not only because I was exposing their hypocrisy but also because they wanted to know how I had managed to smuggle a letter out of jail.

Now take these *okes* in the trunk. Very few are genuinely gay. But so many prisoners seem to abandon all hope, get careless and toss away their lives with gay abandon, so to speak. Why some prisoners go crazy and destroy their lives with Aids because of their promiscuity I could never fathom. So often the three-wheeled (one wheel is missing) mobile push-stretcher from the hospital could be seen and heard wheeling out Aids corpses from the prison hospital to the morgue. This was living—rather, dead—proof for them all to see, several times a day as it traversed the prison centre court with its pathetic little bundle of emaciated bones, wrapped in an old hospital blanket, on its final journey to the prison mortuary.

"We get thin because of the poor food, not because of this thing Aids, and we get TB because of the cramped cells, not because we share one cigarette stub between six people."

Aids tests are done in prison. Many refrain from being tested with the 'I'd rather not know' excuse. Those who do have the test and are found positive often seem to go downhill full speed—a mental thing? And that downhill slide is inducement enough for any of the fence-sitters to want to stay away from the test needle, believe you me.

But just watch what happens when a prisoner, and especially one who was promiscuous in the outside world and who has remained promiscuous inside, proves negative. The change in that person is immediate—they share no more stubs, there is no more 'snooker' on his knees in the toilet, and they rather smuggle food than *boom* (ganja) and cigarettes—a complete *volte-face*! Hope, longevity and self-respect is restored.

And hope can give you amazing willpower and inner strength. I know, I've been there—with hope, and totally bereft of it too.

The prison officers carry out periodic searches of the cells where the prisoners sleep, and of the prisoners themselves. As normal, when you have a young whipper-snapper prison officer straight out of training, he has to flaunt his newfound power. The result during these searches is brutal beatings of the prisoners, wanton destruction of the meagre prisoner-made possessions such as draughts and chess boards and pieces (made painstakingly from papier mâché—some were quite exquisite too) which are trampled into the concrete. Even the prison-issue chessboards which are few and far between are regularly broken during these searches replaced only years later when another donation is made by some civic group.

All this is done during the searches, under the guise of security checks, with as much degrading treatment the guards can muster. One such measure was to have all prisoners strip naked before being searched. You then have to stand around, carrying your little bundle of clothes and whatever else you may possess and when your turn comes you're expected to sit at the guard's feet while your belongings are being searched and tossed all over the place. You are then expected to stand and star-jump just in case you are hiding a pistol or something between the cheeks of your ass. Then it's a mad scramble to recover your stuff, which is being trodden on or stolen in a huge mêlée of naked bodies, stamping boots and chaos. If you're lucky you can get your stuff together and hastily pull on your pair of shorts, or whatever, to recover some dignity and make your way to an area already searched.

From day one I had a problem with the naked search, in public so to speak, and I definitely had a mental block with the star-jump. Part of setting one's own standards, I suppose. Needless to say, this stubbornness of mine always caused a fuss at search-time. I flatly refused to strip naked, or to star-jump. The officers, mostly the nippers, would fume and shout and scream obscenities and threaten me while pointing their rubber batons, as menacingingly as they could under my nose, until one of the senior prison officers, sensing trouble, would come across, pat me down as a face-saving measure and send me over to the searched area of the cell block.

This was by no means a display of arrogance and certainly not bravado on my part. I suppose it was just my way of maintaining a semblance of humanity and self-dignity. Quite often I would just select an officer who was a 'connection', go to him for a cursory tap-down and avoid all the commotion. But sometimes a friendly face was nowhere to be seen among the guards and then the stubbornness syndrome would kick in.

During the search, any contrabrand such as razor blades and cigarettes found out of the holiday season are confiscated, ironically, quite frequently by the same prison officer who had smuggled them into the prison for you in the first place, just because he has to put on a show while his fellow guards look on. The seized goodies on occasions amounted to quite a bundle but cigarettes would always form the bulk of it. There are always mounds of cigarettes in prison. They would be taken for incineration. Yeah sure! We all knew they would be used by the officers to get some good food out of the prison kitchen for themselves.

Not once in nineteen and a half years in prison did I see a dangerous weapon, a piece of wire, a knife or anything at all serious being recovered in one of these searches.

ʔʔʔ

Most prisoners' bedding is infested with lice. Not such *lekker* (nice) little creatures, these lice. See one on your blanket and guaranteed, like fleas, there are plenty more. One goes to great lengths to keep one's blankets and clothes lice-free in jail. You can sometimes do this by smuggling lice *muti* (repellant) into the prison, but this gets a little tricky as the prison snitches—and there are plenty of them too—rat on you. Or you can make a plan and could have your clobber and bedding washed with hot water in the kitchens or better still at the laundry, when it's functioning.

Come search time the guards seem to take huge delight in mixing all the blankets about in the communal cells as they walk among the bed-rolls, kicking them left and right. And there goes all your diligent de-licing work down the drain as the blankets get all mixed up. The mess in the cells was always directly proportional to the amount of trouble caused during the strip search. If the whipper-snappers were frustrated, the blankets would go flying all over the place, into the crapper, wherever, and there they stayed until you could get back into the cell to rearrange your stuff, which would usually be hours later, giving the lice on the infested blankets ample time to make new *posies* (homes) for themselves in your own sanitized stuff.

A lot of prisoners did not seem to notice the lice or bugs, and would sleep, snoring and scratching away, as the little critters ran all over them. This was hugely frustrating for me, and often it was enough to reduce me to tears. So now you're locked up in the cell that looks like a tornado has hit it—but no cleaning or changing of blankets till the next morning because there's no room to do it and it's quite unpleasant in the cell while all the *okes* are rearranging blankets because the dust that collects on them is so suffocating. A lot of the prisoners have bleeding open sores, many don't bath, some shit in their blankets, and others with the 'snooker' penchant leave their body emissions on the bedding, and there's your own all mixed up with theirs. I tell you, after you eventually settle down on the concrete, just one little fibre on your blanket has to tickle your leg, arm or shoulder while you're fast asleep in the middle of the night and you've suddenly got visions of millions of these little blood-suckers all over you! Does not make for a good night's kip.

Jail is called 'The Slammer' universally. It is amazing how a door cannot be closed in prison—it has to be slammed, with patently gleeful, brute force *every single time*, day or night. It does not matter if prisoners are trying to sleep, the door has to be slammed. Maybe these whipper-snappers are taught this in their training depot? We the prisoners are lesser beings, you see, and we don't need sleep—the slamming goes on and on, day and night. Some guards have it perfected to such a degree that they can actually slam doors open!

You have to use all your ingenuity and make every single plan you can if you want to survive a stint in Mugabe's jail, all the more so if it's a lengthy sentence.

Bear in mind that Zimbabwe's prisons are about 300% overcrowded.

You have to continuously dig deep into your resolve and your inner-self for strength to face each and every day. For a long while, especially as a condemned prisoner, time and again, I failed to find that strength. I lost all hope, and with it my will to live. But in all of us, whether you know it or not, there is an inner strength that will carry you through, even if it's just for a few hours. Search for it when you are in your darkest moments, maybe it's God's voice or His presence, maybe it's all the people out there who love you and who ache and pray for you, maybe it's plain stubbornness … but it's there.

Many were the times that I fabricated my own hope, so often out of nothing. Especially as I've said, on death row, when I made these imagined 'hat pegs' on my wall where I'd hang my imaginary hats, each one a 'hat of hope'.

Sometimes there'd be a line of hats hanging there, like when Nelson Mandela was released or when he asked Mugabe for my release and I was told things were looking so good, boy oh boy! the hats were there, big time, rows of the fucking things.

Then time would take its toll and the hats would disappear, one by one, and I'd see my inner darkness ever-closing in, relentless and overpowering as the hats were eroded, just like a sand castle on the beach. When the tide is out, you feel good; there stands your hope, your castle, but sure as the tides, just like depression, the waves would be back and your castle of hope would soon all be gone.

Satan is a clever fucker. You know the little *oke*? Red, pointed ears, a tail, pitchfork and all. He sits on your shoulder whispering in your ear. And he never stops. The little shit is relentless. When things are going well and you've a row of hats on the wall, he just sits there sulking. But he knows the hats will slowly disappear and as they do he perks up and cranks up his crap. All the 'if onlies' and 'why me's' in the world will flood in from this Satan *oke* and, as soon as you're on the downhill, he goes crazy with glee. It's nearly an unstoppable fall before you find yourself so down you wonder how you will ever get up again.

Keep your hats up there I tell you, no matter what. Keep them stuck where you can see them, and you will survive. You can survive anything; just keep the hope there. That's what I'd tell myself day in and day out. Even when I was depressed beyond belief. You have to do it or else you will fail.

It was close, so close, so many times I despaired so badly that I would make a rope out of shredded blanket, but somehow I endured, often just till the next day. "Just till tomorrow, Woodsie," I'd tell myself in my death row cell, while taking the 'three-step shuffle' up and down, or just sitting and staring at my grey wall. "Just till tomorrow," and I would hang a 'tomorrow hat' up there, all the while knowing that tomorrow there would be nothing … zilch, zero.

Maybe I made it through those 7,140 days and nights by fooling myself so often. Maybe it was my God. Maybe it was stubbornness and the knowledge that Mugabe and his cronies would want nothing more than for me to die in that dismal place. I did not want to give Mugabe that gratification, and that was serious motivation for me to persevere.

Whatever it was, through all those years of having my hopes eroded time after time, just like the waves, I made it. Whether I am sane or not (I figure this is debatable) I did it. We can all do it no matter how dark things get, no matter how sad, how desperate, how fucking morbid.

Reach inside and strive to get through, even if it's only 'till tomorrow'.

૭ ૭ ૭

As a lesser form of being, a prisoner is expected to *gara pasi* (Shona for 'sit down') when being spoken to by a prison guard. And believe you me, the whipper-snappers who emerge from 'Green Bomber' (youth political orientation camps—in effect Mugabe's goon squads) and prison training camps, seem to take immense pleasure enforcing this unwritten rule.

One has to set one's own standards in prison. As I've said, you have to draw the line somewhere to maintain your personal dignity, if for nothing else. My line of resistance was just this side of the *gara-pasi* spiel. It would totally frustrate the guards as I would refuse to sit even at the threat of a thorough kicking. Ironically, it was only ever a threat toward me but became very real for other prisoners who tried it and had the temerity to query the guards as to why the *murungu* didn't *gara pasi*.

The Green Bomber training, through which any prospective government employee has to first pass, obviously involves a great deal of psychological orientation (brainwashing if you will), during which total devotion toward the 'dear leader' President Mugabe is solidly instilled. After prison-officer training this brainwashing comes together with a superior attitude and mindset you just won't believe. It doesn't take long though, after posting to their respective prisons, for these youngsters to climb down from their perch.

Prison officers are not highly remunerated and the new recruits are quick to dip into the prisoners' food, soap and toilet-paper rations along with the older guards—even plain *sadza* and boiled cabbage can be purchased by a guard off a prisoner for one cigarette, to be hastily consumed out of sight from senior officers, more usually in the toilets. Senior officers, mind you, who due to their standing and rank don't have to purchase rations from the bandits, simply wander into the kitchens and are served from the prisoners' pots … gratis.

Cigarettes are not allowed in prison— "bad for your health," they say, as they lead the condemned man to the gallows. They will kick the living shit out of you, enough to put you in hospital because you didn't *gara pasi*, but they won't let you smoke because it's bad for you.

Unless you are on your death bed in the prison hospital, your relatives or friends are not allowed to supplement your prison diet other than three times a year on public holidays when food and cigarette parcels are permitted.

The diet in prison is always very bland, and everything is boiled. Boiled and boiled until all nutritional value is destroyed. There are constant electricity cuts and shortages of coal for the boilers that produce the steam used for cooking so all the food is cooked in one go. Between 2.00 and 4.00 a.m. the food for all three meals that day is prepared and then left in plastic dustbins, used as food containers to deliver the food to the halls. It's no wonder malnutrition plays a huge role in prison deaths. The food was poor when I was there, and if recent reports from Zimbabwe are anything to go by, it's worse still today.

A Zimbabwean internet report has recently revealed that in Chikurubi alone an outbreak of pellagra has killed 23 prisoners already this year (to June 2007). Dozens more are said to be seriously ill as a result of this disease, which is a terrible skin infection caused by the shortage of vitamin B and proteins that contain the essential amino acid trypophan. Trypophan is apparently found in meat, eggs, poultry and fish, all of which are like rocking-horse shit in Zimbabwe's prisons— extremely rare! Victims can suffer from diarrhoea, dementia and finally death. When I was in jail prisoners often had to survive on just one small meal a day, and still do. "On a good day prisoners will get *sadza* and beans but the amount is insufficient to survive on," said a prison source in the internet report.

A parliamentary committee that toured Chikurubi and other prisons last year found inmates clad in torn, dirty uniforms and crammed into overcrowded cells with filthy overflowing toilets that went unflushed for weeks as the water was cut off due to unpaid bills.

The report continues: "Prisoners are denied any privacy when relieving themselves and have to use torn strips of blankets or pages from the prison Bibles as toilet paper. Prisoners lacked soap or facilities to wash themselves or their prison clothes."

The parliamentary committee described conditions in some prisons as inhuman and said epidemics such as diarrhoea, pellagra and other diseases swept through prisons due to unsanitary conditions and prisoners' chronic malnutrition." (Zimonline, 5th May 2007.)

And it was exactly the same for the twenty years I was there. The unsanitary conditions were a big problem, and were especially compounded by the constant water cuts. Sometimes there would be no running water for weeks on end and the toilets would overflow, leaving effluent and pure shit all over the place, which would be swept into corners or drains until the water suddenly came on again for a few hours—when there was feverish activity as we all tried to clean up and wash ourselves before the water went off again.

It was very distressing having to sleep in an overcrowded cell with an overflowing toilet hole.

There is a large fish pond in the centre court at Chikurubi. This precious few-thousand litres would serve as toilet flush for nearly 3,000 prisoners for days on end before prison bowsers could be found to deliver water. This megre amount was also needed for the kitchens, and more importantly for the prison hospital, yet in all the years I was at Chikurubi and through all the water problems, the prison service never ever got around to putting down a few boreholes, or installing a few pumps to deliver water from the nearby dam.

৵ ৵ ৵

Visits from my wife (now ex) were restricted to one a month for fifteen minutes (if I was lucky). I didn't see or speak to my children for 7,140 days. Somehow my wife managed a beautiful smile for each visit, yet the trauma of all of it and of seeing my weight loss and deteriorating health must have been quite unbearable for her. This is only one small aspect of my family's suffering that I have become aware of since my release in July 2006. The true victims in this whole cock-up are undoubtedly my wife and children.

Not me.

I went in with my eyes wide shut, whereas they didn't have a clue.

My wife moved to South Africa in 1994 soon after I was reprieved. She never missed a single visit to me for those full five years I was on death row. I'm sure it must have been a pain in the ass for her to travel from Bulawayo to Harare and back again just for 15 minutes of time looking at my sorry face through dirty, barred glass. She moved to South Africa because life in Zimbabwe had become unbearable. She had been ostracized from society, no one would employ her and she lost her position on the Zimbabwe polocrosse team, all because of me.

Once living in South Africa, it was just too expensive for her to come and visit and so I would see her once a year or less. I had maybe three or four other visits from people during my whole time in jail. But I didn't like visits, I used to find them too upsetting.

My wife and kids would write to me and I saw my kids grow up by photograph, but only after death row. On death row you can receive the odd photo but you are not allowed to keep them.

৵ ৵ ৵

If you want to supplement your diet in prison, you have to smuggle in food. Either that or give yourself years of stress and try to get the prison doctor to recommend you be allowed certain foodstuffs from outside. In which event the authorities will do you a great favour and allow you some externally prepared nourishment.

It's typical of their total fixation in maintaining command and control of the prisoners, mentally and physically. No matter what effect the economic situation has on the quality of food supplied to the prisoners, the authorities seem terrified of losing their absolute hold on prisoners and are relectant to accept any form of advancement out of the Middle Ages. They don't even allow regular food to be brought in from relatives so that prisoners can occasionally get half-decent food.

Even basics such as multi-vitamin tablets, sealed in their original containers, are not allowed. Prisoners are reduced to walking skeletons and yet the prisons remain doggedly stuck in their ways. Bear in mind that the basic food-ration scale administered today still dates back to the colonial era. Food is never properly prepared as the regime is broke and can't afford decent food or the means to cook it properly. Ironically, some cooks who were jailed back in the days of colonialism say the food was immensely better. "We even had tea with milk and sugar," they gush. Nowadays you are lucky to get black tea with a touch of sugar for six months of the year, and only half a cup a day, mind you.

There are no prison-shop facilities in Zimbabwean jails. When the maize meal or other food in the kitchen runs out, you can't just go and get a slice of bread from the local prison store—you simply go without and sadly that is an all too regular occurrence.

For all sorts of reasons the staple maize meal is frequenlty unavailable in prison, be it shortage of diesel to collect the mielies (maize), or no maize available at the prison farm. Drought? Yeah sure. Often the meagre crops produced on the prison farms are sold to the commercial millers, who then supply and deliver the milled maize back to Chikurubi, most of which however is filched en route by the prison brass for sale in their own private stores and outlets.

This is Zimbabwe, a country that a few years ago was a net exporter of maize, now, due to 'the land question' is a net importer.

It is not uncommon for milled maize to be unavailable in commercial outlets throughout the country, but it is very common for government ministers to buy tons of maize from the Grain Marketing Board to export *in their own private capacity,* with any money earned, especially foreign currency, being deposited in external banks.

ৡ ৡ ৡ

Frequently the colonial-era steam boilers at the prisons pack up, or there is no electricity or water, or simply no maize, due to the 'illegal sanctions' currently imposed upon Mugabe's regime by the West—the 'West' often being a generalization for any country, *anywhere*, which disagrees with the Zimbabwean government's policies, and says so.

To put you in the picture on the aspect of the 'illegal sanctions' that President Mugabe is always chirping about, I can tell you that he and about 180 of his gravy-train cronies are presently subject to a 'travel and investment ban' by Europe and a number of other countries worldwide, which precludes them from shopping jaunts to the world's fashion capitals. There are NO economic sanctions imposed, by anyone, on the people of Zimbabwe.

As I write, the Mugabe regime and the MDC, the only opposition party in Zimbabwe, have started talks in South Africa that are being mediated by the South African president, Thabo Mbeki. These talks are supposed to lead to a solution of the political problems within Zimbabwe, and pave the way for 'free and fair' elections in the country in 2008. There have never been free and fair elections in Zimbabwe. Be that as it may, one pre-condition by Mugabe for these talks to get out of the starting blocks is for the MDC to call upon the West to lift sanctions. He is simply desperate to get back into the shopping malls in the world's fashion spots. Never mind issues like a new constitution for Zimbabwe, or removing other laws that seriously contribute to human rights abuse. No, we want to be able to go shopping.

Mugabe often infers that everything going wrong in Zimbabwe today is a result of these 'illegal sanctions'. He never lays the blame on his own economic policies, his destruction of commercial agriculture, his government's corruption and plain plundering, which are surely the main causes of all this suffering in Zimbabwe.

Mugabe's regime likes to portray Britain as trying to re-colonize the country. He says this persecution by the British, the Americans and former Rhodesian allies is directed at him, "simply because he wants to return the land stolen by the settler-occupiers in the 1800s to its rightful owner".

Another point to remember is that many formerly productive farms, repossessed and given mainly to Mugabe's cronies, and which now lie fallow, were bought by these evicted white farmers *after* independence in Zimbabwe in 1980.

By destroying Zimbabwe's agricultural infrastructure, Mugabe has effectively closed over 4,000 viable businesses in the agricultural sector alone. No country in the developed world can close 4,000 businesses and not feel the pinch. What more a struggling Third World country like Zimbabwe? And if that is not bad enough the regime now has its eyes set on 51 per cent of all businesses, companies and banks in Zimbabwe. By seizing this 51 per cent the economy will now be in the hands of Zimbabwe and not in the hands of Zimbabwe's enemies. You see how it works?

This once 'Jewel of Africa', an expression coined by former Tanzanian president Julius Nyerere when he congratulated President Mugabe on the occasion of Zimbabwe's independence in 1980, has been reduced to indigent impoverishment, chronic instability and mass unemployment. This is all the more ironic when you remember that Robert Mugabe was, in the early 1980s considered Africa's shrewdest and most sophisticated ideologue.

In those early days, despite his professed Marxism he continued to court capitalist donors. Was he a converted capitalist or just opportunitistic? Maybe he was just adhering to Lennin's doctrine of exploiting the capitalistic system to further his socialist ideas?

President Mugabe well knew that nowhere in Africa had socialism produced a viable economy. He realized, soon after his election triumph in 1980 (and likely even before that) that he needed the skills of the whites who remained in the country, especially in the big business and agriculture, to keep the country going.

He went to the extreme of reassuring white Zimbabweans in late 1980, after he had fired the army supremo General Peter Walls on the grounds that he was "out of step with the government and the rest of the people of Zimbabwe". He had used his emergency powers inherited from the Rhodesian era to promulgate a Deprivation of Citizenship Act, specifically to deprive Salisbury-born General Walls of his citizenship.

General Walls had been away on holiday at the time and had given a press briefing in London on 11th July 1980, where he had said that he had asked Prime Minister Margaret Thatcher to declare the February 1980 election in Zimbabwe null and void on the grounds of the massive intimidation and violence perpetrated by President Mugabe's followers. General Walls had in the same interview dismissed the rumours that he had been planning a coup d'état, a point President Mugabe apparently chose to ignore in preference to getting rid of the general. Robert Mugabe told Zimbabwe that this law was specifically to apply to General Walls only and that the rest of the white population had nothing to fear.

At our commissioned-officer level, and especially for those of us who commanded large numbers of policemen, we knew that there was a plan, just in case Robert Mugabe won the election. There were never any briefings where the complete details of this plan, which was essentially a military takeover, were given out. I had 150 men on my section, including twelve whites, working for me. The black members made up the majority of the Crime Prevention Unit, the CPU, but in those last confusing days one was never absolutely sure just which way they would turn if push came to shove. We, as part of a general police contingent, were to attack the liberation guerrillas' assembly points, which were guarded by the Commonwealth Monitoring Force but who, we knew, didn't care a toss who won and who killed whom.

There were a few companies of Support Unit troops continually in and out of the Bulawayo control-room area, and I knew that there would be some serious back-up from those guys, should they be issued the instructions to attack the former ZANLA and ZIPRA forces that, even with their personal weapons, were sitting ducks in the assembly points. The full operational briefing for this attack was to be given from the Stops Camp operational control room, who would receive their orders from the Joint Operations Command at Brady Barracks in Bulawayo.

In those dying days we all hung around the control room in Stops Camp, not doing much, but with our respective armouries being carried in the boots of our vehicles, and ready at a moment's notice to do what we believed had to be done.

But nothing happened.

On the day the election results were announced, 4th March 1980, and Robert Mugabe won 57 of the 80 seats up for grabs, we were all as tense as cats, waiting for some sort of reaction. Robert Mugabe himself appeared very surprised at the enormity of his victory, and Joshua Nkomo was in tears, having perceived himself winner, being the self-proclaimed 'Father Zimbabwe'. Bishop Muzorewa, who we all thought was going to do quite well, gained only three seats and Ndabaningi Sithole none.

The British-installed governor of the country, Lord Soames, annointed Robert Mugabe as the winner and the Commonwealth Monitoring Force extricated itself with indecent haste. The whites, who had expected so much more fom this whole thing, were left to vote with their feet and Zimbabwe was left to endure the 'scientific socialism', whatever that means, as espoused in his doctrine by Robert Mugabe, the new Zimbabwean prime minister.

At the end of the day, the heads-up to report for briefing and attack on the assembly points never came and it all just fizzled out. Perhaps it was all just a scam that kept us holding our fragile shit together. It's a lot easier to go through something like that knowing that there was some sort of plan should everything fall on its face than to have no plan at all.

President Mugabe has the ability to face both ways when it suits him. In his original appointment of General Walls to command the intergrated army he displayed his exceptional intelligence and considerable political skill. Not only were his own generals incompetent and incapable of running a modern army, but he could not afford to alienate them by appointing one of the better-trained ZIPRA generals from Nkomo's army. President Mugabe had to buy a little time, which he did by appointing Walls, while continuing with his reassuring, soothing speeches of reconciliation to the whites. He was also under a modicum of stress, worrying about 5,000 of Bishop Abel Muzorewa's troops who had been moved south across the border at independence and based in camps near the Limpopo River.

Just a few years earlier, while commanding the ZANLA liberation-war effort from Mozambique, Mugabe was very clear on his thoughts of a multiracial society and capitalism: "We sincerely believe that a multiracial system is a luxury in a state, and capitalism is the main enemy of the people."

Perhaps he had advice from some senior CIO remnants of the Rhodesian war, or from his own intelligence sources, that the majority of the ex-Rhodesian army and police members that were still in the country were totally loyal to Walls, or maybe he had more sinister motives. Some say he was using Walls as a smokescreen to divert attention from the murder a month earlier of a 68-year-old white commercial farmer, Gerald Adams, on his Stamford Farm in eastern Zimbabwe by Edgar Tekere. At the time Tekere was one of Mugabe's senior cabinet ministers and the secretary-general of ZANU (PF).

Tekere, who was considered to be the third-most powerful man in ZANU (PF), coincidentally hated Walls and had totally rejected President Mugabe's hand of reconciliation and the appointment of Walls as the army supremo to oversee the intergration of the former Rhodesian army, Mugabe's ZANLA and Nkomo's ZIPRA army.

The murder of Gerald Adams by Tekere and seven former ZANLA guerrillas had attracted bad international attention and had the potential of negatively influencing donor aid. Walls was therefore a convenient scapegoat. A few months later Mugabe, in true Machiavellian style, dumped Edgar Tekere saying, "He needed a rest." Tekere subsequently became one of Mugabe's fiercest critics and even stood against him in a later presidential election.

After the enactment of the Deprivation of Citizenship Act when Walls had been prohibited from returning to Zimbabwe, President Mugabe reassured whites that, "This is going to affect General Walls. The government does not intend to act arbitrarily." These were sweet tones from Mugabe which turned full circle in latter years when he declared that he wanted all whites, who were now the enemy, to leave Zimbabwe. (All whites except the few amoral bottom feeders who bankroll him and his party to this day and who are responsible for vast amounts of money laundering, diamond- and gold-dealing and fraud in South Africa—not to mention milking the mineral wealth of the Democratic Republic of the Congo during the war there in the late 1990s—rats who hide behind Mugabe's skirts from extradition to face justice. Their day will come …)

ڡ ڡ ڡ

In Chikurubi there are no radios or televisions, no telephones and the 'library' joins the misnomer brigade. The lack of public-telephone facilities places enormous burden on the relatives who live a long way from the prison. Instead of simply being able to make a phone call to their jailed relative, they have to travel to and fro. They have to go through the whole schlep of getting to Harare, and once there being messed about by the guards who take pleasure, it seems, in making a family's visit as unpleasant as they can.

Once you get to Chikurubi, visits with relatives last fifteen minutes, twice a month. Prior to 2002 it was only one visit a month for fifteen minutes, maybe. The visit is conducted on a telephone-intercom device through heavy steel mesh and double-thick glass. You're lucky if you get a glimpse of your visitor, what with the glass being filthy or the lights in your booth out. If your luck is really in, the intercom will be working and you will have a few words with your loved one without the lines becoming crossed and you end up talking to some old toppie from Mukumbura in the next booth, instead of your wife from Bulawayo sitting opposite you.

And while you're arguing with the guards that the lines are crossed or not working, your fifteen minutes dribbles away. A most frustrating and heart-wrenching time is usually had by all, as you try cram as much as possible into that fifteen minutes by talking, making eye contact, often with tears of frustration pouring down your face. The only contact being you and her placing your open palms opposite each other through the glass and steel, a distance which could just as well be across the ocean, for all it is worth.

On two occasions while I was on death row, my wife arrived during a power cut and the stand-by generator was also broken, which meant the intercom, together with nearly everything else in the prison did not work. For those two visits I was taken to the lawyer's interview room where the only partition between my wife and me, for the first time in years, was just a steel mesh.

My heart broke as I sat there, smelling her perfume, seeing her clearly for the first time in years, hearing her voice without distortion, and most of all being able to hold onto her little finger which she stuck through the mesh. For dear life I clung to that pinkie, the only contact with another human being in all those years, the tip of her pinkie, and I was like the proverbial drowning man, clutching to that straw for all I could.

To place this into perspective and to compare these visiting conditions, I have recently visited Pollsmoor Prison in Cape Town, where to my huge relief I saw that the visiting area comprises a large hall with plastic chairs where visitors can sit and talk face to face with their loved ones, holding hands … touching.

❧ ❧ ❧

I have also recently visited Eugene de Kock in Pretoria Prison. Here we have the former Security Police commander of the so-called death camp at Vlakplaas, and supposedly South Africa's most feared killer, 'Mr. Prime Evil', sitting with me on a bench, in an open courtyard, having a chat. We spoke for a while, I brought him a Coke and some chocolates from the prison café, while quite a few of the other prisoners, blacks, coloureds and whites who also had visitors, were sitting on benches around us with their families, including, most importantly, their children—toddlers included.

What a difference to the absolute clampdown, frustration, isolation and degrading treatment visitors have to endure in Zimbabwe's prisons. And I was most pleasantly surprised to see a few black prisoners come over and ask Mr. de Kock "if he would please say hello to my wife and family who really want to meet you". And he was most gracious too, standing, shaking hands and exchanging a few pleasantries and words of encouragement with these people, whom he had supposedly murdered willy-nilly, and who should have shied away from him, if all the horror stories told about him were true. A finer gentleman I have yet to meet. Mr. Prime Evil—yeah sure! I don't think so.

Eugene de Kock and I have communicated since soon after he was first jailed for his work for the apartheid government in 1994. We are close friends I suppose—kindred spirits and all that. Both of us were used and both abandoned once the shit hit the fan.

By the time you read this I can only hope that the morally correct political decision has been made for Eugene and others, who remain jailed for apartheid-era crimes, especially for those who went the extra mile and, like Eugene de Kock, bared their souls and skeletons from their closets to the Truth and Reconciliation Commission. No matter if he failed with amnesty from the Truth Commission, the fact remains that his activity was directly related to the liberation struggle in South Africa, and there was no personal enrichment motive for him. Just his duty.

People like Eugene de Kock are relics of the apartheid era, and they continue to suffer in South African prisons, while so many from that era who didn't care about the TRC, or who are not political sacrificial lambs, or token publicity stunts, roam free on the streets of South Africa. A few names of others sitting in jail for apartheid-era crimes are Koper Myburg, Stephanus Coetzee, Ferdie Barnard, Cliffie Barnard, Clive Darby-Lewis and Janus Waluz, to name but a few—and I could give you pages of names of those who did the same or worse, and who are free ... including me ... but I've done a bit of time.

There is talk now of opening that TRC can of worms with selective prosecutions for people who failed the test; poison cases and so on. Will these prosecutions be in the public interest and involve both sides of the political spectrum? Will they serve any purpose or should our understaffed and overburdened justice system rather concentrate on the thousands of outstanding current criminal cases which clog the court rolls and remand prisons? Can we move forward as a nation with one foot stuck in the past?

Yes, many people lost loved ones, and the scars and tears will never fade, but does keeping the people who were just following orders from higher authority in jail, serve any personal gratification for those who mourn?

Reparations as recommended by the TRC must of course be made, but you can't get blood out of a stone, and holding onto these prisoners surely serves no purpose.

Like me, most of these prisoners were involved in a war that is long past. Their activity was directly related to that war and there is no conflict in South Africa that they would or could return to. I feel it is inane for the Zimbabwean justice minister, Patrick Chinamasa, to refer to me as a serious threat to the stability of Zimbabwe, ten years after independence in South Africa and I think equally crazy to keep these prisoners behind bars when they are no longer a threat to anyone.

I applied to the TRC. I went through the full motions, completed and submitted the forms etc. My application was given the official number 7303/97, and reached the TRC in mid-1997. Deputy chairman, Dr. Alex Boraine, applied to visit me in Chikurubi to go through my application with me, as I would obviously not have been allowed to attend in person in South Africa.

I have since learned that the former justice minister in Zimbabwe, Mr. Emmerson Mnangagwa, who used to be my boss when I worked in President Mugabe's Central Intelligence Office, gave Dr. Boraine the go-ahead to come up to Zimbabwe and visit me. Dr. Boraine went through the motions, obtained written authority and all was arranged when suddenly someone went and snitched to President Mugabe who then torpedoed the visit with one shot.

So there I sat, with my TRC confession more or less public knowledge, and Doctor Boraine was denied access to me by the Zimbabwean government. Even if the TRC had heard my application on video in my absence, which their rules forbade, they still did not have the authority to grant me amnesty for crimes I had committed outside South Africa. That's what I was told, any rate.

As Dr. Borraine subsequently told the Truth Commission: "Mr Woods applied to this commission. He wanted to come clean and say 'Here, this is what I did'. Unfortunately we were denied access to visit him in prison him by the Zimbabwean authorites, so his testimony was never heard before this Commission."

Strangely, a few amnesties were granted to some other *okes* for South African raids into Botswana and Swaziland. Not that I mock those amnesties; they were good decisions. What makes me angry is that South Africa could not approach Mugabe and achieve the same thing for me. He would not hear of it! Perish the thought! "Zimbabwe is an independent and sovereign state and will brook no interference in its internal affairs," to quote Robert Mugabe, ad nauseam.

Quiet diplomacy, or any other sort of diplomacy, does not allow anything like that—old Robbie has a bit of a whiplash tongue too, for so-called friends, presidents even, who have the cheek to disparage his tight-fisted dictatorship. Maybe the TRC didn't read my application just because I couldn't make it to the party?

Dream on Woodsie …

South African President Mbeki, in an ANC Today website, 10th October 2003 said: "When we took the decision to achieve reconciliation, rather than retribution and thus established the Truth and Reconciliation Commission (TRC) we decided to forgive all those who might have caused unspecified harm to anyone in our country, and elsewhere, in pursuit of the objectives either to perpetuate apartheid or to achieve the liberation of the oppressed."

It was extremely depressing when South Africa did not pursue this policy with President Mugabe regarding my case. Throughout my entire prison sentence President Mugabe refused any plea from any quarter for my release, be it from Nelson Mandela as South African president, religious leaders in South Africa, politicians such a Marthinus van Schalkwyk, Tony Leon, Pieter Mulder, or

Amnesty International etc. Even F. W. de Klerk and Pik Botha tried to speak to him.

Mugabe refused to even consider these approaches, dogmatically insisting I was a Zimbabwean citizen who had committed crimes in Zimbabwe, and this was a Zimbabwean sovereign matter and he would stand for no interference in the internal affairs of his country. This was all bullshit of course.

He was accustomed to being the main man in the alliance of Frontline States that were supporting the ANC in its quest to liberate South Africa. However, when Nelson Mandela was released in 1994, Mugabe's status diminished considerably. His foreign-exchange inflows took a huge dip as he could no longer claim support from the West on the basis of his defiant and perilous stance against the apartheid regime.

As Mugabe became more frustrated he became more and more megalomaniacal, blaming Zimbabwe's failure on anyone and anything. And of course, any sort of agreement like my release, as a result of a request from Nelson Mandela would look like he was now taking instruction from Mandela … and that would not do. No ways!

President Mugabe interpreted an approach for my release, be it on humanitarian grounds, fairness or whatever, to be interference in the internal affairs of his Zimbabwe. However, amazingly, on the day of my release in 2006, I found myself deported to South Africa as a South African citizen. I was also prohibited re-entry to Zimbabwe, the country of my birth. The fact is that I am a South African citizen by descent, but it suited President Mugabe to maintain that I was a Zimbabwean and nothing else.

It suited him until the day I was released from jail, that is.

Transfer to
Harare Central Prison

"If there were no fault,
There would be no pardon"
Egyptian

In early 2004, we three were suddenly transferred from Chikurubi Maximum Security Prison to Harare Central Prison, which is basically a medium-security facility notwithstanding the presence there of Zimbabwe's main death-row block, which holds some 100 condemned prisoners.

My first reaction at this massive reduction in the personal security surrounding us was to hammer another huge hope peg into my imaginary hope wall.

I couldn't fathom the reason for the move. Only a few months earlier Chinamasa, the minister of justice, refused to allow me to go for heart treatment in South Africa and rejected any reduction in my security due to me being such a hugely dangerous security threat to Zimbabwe.

In his affidavit to the Supreme Court justifying his refusal to allow me transfer to a South African prison for heart treatment, Chinamasa said that:

1. *The applicant had not been in solitary confinement on death row.* (I had argued in my application that I had in fact been in solitary confinement for five years. I had been locked up for twenty-three hours a day, naked, in a 1.2-metre x 4-metre cell, without natural light but, according to him, that was not solitary confinement.)
2. *He has no rights whatsoever to be released or transferred on grounds of health.*
3. *In all his petitions he has not deserved clemency.*
4. *It is my firm submission that he should serve his term of imprisonment.*
5. *Woods changed his citizenship in 1994 in order to benefit from arrangements made between former South African President Nelson Mandela and President Mugabe for his release—he is therefore not a bona fide South African. He has been making noises about transfer to South Africa where his former masters are and where he knows he will*

be released. (This is pure fiction and blatant lying. Here was the justice minister swearing under oath to the Supreme Court, and lying through his teeth. No one has ever been released from Mugabe's jails as a result of negotiations with Mandela, so to this day I'd love to know whom Chinamasa was referring to.)

6. *His alleged stress is self-inflicted.*

7. *Public interest demands that he remain in prison for life.*

8. *Release is out of the question.*

9. *It cannot be forgotten that he is a murderer.* (The pot calling the kettle black—how many people have blood dripping from their fingers in Zimbabwe, who are well known to Chinamasa, and who walk free—from Mugabe down?)

10. *He has no heart problem.* (This is despite me producing conclusive test results by a Zimbabwean radiologist, Dr. Jonker, concerning my heart condition and an assessment from a heart specialist in South Africa, Dr. Basson. Jonker said I had restricted blood flow in the heart muscle, and Basson said I had damage and needed an angiogram heart test, which was not available in Zimbabwe. Both were eventually confirmed at Luthuli Hospital in Durban after my release in 2006.)

11. *Release is unthinkable and must be denied.*

And just to show how personally subjective and vindictive Chinamasa was, and is:

12. *He must be grateful to fate that his death sentence was not carried out.*

I didn't need to be a brain surgeon to realize that these people wanted me in jail until I died.

And here I was, with the security threat accusation still not dry on the paper, and transferred to a medium-security prison, right on the edge of Harare's central business district. Surely this was preparation for our release? Yeah sure—dream on. A few weeks passed and the hope diminished proportionately, back to its normal level, where each day might, just might, finally be the day for something good to happen. Maybe it would—but probably not.

Hope can be a killer when you're being held in jail at the whim of a dictator, but you can't just go on indefinitely without hope. Like prisoners of war in the German and Russian camps during the Second World War, and in Stalin's gulags after the war, any change in the routine would tease the prisoners' thoughts and hopes, where sad tales like a piece of carrot being found in the swill would get everyone thinking they were being fattened up in preparation for release.



A month or so later, completely out of the blue, and still with absolutely no idea as to the reason for our transfer to Harare Central, I received the news on my little transistor radio, of the sixty-seven mercenaries being arrested at Harare International Airport and being detained at Chikurubi Maximum Prison.

The pieces fell together as I realized this mercenary arrest was obviously a pre-planned event and I had been moved to avoid any possible communication between the mercenaries and myself. The prison and CIO authorities were obviously worried that I would be of assistance to the mercenaries because of my experience in jail and my knowledge of basic human rights, especially in prison, and could tell them what they could demand. Of course I also had intimate knowledge of the physical layout of the prison and its workings, which the mercenaries would have loved to have learned.

The government immediately mounted their crates, hollering for the whole world to hear that Zimbabwe had thwarted a coup d'état in Equatorial Guinea and that the mercenaries would receive death sentences (*Herald*, March 2005).

For their part the mercenaries were insisting they were en route to a civilian security contract in the diamond fields of eastern Democratic Republic of Congo.

As it transpired, the Zimbabwean security-force esablishment, through heavy handedness, screwed up the proper procedures relative to arrest and detention, access to lawyers, chains of evidence and so on. This resulted in almost all of the mercenaries receiving light sentences for contravening immigration and aviation laws and as I write this they're already out of jail, with the exception of the pilots of their chartered Boeing 707 who got a year or so extra—and the leader of their group, Simon Mann. Mann, still held in Chikurubi, an ill man due to the atrocious diet he receives and the essential medical treatment he has been denied, will probably be snuck off to Guinea under some sort of extradition deal, in exchange for a few drums of oil (The *Zimbabwe Situation,* 13th April, 2007) —or for thirty pieces of silver.

An interesting aspect of this mercenary saga is their belief that their whole operation was actually part of a South African government deal that went balls-up when the South Africans realized they could probably make more from compromising the mercenaries in exchange for oil from Guinea, than by letting the mission go ahead and hope for some favourable deals from the new mercenary-installed Guinean establishment. I have spoken to a few of the mercenaries involved and they all sing from this same hymn sheet.

For its part, the South African National Intelligence Services of course deny any knowledge of, or involvement with, the mercenaries, which you'd expect, but who knows? These are murky, unchartered waters.

In a rather touching twist I was phoned by one of the mercenaries after I had been out of jail for a few weeks, while walking around Brightwater Commons in Johannesburg. It transpired that this mercenary, let's call him Louis, was in the small group of mercenaries who had been locked up in the condemned section of Chikurubi, while the rest of them, also in small groups to prevent conspiracies, were in other sections of that jail. Locked up, alone and in the very cell I had occupied for five years, he found himself staring at a fourteen-month sentence for immigration offences. Feeling absolutely dejected and depressed he found my name and date of my death sentence scratched on the wall. He went on to tell me that this had greatly encouraged him and he dispelled all thoughts of taking his own life by saying to himself, "If Kevin Woods can survive twenty years of this, I can do fourteen months."

બબબ

During my first month at Central, an old friend of mine was convicted of murder, sentenced to fifteen years and jailed at Chikurubi. Rusty is a professional game-hunter and owned a fishing concession and camp on the Zambezi River in western Zimbabwe. A lovely friend and a true gentleman, I'd watched his outfit develop and grow into a major contributor to the tourism industry in Zimbabwe in the early 1980s.

His transgression it seems was to try and chase away fish poachers who were using canoes and nets in his fishing safari area. A fisherman's dugout canoe suddenly capsized and the fisherman was never seen again. Despite frantic efforts by Rusty to dive for him, his body was never located. In anybody's book and in any civilized country where the rule of law is not the personal domain of the politicians, that is not an intentional murder. But in Zimbabwe, nearly every facet of life is embroiled in politics—in particular politics and policies which benefit the ruling elite.

Unfortunately for Rusty, his main business partner was Benjamin Paradza, a Zimbabwean high court judge and liberation-war ZANLA guerrilla commander, who had recently fallen out of favour with Mugabe because of his independent judgements he had made regarding the government's theft of commercial farms and property thereon—judgements which did not dovetail with Mugabe's policies.

Paradza had made the mistake of opening himself to attack by asking a fellow judge to relax Rusty's bail conditions. One of Rusty's main sales' platforms of his professional hunting business was an annual sale of professional game-hunts in the USA that he needed to attend and as such needed his impounded Zimbabwean passport. His passport had been surrendered to the court as part of his bail conditions. Paradza, without offering any bribe or soliciting any favours of the judge, asked for Rusty's bail to be relaxed so that he could travel to the States.

This is not unusual in Zimbabwe and certainly does not amount to corruption. There was never the risk of Rusty fleeing while on bail. He firmly believed he had not committed any serious crime and thought he was merely looking at a fine for a culpable homicide charge. In addition to that, he possessed huge fixed assets in Zimbabwe which he would have been foolish to abandon. The judge that Paradza had spoken to scurried off to his political mandarins with this little story, embellished it a bit and together they plotted to get rid of Paradza.

The result was predictable. Paradza was duly suspended, tried for corruption and found guilty by his peers. Paradza was then out on bail and awaiting sentence when he decided that discretion was the better part of valour and vamoosed before he could be thrown into the stocks, not because he was trying to avoid facing justice, but simply because there is no justice in Zimbabwe and he had committed no offence.

So there sits Rusty, pushing fifteen years in jail, which should have legally and logically been reduced on appeal, but wasn't, simply because the ruling party was out to get his business partner.

For many years and especially since the farm invasions in the early 2000s Mugabe has had a serious problem with independent-thinking judges.

At one time when Mugabe was advised, during one of his birthday television interviews, that he didn't actually have the authority to fire the judges, he looked quite surprised and said, "Really? We have not looked into that."

In 2000, after the Supreme Court had ruled that proper procedures *according to Zimbabwean law* needed to be followed when appropriating a commercial farm, Mugabe with special reference to the Zimbabwean chief justice, Anthony Gubbay, retorted: "The courts can do whatever they want, but no judicial decision will stand in our way. My own position is that we should not even be defending our position in the courts."

I suppose that is clear enough.

Following this a Harare war veteran, Joseph Chinotimba, employed as a municipal security guard, was sent to Gubbay's office where, with support from a few other vets, threatened Zimbabwe's top judge with death should he not immediately retire. As Chinotimba told some journalists who had gathered outside the judge's chambers to witness this further spectacle, "He is a British imperialist agent and he must go. I have told him in no uncertain terms that he is putting his life at risk by remaining in his office when we have made it very clear we no longer want him. I told him to vacate his office today. If he does not go, then we declare war!" Subtle stuff.

For this bravery and other such daring acts which resulted in a number of judges taking early retirement, Chinotimba was rewarded with a government Pajero SUV, so that he could perform his duties in style. That a municipal security gurard can invade the chief justice's office, which is guarded by armed police, and carry on like this is yet another display of the country's utter moral decreptitude.

જ જ જ

Philip Bezuidenhout is a prime example of the rule of law in Zimbabwe being subverted and manipulated to suit Mugabe and his ruling party.

Upon transfer from Chikurubi I had arrived at Central to find Phil locked up, twenty-three hours a day, naked, in a death-row cell, under the prison's condemned-prisoner rules. He had been there for over a year and was completely bewildered when it came to his rights. He had been jailed in 2004 for the murder of a Mugabe-affiliated war veteran in the Mutare area.

As a productive commercial farmer, Phil's land was obviously the subject of much drooling by government officials in the area who couldn't wait to get their hands on his property.

Phil was in possession of at least half a dozen court orders in his favour, all of which prohibited the government from taking his farm, until they had followed their *own rules* regarding land. Mugabe's government is not one to stand on ceremony when it comes to the rule of law especially if it involves rich pickings such as a productive commercial farm. The elite could just see themselves ensconced on Phil's verandah at weekends, reclining in comfortable chairs, with the right tipple in hand and meat from one of all those fat cows roasting on the fire. That is often the perception of commercial farming—no work except driving the odd tractor when you want to check out the *plaas* (farm) and the rest just follows—crops grow by themselves, cattle are simply always there and tobacco seeds sow themselves—the crop reaps, cures and conveys itself by magic to the market. Who needs to know anything about farming after all? If you're short of cash you just kill a few cattle and sell the meat, or shoot some of the wild buck. Easier still is to have the workers chop down some trees for sale as firewood. Why slave away in the blazing sun when it's so much easier just to plunder the farm? After all there are plenty of other illegal-white-settler commercial farms that you can help yourself to when your *plaas* has run its course.

And it's also *lekker* being a farm owner because you can bring your whole extended family from all over the country; they can put up thatched huts to live in and support themselves by snaring all the small animals and you can shoot the larger animals like the kudu and eland and, of course, rhinos and elephants with your AK-47. And now, because you have all your family living on the *plaas* you can chase away all the farm labourers, whom you were not paying anyhow, especially the exorbitant farm wages that your political party had passed through parliament, and which you wholeheartedly supported—which the white settler had to pay just before you kicked him off the farm. Yes, my friend, this farming business is *lekker*! So, in order to dislodge Phil and his wife, the war veterans pitched camp around his house, burned anything that would make a nice fire to cook the meat from Phil's cattle that they had stolen and slaughtered on Phil's front lawn, right next to the swimming pool. They would sell some of the meat, purchase a bit of beer and hard liquor and binge during weeks of debauchery, making a huge racket right outside the lounge and bedroom windows.

During this madness Phil managed to offload a few of his cattle at the local stock-sale pens. The prices had fallen to rock-bottom because Phil was not alone in this—farmers in every corner of Zimbabwe were frantically de-stocking their beef herds before all the cattle were stolen or slaughtered for parties by the pool.

The war vets would cut farm fences and drive herds of cattle onto the main roads from where they would be loaded onto hired or stolen cattle trucks to be taken back to the rural areas from where the war vets originated.

Zimbabwe, just prior to this insanity on the commercial farms, had an annual quota of 9.2 million tons of prime beef for sale to the European Union. However, the uncontrolled and unrestricted movement of cattle across the previous veterinary boundaries resulted in an almost simultaneous outbreak of foot and mouth countrywide—especially in the previously sanitized export-cattle-breeding areas. The European Union immediately froze the import of any meat from Zimbabwe.

The veterans continued with their pillage on Phil's farm, destroying fences, to be sold or taken home, stealing and selling irrigation equipment, with larger plant like tractors and combine harvesters being removed to farms belonging to the ZANU (PF) hierarchy (also 'harvested' from white farmers). There the equipment was parked, to rust in the rain or be sold for cash to unscrupulous dealers because there was no commercial farming on the go and no one knew how to use the equipment anyway. Especially as all the experienced farm labourers, their families and friends had been kicked off the farms, to squat and starve on the sides of the roads. Estimates are that around two million farm workers and their dependents were rendered homeless by this farm resettlement policy. Many of these farm labourers go back generations on the farms from were they were evicted. Experienced farm labour is probably the most valuable asset of a commercial farm. You simply cannot ignore or waste experience like that.

I'm not saying that land reform or redistribution in Zimbabwe was wrong; I am saying it should have been done in a structured, legal manner with due concern to maintenance of food and export production. However, as Mugabe had just lost a referendum for a new constitution in Zimbabwe and desperately needed to play his final ace (joker) to maintain support from the war vets and keep his gravy train happy, he let this madness run amok. The Zimbabwe Republic Police were ordered not to interfere as Mugabe claimed that the occupation of the farms was a spontaneous reaction from a population that was tired of waiting for its rightful property to be returned to it.

Eventually fearing for his wife's safety, and with nothing of value on his farm other than his farmhouse (not even a chicken survived the war veterans' fires) Phil had her move to Mutare, while he chose to stay with what little he had left of his whole life.

Despite numerous phone calls and visits to the police station at Odzi, the police did not attend to the theft, robbery and vandalism on his farm. They flatly refused to react, under political instruction from their self-confessed ZANU (PF)-aligned police commissioner, Augustine Chihuri, who, so the rumour goes, has three prime commercial farms himself.

On that fateful day in 2001, fearing for his life, Phil was evacuating his farm. Trying to dash away from his homestead in his pick-up, one of the war veterans suddenly leaped out in front of his vehicle. Phil panicked at this sudden apparition in his way and swerved left then right as the war veteran did the same. Phil was not about to stop, so with his foot flat he tried to dodge the vet but winged him with his front-right fender before speeding off.

To his credit, which the court scoffed at as irrelevant, Phil went directly to Odzi police station to report the incident. As soon as the cops heard it was a war veteran who had been run over and killed, they threw Phil in the cells. Bear in mind these are the self-same cops who never once reacted in any way to all the atrocious and unlawful things the war veterans were doing on Phil's farm.

The rest is history. Phil was sentenced to fifteen years with labour for murder, with the Zimbabwean chief justice—this time a proper ZANU (PF) lackey, Godfrey Chidyasiku, murmuring that he would have preferred to see the death sentence given to Phil.

ج ج ج

Rest assured, Phil's case is not isolated. Almost every farm eviction and repossession (some 4,000 of them) was just as violent and many just as tragic with loss of life and huge financial losses. Martin Olds from the Nyamandhlovu area is yet another one. When the war vets failed to dislodge him from his farm with their usual shenanigans, they shot him dead in his front yard. This was after a two-hour gunfight at his homestead and only after the veterans had managed to drive him from the cover of his house by setting it alight. And he was alone in his house, having sent his wife and two children into Bulawayo to avoid the terror on the farms.

The police had erected a roadblock on the road leading to Martin's farm. They allowed the convoy of armed war veterans to pass through and stood there listening to the gunfire without doing anything about it. When an ambulance arrived, which had been summoned by Martin after he had been shot and wounded in the leg, it was stopped and refused throughfare, as were the neighbouring farmers who were rushing to his aid.

Martin's bruised, battered and shot-up body was later recovered on his front verandah when his friends eventually arrived—only after the 200 armed attackers had spent a further two hours burning all the farm buildings and collecting as many of their cartridge cases as they could, to cover their tracks, before driving back through the roadblock waving their guns and singing liberation songs. Needless to add that no one was ever prosecuted for this murder.

ج ج ج

Roy Bennett was an MDC member of the Zimbabwean parliament. He purchased his 2,800-hectare farm, Vooruitzicht, which adjoins the Chimanamani National

Park in eastern Zimbabwe, in 1993, some thirteen years after independence. This is mostly mountainous commercial timber country. However, Roy had carved out fifty acres of coffee and fruit trees and had built up a herd of 1,000 prime-beef cattle. He also boasted the purest herd of eland antelope south of the Sahara. His annual turnover on the farm was approximately US$3 million per annum.

Roy is completely fluent in the Shona language, and is very popular among the tribespeople in the Chimanimani area who subsequently elected him as their representative in parliament.

It didn't take long for avaricious eyes to pick out his farm. Being an MDC official made him a prime candidate for a farm invasion—notwithstanding the productiveness of his farm or the fact that he had purchased it well after independence and that he was a one-farm owner. It wasn't long before the invaders arrived. They carried out their full routine of theft, damage, death threats and beatings until Roy was forced off the land with his family, his whole livelihood stolen and destroyed.

A few months later during a parliamentary sitting in Harare and in a moment of rage and utter frustration, Roy pushed Zimbabwe's minister of justice to the floor in parliament after Chinamasa had called Roy's forebears thieves.

This was manna from heaven for the regime's elite and, using parliamentary rules, Roy was rapidly jailed for a year for losing his temper and 'misbehaviour' in parliament.

After serving his full sentence Roy was persecuted and hounded and fled the country of his birth in genuine fear for his and his family's lives. The regime had invented some treason charges against him, and he was forced to take to his heels.

He has now been granted political asylum in South Africa after appeal to the independent Asylum Appeals Board. In South Africa, and at no little threat to his life from Zimbabwean agents, he devotes his life to the freedom of Zimbabwe's people, through peaceful means. He stuck to the legal channels open to him in Zimbabwe and never strayed from his path of peace. Throughout his ordeal Roy behaved with impeccable constitutional decorum while the government's demeanour was grossly improper throughout. I have huge respect for Roy Bennett. Were it me I would probably have shot the people who were brutally and blatantly robbing me of my rights and my personal property.

I would like to quote Roy just before his forced exile: "They can take my farm, but I am still running as a member of parliament. I have faith in humanity and that what the government has done is wrong and the people of Zimbabwe know it and will vote out ZANU (PF) and return the rule of law. I am committed to peaceful change. I am not going back. I realize the implications. I realize the threats. I realize the danger. The people of Zimbabwe are being suppressed by a very evil regime. I am not going to be intimidated by this evil. If I lose my life, so be it. For my children to have a life in this country someone has to make a stand."

Strength to you Roy and all in your movement who are battling enormous odds on behalf of the ordinary people of Zimbabwe.

Please don't ignore the fact that Phil, Roy and Martin all purchased their farms with their own blood, sweat and tears, and with their own money *after* independence in Zimbabwe, as did nearly every other farmer who has had his *plaas* occupied and repossessed—giving truth to the lie by the Mugabe regime that they are repossessing land stolen by the original occupying settlers who arrived in Zimbabwe in the 1890s.

It remains a fact that to this date, not a single farmer who had his land stolen by the regime during this madness, has been paid proper compensation for the development and time and money that he poured into his farm. It is part of Zimbabwean law that farmers who have been dispossessed of their land will be compensated *fully and fairly* for any development on their land. The law clearly states that they will not be compensated for the land itself which the regime says was originally stolen by the whites when they occupied the country in the 1890. As mentioned before most of these farmers, many of whom have been murdered in the land-acquisition process, had bought their land after independence.

The death-row cells at Harare Central where I found Phil are small, pokey little dens, each with a solid five-centimetre-thick wooden door. Each door has a small round peephole drilled though it. When a death-row prisoner needs to draw attention, he sticks his index finger through the hole and wiggles it a little bit. Hopefully one of the service prisoners who hang around in the passageways to keep the place swept will see the finger, check what's up and if necessary call a guard, who may come and talk to the prisoner. A death-row prisoner does not hammer or kick the door to gain attention, lest he wants a thorough beating.

Phil would accordingly stick his finger through the peephole and give it a wiggle and if I didn't see him 'calling' a service prisoner he would call me. I'd wander up and give his finger a friendly shake—that's how it is in the death row at Central—you shake fingers.

It didn't take me long, with my jailhouse-attorney experience, to have Phil up to speed. He started demanding clothes to wear, adequate food and more time out of his cell, as had been ordered by the Supreme Court for us three at

Chikurubi. This court order was supposed to apply to all prisoners on death row, and not just the three of us.

It then didn't take long for Phil to be moved from the death house at Harare Central to Chikurubi so he wouldn't be influenced by this old jailbird. At least at Chikurubi he would find conditions, insofar as being clothed and outside during the day, easier to handle.

 روی روی روی

After Phil was transferred to Chikurubi, I was removed from the death-cell area at Harare Central before I could corrupt any more of the death-row population.

When Roy Bennett arrived at Harare Central to start his year in jail for his 'atrocious' behaviour in parliament he was immediately placed in a section of the prison where I would not have access to him. Being the *skelm* that I am, that attempt of incommunicado by the authorities lasted about five minutes before I started getting messages through to him. It was quite a joy being in comms with Roy. It was really quite fun sending and receiving messages and letters with Roy while the prison authorities thought they had him totally isolated. We struck up a friendship over this, even though it seemed imperative to them that we be kept apart lest I share my jailhouse knowledge with him.

I actually became really good friends with a number of prisoners over the years, of all colours and kinds. Many prisoners are really good people but just get stuck in jail because of politics or circumstance. The majority of the prisoners in Zimbabwe are black, though there were a few coloureds and a few whites while I was there, but not more than about twenty altogether. I was friends with all the whites but a few of them were real skates—habitual thieves, housebreakers, car thieves that kind of stuff. I had a number of really good black friends too. Some were murderers, car-jackers, drug dealers; we saw it all. Some were actually nice people and on holidays and at other times during the year, we would share any food that we could get, either smuggled from the kitchen or from outside. I had a few black friends who used to bring me food on the holidays in exchange for sharing food with them during the year that I was able to snivel from the kitchen because of my heart problem.

You cannot live in isolation in jail and after I left death row it was quite natural to make friends and spend day after day playing chess with a lot of black guys. Yes, some prisoners are just evil scum and I tried to avoid any sort of contact with them but I couldn't really hold myself aloof though as I was also in there for murder, regardless of my case being political.

I had no people in Harare to bring me food regularly and Mike Smith would not allow his sister, based in Harare, to do anything for me. She was willing to help, but he had threatened that if she wanted to help me, he would cut himself off from her. We don't like each other too much, Smith and I.

Many times I stopped the officers from beating the black prisoners for nothing. The officers would pay heed when I started shouting at them as they knew I was Mugabe's personal prisoner and could get letters out to the politicians any time I wished.

I maintain contact with some of the prisoners who are still in there and send them the occasional goodie parcel. The majority of people in prison are poor and are just victims of circumstance—that's why they are there, because there are no jobs in Zimbabwe. Sadly, many prisoners are jailed for such petty theft you wouldn't believe it—like stealing a bunch of vegetables to feed their family and so on. It's quite tragic.

I was also friendly with most of the guards. In general they are just normal people doing an abnormal job. Of course, some of them were evil shits and tried to make everybody's life a misery, but they were in the minority. I still phone and correspond with some of the guards that helped me in jail. They are in a real tight fix up there and earn peanuts, so even the odd R50 that I send them on occasions makes a huge difference, especially when you realize that they earn around the equivalent of R20 a month.

කැ කැ කැ

In comparison to Chikurubi, jail time at Harare Central was a breeze, mainly because you have access to the kitchen service area and also to the prison hospital, whereas at Chikurubi, if you want to make any deals to improve your diet or just get some headache pills, it is a major hassle going through three or four different couriers. Being on the outskirts of the Harare central business district made it quite easy to ask a guard to go and fetch you something small to eat, to post letters and so on.

At Harare Central, with easy access to the steam-fired kitchen, getting rid of bed lice was simply matter of washing your blankets in a few buckets of boiling water. If you were in a crowded cell this would last as long as it takes for one of these little critters to cross from one blanket to another, but in a single cell, so long as you restrict your visitors who might be carrying lice on their clothes, you could be lice-free for weeks. But of course you had to pay for the boiling water from the kitchen, a few smuggled smokes or such like. Such is life in prison. You have to make a plan, always, and every day, if you want to survive.

And I was, if nothing else, determined, somehow, to survive.

♋♋♋

Every day, twice a day, President Mugabe is flown over the prison in his luxury Cougar helicopter, escorted by a Zimbabwe Air Force chopper on his way from State House to the National Military Headquarters near the prison. Regular as clockwork, the two helicopters fly overhead, and it's quite a hoot watching the prisoners making pistols out of finger and thumb and blasting him out of the sky. In reality, the choppers fly slow and low, so they'd make easy pickings for a heat-seeking missile, or plain rifle fire, which at that range and speed wouldn't need much of a marksman. Anyhow, if one of Mugabe's secret service people ever reads this he may wake up and and decide to alter the daily route a bit.

♋♋♋

I had been corresponding with Judith Todd for a few years from Chikurubi and this correspondence and friendship continued after I had been moved to Harare Central Prison. In 2005, she managed to convince a Roman Catholic priest in Harare to have a look at our plight. This was no mean feat for her as she had to go through an intermediary who was a mutual friend of hers and the priest's. Father Fidelis Mukonori, a close friend and confidant of President Mugabe, visited us three in Harare Central in July 2005 and after an hour or so talking with me he left, leaving me hanging up my biggest 'hope hat' ever! He told me that President Mugabe was a personal friend and that he would try to speak with him for some relief for me and my co-accused.

Father Fidelis Mukonori is a man of huge moral strength and standing in Zimbabwe. He is highly respected and because of his friendship and religious closeness to Mugabe (he is Mugabe's confessor) he has some political clout, with most of Mugabe's cabinet paying heed when he speaks. He is frequently asked to intercede between the government and human rights groups when the security forces go overboard and the human rights people find themselves unable to obtain any relief from Mugabe's cabinet members.

The so-called Operation *Murambatsvina* was one such case where his intervention was sought. *Murambatsvina* means 'human filth is not wanted'. The operation involved the security forces destroying urban slum dwellings. These slum-dwellers, of which there are a great many because there is no formal employment in Zimbabwe, are the nation's poorest. That they have to live in makeshift homes while government calls them 'shit' is immensely cruel. The slums and shacks where these people resided, women, children and all, had been constructed mainly in the backyards of the overcrowded high-density-population areas of the country's cities and towns. For building material these people had scavenged pieces of plastic, galvanized sheeting—anything that would keep the elements marginally at bay.

As if tossing thousands onto the streets without any shelter in mid-winter was not enough, Mugabe's ministers then denied them food from human rights groups. The Harare government wanted to politicize food aid to the people they had rendered homeless and keep them beholden to the state—so they were not too pleased when the human rights organizations climbed in with food aid. The best way to sort that out was to flatly deny them authority to feed the homeless. The reason the state gave for this was that the human rights people were themselves politicizing the food aid they were supplying! The state wanted to remain in control of these poor people's stomachs so that they would then be able to control their minds and change their voting patterns which, in the urban areas of Zimbabwe, are universally anti-Mugabe.

The opposition party, MDC, entered the fray and obtained a donation of some 300 tons of food from South Africa which was to be given to the human rights organizations to distribute. At first the government refused to issue a permit for this food donation, so it sat at the border for months until it was returned to its original donor, while the people starved on the streets of Zimbabwe. If that isn't systematic genocide, I'm not sure what is.

But Father Fidelis Mukonori used his influence with Mugabe who subsequently overrode his ministers and at last the human rights organizations were allowed to provide food and clothing and basic canvas shelter to the thousands of homeless—the proviso being that the distribution had to be closely monitored by the government.

The irony here being that the poor took their canvas tents, clothes and food they had been given and went back and pitched camp in exactly the same spots where their little shacks had been destroyed a few weeks prior. Sometimes they resorted to using the leftover scraps of their destroyed homes to reconstruct the new shacks.

Release

"However long the night may last,
There will be morning"
Morroccan

One day I was sitting in my single cell at about 3.30 p.m., mentally preparing myself for another night. In jail you don't just go with the flow, you have to prepare yourself, each and every day, and night, to get through. So there I was sitting on my bedroll on the floor when an officer appeared at the door with the message that I was wanted in the administration block, as the officer commanding—the regional boss—wanted to see me.

As I walked across to his office, with heart hammering furiously in anticipation of something bad going down, I couldn't fathom why on a Friday afternoon I was being called in by the big shot. Smith and Conjwayo had also been summoned and we made an apprehensive trio as we mounted the steps of the administration block.

An hour later, having been told that President Mugabe had granted us a full pardon, we floated down those same steps—feet light as air …
The 30th June is a day that will be engraved in my brain forever. For two reasons. My botched escape was planned to go down on 30th June 1988 and exactly nineteen years later I was reprieved.

We were told that the clemency order had been signed, but the papers had not yet come through from State House and so we were to spend that night in our cells to be released the following morning.

I asked the officer in charge to phone the news through to our lawyers, which he did. I have since been told that from that moment on the news hit the internet and the phones didn't stopping ringing across the globe that night. It is one of the most humbling things ever to have so many people worldwide, who had cared and prayed for us for so many years, rejoicing and passing the news on at lightning speed. In jail news travels just as fast!

While still in the administration office, I began to get very tearful because suddenly all the prison brass started to shake my hand and pat me on the back and as we emerged and made our way back to our cell blocks, the prison windows and doorways were a sea of waving arms, all screaming "Bye bye *murungu!*" Even the guys in death row had heard the news and were shouting salutations through their little barred, grill-covered windows.

The section I was in at that time was an old death row, consisting of two rows of solid doors and finger-sized peepholes. with a wide passage down the middle. As I walked in, I was greeted by the sight of every single peephole with a black wiggling finger sticking out—each occupant eager to wish me well and say goodbye. After twenty years of such heartache and stress, and on many occasions consoling, or being consoled by, the owners of those wiggling fingers, I was enormously choked up as I went from finger to finger to 'shake fingers' and say farewell.

Even though I'd still be there at unlock in the morning, each and every one wanted the full story. The prison guards too, were full of smiles and handshakes: "You don't belong to us anymore, *mandebvu* [bearded one]. Lock your cell or don't lock it, it's up to you."

The doors have huge spring-type activated locks which shut upon closing, so I just had to slam the door to be locked inside for the night. I finished my goodbye rounds, had a cold shower and locked myself in my cell at about 9.00 p.m. that night, later than I'd ever been outside a locked cell in twenty years.

My imminent freedom only fully registered a little bit later as I was sitting there tearing up all my papers, getting ready to leave. I felt indescribable relief but also a deep-down fear of the unknown, not knowing what to expect when I got out, what to expect when I saw my kids and my wife for the first time.

Early Saturday morning on 1st July 2006, I was unlocked to the same huge fuss from all the other prisoners. Then it was over to the hospital to be medically checked out of the prison. An hour's wait later and a civilian doctor arrived and gave me the best medical check-up I'd had in twenty years.

"Any medical problem for Woods?" he asked. "Any illness?"

"No," I said, "absolutely nothing, doc. Just sign that paper because I'm outta here."

"Can I take your blood pressure?" he asked.

"No doc, just sign—sign!"

Time for Conjawayo's final medical and the old guy started complaining that he had back pains and some urinating hassles dating back ten years and could he please have some pills to take home. I nearly had to drag him out of the doctor's room!

৵৵৵

Once outside we were approached by brass-looking men in suits. Trouble! I thought. There is always trouble.

"Mr. Woods, you are a South African citizen?" their leader enquired.

"Yep," I said.

"Fine. As such you are going to be deported to South Africa and will be a prohibited immigrant."

"That's okay, I want to leave anyhow," I replied, tongue in cheek. I wanted to spit out all the presidential bullshit about me being a Zimbabwean citizen that I'd had to endure for nearly twenty years.

I was subsequently issued a prohibited-immigrant declaration, photographed and fingerprinted, as was Smith, while Conjwayo, who had been born in the Transkei area of South Africa, walked out the gates of the prison, free to stay in Zimbabwe!

A while later, outside the huge brass-studded doors of the prison into the free world I stepped—to be greeted by a forest of microphones and flashing cameras from the local and international press.

It didn't end there.

The immigration department had been caught on the hop by the deportation order. They had received orders which specified that Smith and I be conveyed to the South African border some 600 kilometres away, by road. My lawyers were right there and had an air ticket in their possession for me to fly to Johannesburg later that day. They had also been caught unawares by the deportation spiel, but were not making a fuss about citizenship, preferring to get me out of Zimbabwe as quickly as possible before the fickle hand of fate once again screwed it all up.

৵৵৵

Immigration meanwhile were in quite a tizz. Saturday morning and they had no vehicle to drive us to the border. An hour later they found a twin-cab, but it required new tyres. Two hours later they found two different wheels which they fitted on the front with the better two of the original four being placed on the rear. Now came the hard part, perennial in Zimbabwe then as it is now—fuel for the vehicle and money to buy some diesel on the road to Beitbridge.

As midday approached, while we were standing around outside in the free sun near the huge brass-studded double-door entrance, the butterflies were going crazy in my stomach and a huge premonition came over me that all was not quite right. While the immigration people were off looking for cash and fuel a police

TIGHT SECURITY AS TWO APPEAR IN HARARE COURT

Court Reporter

TWO of the 17 people arrested after the bomb blast in Bulawayo last month had their warned-and-cautioned statements confirmed by Harare provincial magistrate Mr Ephraim Chiwara in the city yesterday.

Senior public prosecutor Mr Tadius Karwi said the statements by Michael Smith and Kevin Woods had not been challenged.

More of the people picked up by police will appear soon, including Rory Maguire and some members of the family of Thomas Bawden.

Confirmation hearings are heard in camera.

Woods, a former CIO officer; Maguire, a Bulawayo company director; and Smith were brought to the Harare magistrates' court shortly before lunch.

There was very tight security both inside and outside the court building at Rotten Row. No one other than security men, judicial officers and other court officials and employees were allowed in or near the courtroom where the hearings were being held.

KEVIN WOODS (left) entering the Harare Magistrates' Court yesterday for his confirmation of statement hearing. Rory Maguire (right) being escorted into the court yesterday. His confirmation hearing will probably be next week.

Pictures by Reuters.

Top: Woods and Maguire appear in court, February 1988.

Above left: Woods' sketch of a prison search.

Above right: The author with retired General George Meiring. Pretoria, July 2006.

Top left: Reunion of four former BSAP Support Unit commanders. Standing: a friend Gary is flanked by Gus Albertson (left) and Tony Merris. Seated are Barry Woan (cap) and Kevin Woods.

Top right: Reunited after twenty years with son Clinton. *Photo: Waldo Swiegers/Beeld*

Centre left: With Ian Smith, 2006.

Centre right: The author (right) with Barry Bawden and Jacob Zuma.

Above left: 'The Rat Pack' celebrates Woodsie's first year of freedom. Left to right: Woods, King, Mrs. Wasserman and Joan Robey.

Above right: Kevin Woods and Barry Bawden.

Woods with Nelson Mandela.

Former RLI Sergeant Dave Hoskins being delivered at Durban International Airport by Sergeant King. Dave's wife, Roach, is on the left.

Impressions by Craig Bone.

Impressions by Craig Bone.

An impression by Craig Bone.

vehicle arrived. Four suits alighted and sought out my two lawyers who were also standing around with us.

After a serious conversation between the police and my lawyers I was called over. A chief superintendant who introduced himself as the Officer Commanding Harare CID Homicide told me: "We have found a human skull in your old office and need to know whose it is."

I was now experiencing serious anxiety. I'd had misgivings from the previous evening, worrying that this was all too good to be true. This had been compounded that morning with the immigration bullshit, but I never expected this histrionic crap. It took me a few heartbeats to get my head together and think clearly. I told him, in the presence of my lawyers that as an intelligence-gathering organization, we, as the CIO back then, didn't collect skulls, and furthermore the CIO in Matabeleland had moved their offices to new premises in 1988 anyway, which was after my arrest, so how could I possibly know anything about an office I hadn't seen—or even occupied for over twenty years.

"Good point, Mr. Woods," he replied, obviously shamefaced, about having been sent on an errand without substance that he was not really interested in performing.

"Please wait a little while," he asked, as off he and his colleagues went.

The South African high commissioner then arrived. He is a remarkably sensitive and considerate man. As soon as he heard all about these shenanigans he at once declared that he would escort our immigration convoy to Beitbridge. Our lawyers also volunteered to come along.

In the bad days of yore, it was not uncommon for a person who was a bit of a thorn in the side to be 'shot while attempting to escape' and such thoughts were apparently somewhere in the heads of my lawyers and the high commissioner. Just imagine that! Kevin Woods shot trying to escape while being driven to the border and freedom! Stranger things happen in Zimbabwe so this is not as far-fetched as it sounds.

Toward mid-afternoon the immigration people arrived back with a sack (literally!) full of Zimbabwean dollars, for fuel en route, which would have to be bought on the black market. The twin-cab also had a full tank—again of black-market fuel.

And there we all sat, waiting for the final all-clear from the CID.

The lawyers were busy drafting an urgent court order for me to depart, after all I'd just received a full pardon from the Zimbabwean president, when the CID *okes* returned, all full of smiles.

"No problem! You can go," they beamed.

❧ ❧ ❧

Our little convoy consisted of three vehicles—immigration's, the high commision's, and a prison's truck for good measure. I'd just been given three and a half million Zimbabwean dollars by my lawyer in case we got separated. Whoopee! I was loaded! The large top pocket of my shirt was jammed full of Zimbabwean fifty-thousand-dollar bearer's cheques.

(I'm repeating myself to highlight Mugabe's idiosyncracies He will not allow the Zimbabwean Reserve Bank to print notes in larger denominations than one thousand dollars. Even with inflation heading like a shuttle into outer space, no bank notes above Z$1,000. So the Reserve Bank is forced to print other forms of currency, the latest being a bearer cheque, which looks just like real money, with a serial number, security thread and all. But it's not a bank note. So that's okay. Mugabe feels that having large-denomination notes will make him look silly and make Zimbabwe appear like a typical banana republic. Talk about stable door …)

So eventually, with a churning stomach full of acid and much apprehension, we set off for the border. My South African passport was snug in the pocket of my jeans, with my other pockets bulging with loot. What more could a man want?

Chivu (formerly Enkeldoorn) is a small village 190 kilometres south of Harare on the main road to Beitbridge. Things were a little tense in the vehicle, where I sat outside without leg-irons or handcuffs for the first time in twenty years, in the back seat with my lawyer. The two immigration officers were in the front. As I was now extremely wealthy, I offered to chill things out and offered the two officials a little refreshment and a snack, which they said would be nice.

At a service station in Enkeldoorn, walking around the forecourt free, unrestrained and on cloud nine, I ordered two Cokes and a small bottle of spring water. To show these guys just how flush I was, I added a packet of mixed biscuits, and like a real Arab sheik, dumped the loads of both pockets on the counter for the attendant to count out the required few notes. She very efficiently, just like a bank teller, flipped through pile after pile of notes and with some consternation on her face asked if I had anything smaller than a fifty thousand as she was tight on change.

"How much change?" I asked.

"Forty-five thousand."

So that meant she would use some of my loot and only needed an extra five grand. No sweat. This was chicken feed for Zimbabwe's newest millionaire.

"No problem," I beamed, "You keep the five thousand. What have you got on your shelves for forty-five thousand?"

She turned around with a bemused look on her face, plucked something out of a bottle, handed me two small toffees and, with a flourish, swept every single note off the counter into a box on the floor at her feet—obviously a makeshift till. The normal till was far too small to hold all the cash needed for normal daily business.

Two fucking toffees! Good grief! Forty-five grand for two toffees. Three and a half million for a couple of Cokes and some biscuits. Welcome to the real world, Woodsie.

With a shit-eating grin, just as if I had known all along exactly what the prices were and what was going on, I handed her back the two toffees. "Have these my sister," and we were out of there.

To put a little perspective on this I will tell you that in 1980 I bought my house in Bulawayo for twenty thousand Zimbabwean dollars. Now, suddenly my house—five acres, stables for the horses, servants' quarters etc., is worth less than two little toffees. There must be a better description than banana republic.

The rest of the trip was uneventful other than a major hassle halfway to Beitbridge when we had fuel trouble, which once again had to be sourced on the black market late that Saturday night.

A vivid impression of Zimbabwe's desolate and barren farmlands flashing by as we travelled toward the border, sticks in my mind. Farmland I remember from all those years ago that was always green and productive with irrigation sprinklers going full blast. And now there's nothing but dry, dead fields. Crossing into South Africa the difference is like night and day, with lush, green fields of maize, sunflowers and everything else stretching far into the distance in every direction. Anyone who wants to make decisions on land usage and distribution should make that trip, in either direction—it will take your breath away.

I had an attack of the 'jeebs' and bad vibes as we approached Beitbridge. That little episode with the skull at the prison had unsettled me, even though I'd assessed the whole charade as just a final twist of the knife by Mnangagwa or Chinamasa sitting in the officers' mess at the army barracks deciding to put the shits up me … just one more vindictive time. Irresistible.

I mentioned to my lawyer that I doubted there would be an easy passage for us through the border. Thank God I was wrong.

At half past two on the morning of 2nd July 2006, as I was driven across the 'new' bridge over the Limpopo River at Beitbridge between Zimbabwe and South Africa, the high commissioner cranked open the sun roof of his Land Cruiser and I watched a crystal-clear Milky Way drift by—all so beautifully crisp, cold and clear as you only get on a lowveld winter's night.

"Thank God for that," I whispered to my lawyer sitting behind me.

She gave me a reassuring pat on the shoulder. "God bless you too," she whispered.

I'm sure she heaved an equivalent sigh of relief as my other lawyer in the vehicle behind us who had also fought for me, bullied government departments for me, prayed for me and cared about me for many years …

❧❧❧

Vincent van Gogh painted the picture that inspired Don McLean to sing *Vincent* with its haunting lines 'Starry starry night'. I have always loved that song and it holds many memories for me—none more poignant than on that night when after midnight on the second, I looked at a crystal-clear sky filled with stars so near and so bright … for the first time in twenty years.

Tie a yellow ribbon ...

"I pointed out the stars and the moon,
And all you saw was the tip of my finger"
Swahili

Thanks to the Zimbabwean government, it was well after 2.00 a.m. on the morning of 2nd July 2006 before I crossed over into South Africa to be met by Barry Bawden and a television crew from the SABC. Barry had been waiting for us since early afternoon as he, like everyone else, had been caught unawares by the deportation order and by the skull-in-the-cupboard nonsense. He had brought along a dozen beers and a bottle of brandy as a bit of a celebration. Our delay and the cold weather meant that there were only two beers left awaiting us!

Nothing has tasted as good as those two cool draughts, at 2.30 in the morning, with so many conflicting emotions running wild through the very core of my being.

What was I to expect?

What would my kids have to say?

Where would I go? What would I do?

I had no home, no furniture, no car, no nothing. Even my old clothes had been stolen during one of the moves my wife had made. I had the clobber I was wearing. And that was it.

With nerves jangling, we checked into reserved rooms at a hotel in Messina (now Musina), a small *dorp* a few kilometres into South Africa, just to chill for a few hours and await the dawn of what was expected to be a day of enormous emotion. All I could be absolutely sure of, was that a part of my life was over. The hardest part.

I didn't even try to sleep those few hours. Rest was impossible, not with all the thoughts screaming in my head, so I attempted a little solitary contemplation. Revenge was something that was always so close to my thoughts while I was in jail—revenge for my wasted life; against those who were holding me there and against those who, through my pinhole of perspective, had abandoned me. But now that I was free, that desire for revenge seemed to ebb further, as it has been doing ever since my release. A little each day and in its wake I think I've developed the potential for renewal, and an attempt to acknowledge my failings in the past and to atone for them in some small way to make a better present and future.

I am quite fortunate that I don't dream too much. I never have, and don't much even now. I am not haunted in my dreams by the things that I have seen and done in my life. If I am haunted at all, it's while I am awake. Interestingly though my dreams are always the same, the ones where you try to shoot someone and the gun does not go off, you try to run and your legs won't move.

Anyway, in this sort of philosophical mood Barry's cell phone (a what?) rang and I spoke to my brother, Mike, my personal crusader in Australia. We didn't make much sense and I handed the phone back to Barry who, expecting a flood of calls promptly switched it off and lay down for a short kip! After all, he was playing taxi driver and had to drive us to Pretoria, some 500 kilometres south, in a few hours.

At about 5.30 a.m., after a cup of coffee, which in itself was a massive novelty (you don't get early-morning room service with coffee in jail in Zimbabwe!) we saddled up and hit the road in Barry's sedan. With my throat choking and my emotional strength paper thin, my first free sunrise in twenty years rose off to the east, casting long, undulating shadows as we let the fresh air wash away some of the cobwebs inside our heads. Today was going to be another story, that's for sure. Barry handed me a cell phone.

Ja well, no fine!

"What do I do with this?" I asked. At 53 years of age, July 2006 was the first time I had ever held a cell phone in my entire life. (The technological shock for me after twenty years in jail was mind-boggling. Even the basic things in life, like walking into a bank through its security doors, to using a computer were quite beyond me and I had to be led through most like a newborn child.)

Barry showed me how to switch it on and the rest of that day dissolved into phone call after phone call, starting with my children, whom I hadn't spoken to for nearly two decades. The conversations with my son and two daughters amounted to a few minutes each of suppressed sobs and choked-up throats. Barry kept telling me to let it out and I sat there covering the distance to Pretoria sniffling and sobbing love and relief to all who phoned.

During my time in jail, my wife received an allowance from the South African Military which was a life-saver and helped care for her and educate my kids. But she'd had to offload all my assets one by one to survive. My Mercedes, my boats, my cattle and house all went under the hammer over the years; and so I came out of jail to nothing. I have no wife and no assets, but I have three kids who love me. And that is what I survived for.

Within a few days my children were in Pretoria. I am surely blessed. They call me dad. I can hug them. They love me. What more can a man want?

Sometimes though, when I think of them in my mind's eye, they are still little children. Even now, after having seen and spent time with my kids all grown up, it's quite hard for me to realize that these are my kids because of the huge gap. Nonetheless, my time with them is absolutely magic and I can't thank God enough for that.

✍ ✍ ✍

I asked Nelson Mandela's office if I could see him—just to thank him for all he had tried to do to get me released. I was overjoyed when this was granted. My wife accompanied me on that visit. It was a massively humbling occasion to meet Nelson Mandela. We spoke for over half an hour and laughed a little at Robert Mugabe's vanity which has him aged over eighty without a grey hair on his head or any wrinkles on his face. All at the expense of the Zimbabwean taxpayer, who pays in blood, sweat and tears for cosmetic surgery and hair dye. The most profound comment was when Nelson Mandela told me that Robert Mugabe has an inferiority complex. There's nothing closer to the truth, for sure.

The security surrounding Nelson Mandela is good but not intimidating, although it worries me to think how lax some aspects are. As I departed Nelson Mandela's office I joked with the security agents sitting outside his door that they hadn't searched me on the way in.

"Ha ha. You don't look dangerous," they replied.

I met with Mr. Jacob Zuma who had also tried to get us released and was a refreshing experience to listen to his views on how bureaucracy in South Africa, and throughout the continent, was stifling development and investment.

I met with former Rhodesian prime minister Ian Douglas Smith in Cape Town and also with retired Colonel Ron Reid-Daly of the Selous Scouts.

I have spoken to Tony Leon and Marthinus van Schalkwyk on the phone and also to Dr. Pieter Mulder's number two, and look forward to the opportunity of meeting these luminaries of the South African political scene.

A few days after my release, while walking around a shopping mall in Pretoria, with Phillip Albertyn who was my mentor and guide for a few days, I met with retired South African General George Meiring. He expressed his profound relief at my release and told me that had they had their way, I wouldn't have spent twenty years in jail. He added that it was the political leaders, especially Robert Mugabe, who had been intransigent throughout. That's a thing about President Mugabe—in addition to his vanity, which at 84 keeps him without a single grey hair on his head or a wrinkle on his face—he enjoys the dubious distinction and reputation of never yielding to pressure, internal or external. He considers himself to be Zimbabwe's only liberator and as such should rule in perpetuity.

And don't for a second think that because there are travel bans on him, that he is without his Saville Row suits, Gucci shoes et al. He simply shops by catalogue these days. And you can bet that the tailors who hand-make his suits for him visit him at State House or at his new villa in Borrowdale in Harare's affluent suburbs, which reportedly cost US$10 million to build.

I suppose I'm getting a little petulant about my feelings for Robert Mugabe. The best is to have no feelings at all. No love, no hate. I have to use the power of my mind that got me through twenty years in his prisons to get me through my future, and not waste my fortitude on him.

❧❧❧

On my arrival in Pretoria I stayed for a while at Barry's home and the first impression of the new South Africa I had was the amount of barbed wire, razor wire and electric fencing people have around their homes. I had just spent nearly twenty years inside a maximum-security prison surrounded by razor wire and electric fences meant to keep the crooks in. And here I stood, in Barry's front garden, surrounded by razor wire and electric fence meant to keep the crooks out. And it wasn't just Barry's home. Every single house I've visited, and nearly every one you drive past is like Fort Knox. With all the housebreaking, robberies, rapes and murders going on all the time in South Africa the country is a security provider's dream.

A month or so later I was in Durban. Early one morning at about 2.00 a.m. I took a walk on the Esplanade. I am told this was madness and that I am lucky to be alive. True, there were a lot of people, dressed up in a lot of creaking leather and adorned with chrome and gold trinkets, sitting in the deep shadows of the beach, where I walked alone.

I could feel their animosity and maybe their fear. Maybe I gave off some sort of aura that said best leave this *oke* alone. Something like, "He must be nuts walking here, or else it's a major bust going down. So *los* him [lit. ignore him]." Because I did my stroll full of bottled bravado, stimulated with the thought that I really didn't value my life too much, that I was not worth anything anymore and that life or death was cool to me. These thoughts are a one-way street to where I'd been for twenty years. Self-pity, a one-way street. I had a lady along with me, although she was wise enough to decline my offer to walk on the beach, choosing rather to stand next to a police cruiser that was parked up on the road.

The cop, a young coloured *oke*, was quite shocked when I told him I was taking a walk on the beach down to the water's edge on my own. "Leave your watch here with me, sir. It's dangerous down there."

I couldn't believe an attitude like that from an armed cop. In my day and especially as an undercover cop in the CPU, I would not have cautioned a member of the public against walking somewhere. I would have considered it my duty to make that place un-dangerous. Times have changed. We as cops were never well paid, but we had some esprit de corps. These days most cops are paid shit and they work eight hours a day and it's all about getting through those eight hours without getting shot, and then going home. A better wage for the cops in South Africa would be a good place to start.

లలల

The world is a different place than when I was living in it twenty years ago. Everything seems different, especially with science and technology having progressed so far while I was away. Every day is a huge learning curve for me. Just using a cell phone, it's truly amazing what you can do with them. Ironically, if we had them back then, I probably would not have been arrested. Communication is just so easy these days. I also love all the high-tech stuff in motor vehicles— truly amazing. One day I am going to have a larney car—just watch.

Going around the new South Africa with its enormous mega-cities is such an eye-opener to me. The lights of Jozi, Durban and Cape Town just seem to go on forever. Even the smaller towns, like Pietermaritzburg used to be when I last drove through it over twenty years ago, have mushroomed into huge cities.

The presidential convoy in South Africa, which everyone seems to complain about, is piss-willy compared to Robert Mugabe in action. Mugabe was warned by the CIO that with so many people keen on assassinating him, the last thing he should do is announce his whereabouts, passage and arrival with such fanfare. But he seems to take satisfaction at this display of opulence. Here in South Africa, if the convoy is approaching in an opposite lane, well, you jusy carry on with your journey. Just try that in Zimbabwe and you'll be lucky if you only get a thrashing—unlucky and you get shot. There is no vehicle movement on any road or highway in any direction when President Mugabe is approaching or passing through. So those of us in South Africa who take exception to the odd speeding convoy should be grateful that we don't have the circus that Zimbabweans have to put up with on their roads, every day of their lives.

South Africa is a fantastic place with such huge potential. It's humming, it's jumping, and it's moving. I believe that Jacob Zuma could be the next president of this country and I also believe that if he has enough decent advisors, then everything is going to be *lekker*. Potential in South Africa is massive and has a solid foundation. Everybody just has to watch out for the tell-tale signs that have already happened, like shortages of Coke, beer, electricity, and most recently, petrol. These things should just not happen. The ministry of energy should not tell us to use less electricity, they should make more. Yes, crime is a huge problem in South Africa, I live as a free man behind more concrete and razor wire than there is in jail, but for now I think South Africa is okay.

Over the years that I was jailed in Zimbabwe I had many legal representatives. Mostly they were paid for by Military Intelligence as we certainly couldn't afford them ourselves. Some came and went, like will-o-the-wisps concerned only in the payment of their fees. Two men, Robin and Adolf, stuck with us for many years, determined and resolute, and are an exception to the rule that I apply to the legal fraternity. For me, male lawyers in general have no heart. They do the job, and then they're out of there.

In later years and from 2000 onwards I had a female lawyer introduced to me by Judith Todd. Julia is indeed a jewel. For my last two or three years Maggie also came on board. What a life—two lady lawyers and both who cared. And that's the difference—ladies CARE. As for me, if I ever need to engage a member of the legal fraternity, it's going to be one of the female sort! I suppose the male lawyers' association of South Africa will now sue me for discrimination. Join the queue, my brothers!

I bumped into singer-songwriter John Edmond in Durban a few months before finishing this book and after telling him a bit about the past twenty years, I related the story of the mercenary who had phoned me about my name and death-row date scratched on the wall in Chikurubi. John then wrote this song:

Chikurubi

Chikurubi, you took away my day and my night
My dignity, my soul and you tried to take my life
You're a monument to hell and evil and each day I pray
That the Lord split you asunder on His mighty judgement day
Judgement Day

I lie naked on the concrete; there's no window just a door
And the only air is odour from a foul hole in the floor
The cell is claustrophobic and it measures one by three
Three steps forward three steps back is exercise for me
There's no pen, no paper, books or news or letters from outside
And I wonder 'bout my friends and folks, my children and my bride
And the loneliness of spirit makes me crave for company
A cockroach or a spider or an ant or just a flea

I don't know date or month or year or if it's day or night
I'm in darkness all the time and there's no natural light
The gallows are adjacent to the so-called sick-bay block
The innocent are hung there; they've got no chance in the dock
And the torture of emotions is my persecutor's plan
But the spirit that God gave me is unreachable by man
He's my counsellor, protector, my confidant and friend
And it's Him that's gonna keep me going to the very end

They beat someone 'til he confessed a crime he didn't do
Just like they did to Jesus when he died for me and you
And then despair engulfed me, would have taken my own life
If I only had a length of rope, some poison or a knife
Then I saw a name was scratched into the concrete of my cell
And I saw that one before me suffered twenty years of hell
Must have been the Holy Spirit that kept his head up high
"If Kevin Woods could do it," I said "So the hell can I"

One of the most touching things to happen was my arrival at my sister's house in Durban. I was driven from Jozi to Durban a short while after my release. My sister and brother-in-law had already been up to Jozi to say hello and meet me so it wasn't that aspect which affected me so much. You know that old song by Tony Orlando and Dawn—*Tie a yellow ribbon round the ole oak tree*? Well, sitting in the front passenger seat of the car and about half a kilometre from my sister Jo-Ann's house I suddenly saw that the trees on both sides of the road were adorned with these huge yellow paper ribbons. Boy, did that have me in tears! Both sides of the gate, yellow ribbons … and all over the trees in her driveway … yellow ribbons.

"I'm coming home I've done my time" … for sure.

The end

Glossary

ANC: African National Congress
APC: armoured personnel carrier
APL: African Purchase Land/s

Blue Job: airman (slang)
bomb-shell: to flee or scatter in all directions (insurgent dispersal tactic on
    contact)
Brown Job: soldier (slang)
BSAP: British South Africa Police (the Rhodesian police force)

c/s: call sign
cadre: insurgent rank and file
casevac: casualty evacuation
Charlie Tango: Radio-speak for communist terrorist
Chimurenga: Shona term for the Rhodesian bush/civil war. ZANLA's 'Second
    War of Liberation', first used in the Mashona Rebellion of 1896, or 'The First
    War of Liberation'
chopper: helicopter
CODESA: Convention for a Democratic South Africa
CO: commanding officer
COIN: counter-insurgency
ComOps: Combined Operations Headquarters
CT: communist terrorist

dagga: ganga, marijuana (Afrikaans)
doppie: expended cartridge case (slang)

ek sê: I say (Afrikaans)

Fireforce: airborne assault group
frag: fragmentation grenade
Frantan: Rhodesian euphemism for napalm
Frelimo: Mozambique Liberation Movement (*Frente de Libertaçâo de Moçambique*)

G-car: troop-ferrying helicopter, normally an Alouette III, armed with twin
    .303 Brownings or 7.62 MAGs
gomo: hill or *kopje* (Shona)
gook: insurgent (American military slang from Vietnam)

HE: high explosive
hondo: war, conflict (Shona)

Intaf: Ministry of Internal Affairs (abbreviation)
IO: intelligence officer

jesse: thick thorn scrub
JOC: Joint Operations Centre
Jozi: Johannesburg (street slang)

K-car: 'Killer car', helicopter command gunship, normally an Alouette III,
    equipped with 20mm cannon
kopje: hill (Afrikaans—pronounced 'copy', also *koppie*)
kraal: African village (South African corruption of the Portuguese *curral*
    meaning a cattle pen or enclosure)

lemon: term for an aborted or botched-up call-out/operation. (Rhodesian
    security force slang)
loc: location or position
locstat: positional co-ordinates
LZ: landing zone

MDC: Movement for Democratic Change
mielies: maize (Afrikaans, also mealies)
MK: Umkhonto we Sizwe (armed wing of the ANC)

NCO: non-commissioned officer
NS: national serviceman

OC: officer commanding

OP: observation post

op/s: operation/s

PATU: Police Anti-Terrorist Unit (BSAP paramilitary COIN specialist unit)

PF: Patriotic Front (ZANU/ZAPU alliance)

povo: people (Portuguese, and now commonly Shona)

PRAW: Police Reserve Air Wing

PV: protected village

RAR: Rhodesian African Rifles

RF: Rhodesian Front

RLI: Rhodesian Light Infantry

SADC: Southern African Development Community

SADF: South African Defence Force

SAP: South African Police

SAS: Special Air Service

SB: Special Branch (of the BSAP)

SF: Rhodesian security forces

sitrep: situation report

Sneb: air-to-ground attack rocket

stick: four-man battle group, an Alouette III helicopter troop-load, originally
    five men but the fifth man made way for helicopter machine guns; originally
    from a 'stick' of paratroopers

taal: language (Afrikaans)

'take the gap': Rhodesian security force expression used to denote a rapid exit
    from a location

TF: Territorial Force

TTL: Tribal Trust Land/s (Rhodesian Land Tenure Act)

UANC: United African National Council

UDI: Unilateral Declaration of Independence

vlei: swampy, open grassland (Afrikaans)

WO: warrant officer

WP: white phosphorus

ZANLA: Zimbabwe African National Liberation Army, ZANU's military wing

ZANU: Zimbabwe African National Union

ZAPU: Zimbabwe African People's Union

ZIPRA: Zimbabwe People's Revolutionary Army, ZAPU's military wing

ZNA: Zimbabwe National Army

ZUPO: Zimbabwe United People's Organization

Appendices

Diocese of Bulawayo

—AFRICA
ZIMBABWE

OFFICE OF THE BISHOP:
LOBENGULA STREET/9TH AVENUE

PHONE 63590

REFERENCE.....................

P.O. BOX 837
BULAWAYO
12.2.-83

The Honourable, the Prime Minister,
          Robert Mugabe

Dear Prime Minister,

          I have been receiving reports of violence perpetrated by the 5th Brigade against civilians in those areas of my Diocese under marshal law.

          I have received details of casualties from the doctors at our hospital and at missions, and have travelled to Regina Mundi Mission, to assess the situation, and have met people who have witnessed and experienced atrocities. Some witnesses have approached me here in Bulawayo.

          Reading the statement of Mr Sekeramayi made in Parliament, and reported in today's Chronicle, I was surprised that the Government was not aware of the behaviour and brutal approach of the 5th Brigade who terrorise and intimidate the population through murder of men, women and children, and beatings administered to innocent people of the community. At no time has there been a mention of killing innocent people in cross-fire.
Many cases of rape, even of Primary School girls, were brought to our notice.

          It seems to be the deliberate and indiscriminate revenge on the Matabele people.
People have spoken already of a policy of genocide, as this has been expressed by some of the Brigade.

          The fears of people in other areas that this Brigade will be deployed there has already been expressed. Such deployment would confirm our fears that a policy of genocide is being contemplated.

2/..

257

The Government's stated policy of reconciliation and peace
is not being persued in this area, and the present violence
against an unprotected people - even the Police Force of the
State cannot protect them - can only lead to lack of trust in
the institutions of Government, to further violence, hatred
and revenge.   We fully realise that a Government must take
firm action against banditry and unlawful armed resistance to
the State. Dissidents must be eradicated, because they terrorise
and intimidate the ordinary people and interrupt the peaceful
progress of the country. We do know that various appeals by
the Government to the dissidents to surrender have fallen on
deaf ears. However, a policy that strikes at the innocent
"Man in the Middle" can in no way be justified, and can only
lead to further bitterness and violence.

         As in the past we reiterate the policy of the
Church to defend the innocent people, and take a firm stand
where basic human rights are violated.
Basic supplies of food and freedom of movement to and from
hospital have been denied through the closing of stores and
the banning of transport in these areas.

         The Church has always taken a stand for Peace
and Justice and Reconciliation in so far as possible with the
lawful Government. As in the past the Church is prepared to
mediate to seek peace. Negotiation and Dialogue are the only
means, it seems to us, that can lead to a just and lasting
peace and reconciliation which will bring prosperity and
harmony to our nation.

         I hope that you will accept the points I have
raised as offered in the constructive spirit in which they
were intended.

         In this spirit and on behalf of the innocent,
but suffering people, may I appeal to you and to the respective
Ministries to let the rule of law prevail in this part of
our country.

            Yours faithfully,

                   + Henry Karlen

            + Henry Karlen, Bishop of Bulawayo

ST. BERNARD'S SEMINARY

P.O. PUMULA

BULAWAYO

73003

TELEPHONE 6211770

REPORT ON INCIDENTS INVOLVING ATROCITIES COMMITTED
BY THE GOVERNMENT FORCES IN THE GWAAI SIDING AREA
BETWEEN 30th JANUARY AND 1st FEBRUARY, 1983.

This information is a mere summary coming from 4 eye witnesses
and presented by a man resident at Gwaai area who did not
like his name, habitation or profession to be named except
that he is resident near Regina Mundi Mission near Gwaai
Siding.

The soldiers deployed at Gwaai Siding, thought to be
the Fifth Brigade "Gukurahundi" are cruel and ruthless on
the civilians. They inquire from the people and want to
know from them where the dissidents are. Since the dissidents
are mobile the people often reply that they do not know where
they are. At this response they beat the people mercilessly or
shoot them. Very near Gwaai Siding less than 20 kilometre radius
in Lupane district where curfew has been imposed civilians have
been shot dead, by the soldiery.

At Sikali Village more than 5 civilains were shot dead
At Nkwalini more than 3 were shot dead
At Mlagisa North of Gwaai Sdg more than 50 were shot dead

Anyone getting onto the train or getting down at Gwaai siding has to join the queue and almost all were being
ruthlessly beaten or maltreated. The soldiers ask people
questions in Shona and since the people only know Sindebele
and reply in Sindebele there is great resentment of this
by the soldiers and this makes them even more aggressive.
The police cannot help the people because they have to keep
within their camp. There is much hunger and starvation in
the whole area because they have forced all stores to close.
No wagon, cart or donkey may be used to carry mealie meal,
it must be carried by the person only.

Report given at Bishop's House in the
presence of Bishop Karlen on 3rd February
1983, in Bulawayo, at 9.00 hours.

Compiled by Fr. Pius A. Ncube.

Pius A. Ncube

REPORT BY 2 EYEWITNESSES AND AN AFRICAN SISTER (12.2.-83)

9.2.-83: Two men were killed near Sipepa (Gwaai), one was an
old man.
At the whole line, men, women and children were beaten up.
One woman has a fractured arm.
Behind the Clinic at Sipepa the whole family of 7 was
killed.
About 200 people ran away and went to Regina Mundi Mission.

10.2.-83: The soldiers (10 - 15) came to the Mission. One soldier
told the African Mother General to run to him. Another
Sister joined her. He said: "I can kill you, bayonet and
cut you in pieces just now." He then asked about dissidents.
Two workers were called, they had to sit down and were
clapped and kicked, and hit with the bayonet.

- The other soldiers at the Mission met the Secondary School
boys and the local people.
cf. Report by Fr. David attached.

- The eye-witnesses said: The people left in the evening
and stayed in the bush, because the soldiers told them:
"If you do not leave we shall shoot the people and also
Father".

- At St. Mark's (3 km from the Mission) people were beaten
up and one teacher had a broken arm.
The store at Gwaai Siding is open only for the Mission /
School. All other stores are closed and the people have
to starve. The soldiers said: "We want all Matabele to die".
"We have been sent to kill and to finish you up."

- Near St. Mark's a mother with 3 daughters were raped in
the same room at the same time.

- Women and girls who want to go to Town by train had to
have sex with the soldiers at Gwaai Siding - they were
thratened to be shot.

- The eye-witnesses also said that the soldiers told the
people: "The people are deceived by this "Ibunu" (Fr.David
Fernandez).

+ Henry Karlen,
Bishop of Bulawayo

OTHER REPORTS RECEIVED ON 11.2.-83.

- Bishop I. Prieto of Hwange reported:

  Near Tsholotsho 3 men were killed.
  At Dete 6 people   were killed.
  At Lupane people were beaten up.
  At Kana Mission one man was killed.
  Soldiers are going from house to house. If the people say they
  do not know where the dissidents are, they are beaten up.
  In Hwange Hospital are a number of people who are beaten up.

- One young man who ran away from Gwaai Siding on 1st February
  reported on 11.2.83 that his whole family has been killed.

- A coloured family of 7 from Thorngrove, Bulawayo, working in
  a field near Lupane were killed by soldiers. Only the youngest
  daughter of 3 years escaped alive. This happened on 9.2.83.

                              + Henry Karlen,
                                Bishop of Bulawayo

REPORT BY EYEWITNESSES - - 8.2.83   Page 2.

              - The feeling of the people is that it is a fight
                between Shonas and Matabele.

              - The soldiers talk Shona - if people reply in Sindebele,
                they are beaten; if in Shona, they are told that they
                should not be there now, but should go home.

ST. LUKE'S / ST. PAUL'S (LUPANE).

From 6.2. - 8.2.83 : 27 people with gunshot wounds came or were
                     brought to St. Luke's Hospital as well as
31 assault cases. It could not be established how many people
were killed, but a number of corpses have been seen. Soldiers do
not bother about the injured and the bodies are left lying about.

It seems there is indiscriminate shooting and beating up of women,
children and men.
People have the impression that the Matabele are being crushed.

                    Compiled by + Henry Karlen,
                               Bishop of Bulawayo.

P.S.: I was at Regina Mundi Mission on 8th February 1983.

      Killing and beating up of people are going on also in
      Tsholotsho area, but so far we do not have details.

Telephone: 700501
Our Reference: DDS/48/3
RS/KJW

PERSONAL & CONFIDENTIAL

P.O. BOX 2278
HARARE
ZIMBABWE

<u>PERSONAL & CONFIDENTIAL</u>

29 March 1985

Mr K.J. Woods,
c/o CIO,
PO Box 567,
<u>BULAWAYO</u>.

Dear Mr Woods,

I am pleased to advise you that in terms of a Promotions' Board recommendation and Ministerial approval, you have been appointed to the rank of Senior Intelligence Officer, which is to take effect retrospectively from the 1 July 1984.

2. The approaching General Election and an upsurge of RENAMO activity within Mozambique adjacent to our Eastern borders has made it necessary to transfer a senior detail to Manicaland, and you have been nominated to perform this task.

3. I have accordingly authorised your transfer to Mutare, to be effected on or about the 1 May 1985, which is during the period of the forthcoming school holidays.

4. Please accept my congratulations on your promotion.

Yours sincerely,

D.D. STANNARD
Director-Internal, CIO

CENTRAL
INTELLIGENCE
ORGANISATION
2 9 MAR 1985
P.O. Box 8019
CAUSEWAY

<u>PERSONAL AND CONFIDENTIAL</u>

PERSONAL & CONFIDENTIAL

Ref : B9a/1/115

MINISTRY
~~DEPUTY MINISTER~~ OF HOME AFFAIRS
PRIVATE BAG 7703, CAUSEWAY
~~SALISBURY~~

Telegrams: "LEGAL"
Telephone: 703641-2-3

5 June 1987.

Mr Kevin John Woods
P.O. Box FM 211
FAMONA
BULAWAYO

Dear Sir

APPLICATION FOR A PRIVATE INVESTIGATOR'S LICENCE

Thank you for your letter of 1 June, 1987 and the revenue stamps to the
value of one hundred and fifty dollars ($150,00) enclosed thereto.

Enclosed hereto is your private investigator's licence.

Yours faithfully

M.M.Mudzi
CONTROLLER OF PRIVATE INVESTIGATORS
AND SECURITY GUARDS

MMM/bsc.

Bomb victim identified by his foot

HARARE. — A witness at a Zimbabwe trial of three men accused of staging an attack in Zimbabwe for South Africa told the court yesterday that the only identifiable part of the victim after a car bombing was his foot.

The witness, Mr Victor Ndlovu, was describing how police took him to the scene of the car bomb in Zimbabwe's southern city of Bulawayo on January 11 to help identify the body of his lodger, Obert Mwanza.

"The body was in pieces and parts of the body were in a plastic bag. In it was a foot which I identified . . . he used to walk barefooted so I knew his feet," Mr Ndlovu told the court.

He also identified Mr Mwanza from his identity card and the clothes he was wearing when he left for work the previous day.

The prosecution says Mr Mwanza was forced to drive unwillingly to his death in a boobytrapped car which was exploded by remote control outside a house used by the African National Congress (ANC).

Three Zimbabweans, two White and one Black, are on trial for murder, terrorism and causing an explosion in connection with the January bombing. All risk the death penalty.

Mr Kevin Woods (35), Mr Michael Smith (34) and Mr Phillip Conjwayo (54) have all pleaded guilty to the charges.

At yesterday's hearing, under heavy security guard, a Bulawayo office worker, Mr Francis Kapfidze, identified Mr Conjwayo as the man who bought his yellow Renault 5 car for R7 700 on January 7 under the name Mr James Sibanda.

He also identified the number plate and front bumper of the wrecked vehicle as those of his car, which was used in the bomb attack.

Judge Wilson Sandura told the court he would rule later on a defence application to have the pre-trial statements of the three accused ruled inadmissible in evidence.

The prosecution charge is that Mr Woods, Mr Smith and Mr Conjwayo are South African agents who took part in an undercover sabotage campaign against the ANC. — Sapa-Reuter.

Zimbabwean worry again about whites

Mercury July 6th 1988

HARARE—The claimed divided loyalties of Zimbabwe's white minority are once again being debated there after the alleged spectacular defection of a young white air force officer.

Gary Kane, a helicopter pilot, is the alleged key figure in a plot to rescue six people claimed to be 'South African agents', according to the Zimbabwean Security Minister, Mr Sydney Sekeremayi, who made claims about an aborted operation this week.

Mr Sekeremayi identified Kane as 'Group Captain', but white Zimbabweans who knew him said Kane — who joined the Zimbabwean air force in 1982 as a cadet — was in fact a lowly flight lieutenant.

The objective of the claimed June 30 attempt was to free six men, held since January in connection with alleged bomb attacks on ANC people, as they travelled from prison to a court hearing in Harare.

He claimed the young officer took off from New Sarum air force base near Harare about 7.30 a.m. on June 30 — without a co-pilot or engineer — in an Augusta Bell helicopter.

When the rescue bid was called off — because of tight Zimbabwean security on the road between Chikurubi prison and the courthouse, he alleged — Kane took off from a firing-range with one other.

He was said to have flown to an airstrip near Kwekwe, 160 km south of Harare, then riddled the helicopter with bullets from an AK-47 automatic weapon before taking off in a waiting plane for South Africa, the Zimbabwean minister claimed.

Mr Sekeremayi hinted that Zimbabwe was likely to review the loyalty of its remaining white officers after Kane's alleged defection.

'Obviously confidence in some of the officers is very shaken,' he said. 'It is very difficult to tell on the face of somebody that this one is loyal, and for how long, and that this one is disloyal, and for how long. It is a very tricky situation,' he mused.

Blow

Between 30 and 40 whites are still serving in the Zimbabwe air force, about 10 of them pilots.

After independence the air force, heavily reliant on white expertise, suffered a devastating blow when saboteurs destroyed 13 aircraft at Thornhill airbase near Gweru in July 1982.

Six white officers were arrested, later acquitted but then expelled from the country. The departure of many other whites did more to damage the Zimbabwean air force than the loss of the planes, according to some.

Zimbabwe's white community now numbers about 100 000 people among more than 8 000 000 blacks — compared with 250 000 before independence in 1980.

Most of those who left, including many blacks, sought refuge in South Africa — including an estimated 5 000 people who served in the Rhodesian security services.

Of these, some joined special units of the South African Defence Force — some allegedly specialising in cross-border raids. Others stayed on in Zimbabwe — as a so-called 'Fifth Column working for Pretoria'.

The group which Zimbabwe says South Africa tried to rescue last week — headed, it is claimed, by Kevin Woods, a former senior member of Zimbabwe's Central Intelligence Organisation (CIO) — is claimed by the Zimbabwean State to have been hitting ANC targets since 1981.

Some whites who have remained in Zimbabwe are said to be bitter and afraid that evidence of treachery when the group comes to trial will cast suspicion on all whites.

'Now they can tar us all with the same brush,' one Harare woman complained.

Others, more sympathetic to the arrested men, feel they should benefit from the recent amnesty for black rebels in Matabeleland, and for police and soldiers guilty of atrocities there.

The Zimbabwean Government faces an impossible task in checking the loyalties of the white community. Many whites have relatives and business connections in South Africa, and travel there on shopping trips.

'Give me (President Robert) Mugabe rather than P W Botha any day,' is a common phrase thrown to the wind.

Dr Mugabe made reconciliation with whites a central theme when he took office in 1980, and has stuck to the policy in spite of periods of impatience when he has criticised those with white skins.

Sympathy

Tensions have eased markedly since the political demise of former Rhodesian prime minister Ian Smith and his allies and parliamentary seats reserved for whites were abolished last year.

In their place Dr Mugabe has brought in a sprinkling of more moderate white faces in Parliament. There are two white junior ministers and one full minister, Chris Andersen, who is responsible for the civil service.

But the president, seen as more sympathetic to whites than many others in the ruling Zanu-PF Party, castigated the white community a month ago for 'a lack of political commitment' and 'British arrogance' towards blacks.

He told black American journalists in New York his Government worried about 'white loyalty'. — (Sapa-Reuter)

Wednesday 12 October 1988

Alleged Zimbabwe bombers could hang

HARARE. — A former officer in Zimbabwe's intelligence service and a farm manager could be the first Whites to hang in Zimbabwe since independence if convicted of murder and terrorism charges at their trial which opened yesterday.

Mr Kevin John Woods (37), a former senior officer in the Central Intelligence Organisation, Mr Michael Smith (34), a farm manager, and Mr Philip Conjwayo (50), a Black ex-policeman, are being tried for their part in a car bomb attack on a house in Bulawayo last January.

The house was being used as a hiding place by the African National Congress (ANC), and Mr Woods was said to have masterminded the bombing operation.

All three are charged with murder and two other counts under the Law and Order Maintenance Act covering terrorism. All charges carry the death penalty.

Tight security was expected during the trial at the High Court after Zimbabwe said it foiled an attempt by South Africa to free the three accused and two others when they were being taken to a remand hearing on June 30.

Mr Woods, Mr Smith and Mr Conjwayo were arrested in January, a few days after a car bomb devastated the ANC safe house in Bulawayo, Zimbabwe's second city.

The bomb, big enough to damage houses 200 metres away, injured three ANC members, one seriously, in an isolated single-storey villa in Jungle Road, in the run-down suburb of Trenance on January 11.

The driver of the car, hired from the local labour exchange to take the vehicle to the house, was blown to pieces.

Mr Rory Maguire, a Bulawayo garage proprietor also arrested in January, has turned state's evidence after pleading guilty to failing to report Mr Woods' involvement in the bombing. He is expected to be one of the prosecution witnesses.

According to evidence presented at an earlier trial Mr Christopher Bawden, the man who carried out the bombing with Mr Woods, escaped to South Africa three days after the explosion.

The trial, one of the most sensitive in Zimbabwe since independence, is the first in a series involving alleged South African agents.

Mr Woods and Mr Smith face a second trial in November with Mr Barry Bawden, a relative of Mr Christopher Bawden for their part in an earlier bomb attack in Harare. — Sapa-Reuter.

266

Tuesday 18 October 1988   *Citizen*

ANC witness describes bomb blast

HARARE. — The High Court in Harare was told yesterday that African National Congress premises in Bulawayo, bombed by alleged South African agents last year, were not used by refugees of the organisation to implement ANC policy, the national news agency Ziana reports.

This evidence was given by an ANC refugee who was at the house when an explosion occurred on January 11, killing a man and injuring three others.

The witness, who had been staying at the house for six months, was testifying at the resumption of the trial of three Zimbabweans, alleged to be on the South African payroll for the purpose of committing acts of sabotage on the house.

Former Rhodesian Government employees, Mr Kevin John Woods, Mr Michael Anthony Smith and Mr Phillip Masiza Conjwayo, have pleaded not guilty to the murder of Mr Amon Obert Mwanza.

The three have also pleaded not guilty to two alternative charges under the Law and Order (Maintenance) Act, which relate to the use of explosives without lawful excuse and to committing acts of terrorism and sabotage.

Mr Woods (35) is a former member of the Central Intelligence Organi-

sation, Mr Smith (34), a former member of the Rhodesian Light Infantry and Mr Conjwayo (54) a former member of the Rhodesian Special Branch.

The witness said he and his colleague were playing a game of "monopoly" in the living room of the house when he heard a loud bang which was followed shortly by darkness.

He said he crawled looking for his way out and when he eventually left the house he went straight to a policeman who was guarding the house. He then heard some shots.

The witness, identified as Mr Y, said he and the policeman returned into the house to check for his colleagues.

When he called out, one of his colleagues answered saying he had been injured slightly.

Mr Y said he eventually found that three of his colleagues had been injured, one of them seriously.

He went out of the house and found another colleague of his seriously injured and lying in a pool of blood. He and the policeman rendered first aid, called an ambulance and the injured person was taken to hospital.

Cross-examined by defence lawyer Mr Mike O'Meara, Mr Y said he had heard some of the statements uttered by Mr Nelson Mandela.

He agreed that the ANC has been respon-

sible for attacks in South Africa.

He said he subscribed fully to the policies of the banned organisation, but denied the house which was attacked in Bulawayo was being used to implement the ANC policy in South Africa.

Mercury 19/11/88

Zimbabwe bombers sentenced to death

HARARE—Two white Zimbabweans and a black were sentenced to hang yesterday for the murder of an unemployed Zambian driver who was killed in a bomb attack on the African National Congress.

Kevin Woods, one of the condemned men, told the Court he and his fellow accused Michael Smith carried out the bombing 'on behalf of the people of South Africa'.

Phillip Conjwayo, the third defendant, angrily accused his former colleagues in the Zimbabwean police of making up evidence to convict him. 'I have never in my lifetime seen liars like the police,' he said.

If the sentence is upheld by the Supreme Court Smith and Woods will be the first Zimbabwean whites to hang since independence in 1980.

The victim, Obert Amon Mwanza, a 45-year-old Zambian, was hired for about R60 to drive a booby-trapped car last January to a house in Bulawayo used by the ANC. The car blew up with Mwanza still inside.

The Judge ruled that all three were guilty of murder with constructive intent in their attack on the ANC, but not of actual intent to kill Mwanza.

Woods, 35, giving his final statement before the sentencing, said he was speaking on behalf of Smith and himself.

'We have no quarrel with Zimbabwe,' he said, adding that they were sorry that the victim Mwanza was not a member of the militant wing of the ANC.

'Our only motivation was on behalf of the people of South Africa who suffer mayhem and death on a daily basis at the hands of these ANC murderers.'

All three men are due to be tried again next year accused of taking part in earlier bomb attacks on ANC property in Harare. — (Sapa-Reuter)

Alleged SA saboteurs
Sunday Star Oct 23/88
caught in phone trap

**Lawrence Bartlett
Africa News Service**

HARARE — Intelligence circles in Zimbabwe have been stunned by the apparent flouting of basic spycraft which led to the cracking of an alleged South African spy and sabotage ring.

Three men sat slumped in Harare's High Court dock this week as a disembodied woman's voice asked the bizarre question: "Is it a trap?"

The State says the voice belongs to Mary Baker, a former Rhodesian working for South African Intelligence in Johannesburg, who was recorded while talking on an open telephone line to Phillip Conjwayo, one of the three men now accused of murder in a car-bomb attack on an ANC house in Bulawayo earlier this year.

"It is not a trap," was Conjwayo's reply. At the time he was surrounded by Zimbabwean intelligence officers. They recorded his conversation with Mary Baker, in which he pleaded to be taken out of the country because the police were closing in on him.

In a subsequent call to a number given to her by Conjwayo — which was in fact a Zimbabwe Central Intelligence Organisation number —

Baker told Conjwayo to pick up a thousand dollars hidden in a toilet cistern at a garage in Bulawayo and make his way to Francistown in Botswana.

The owner of the garage, Rory Maguire, was jailed for seven years in July for failing to report the presence of South African saboteurs. The policeman who recorded the conversation between Conjwayo and Baker told the court that without Conjwayo's co-operation they would never have caught his fellow-accused, Kevin Woods and Michael Smith.

He said Conjwayo had told him the telephone call would help catch "the whites" involved. Once Woods and Smith had been picked up other names came tumbling out. Henry Johnson had parachuted on to a remote Zimbabwe farm shortly after Christmas last year with "equipment", Woods said in a warned-and-cautioned statement.

Barry Bawden — who is awaiting trial — had organised the dropping zone, said Woods. Christopher "Kit" Bawden — a fugitive still at large and believed to be in South Africa — pressed the button that blew an unsuspecting driver to pieces as he sat in a car outside the ANC house, said

Smith in a similar statement.

Kit Bawden's brother Guy and cousin Barry are in Harare's maximum-security Chikurubi prison awaiting trial on charges involving attacks on ANC targets in Harare.

At least three more trials of alleged South African agents are due to follow the current one.

They deal with a commando raid on ANC offices in Harare, a rocket attack on an ANC house in the same city, a car-bomb blast at a suburban shopping centre which injured several people and an alleged attempt in July this year to free Smith, Woods and the Bawdens from jail.

Now Woods and Smith, who have pleaded not guilty, face the prospect of being the first whites to be sentenced to death for politically related offences in Zimbabwe's history.

Their defence, led by white-haired advocate Michael O'Meara, himself a former Rhodesian Special Branch policeman is challenging the validity of every statement made by the accused and has appealed to the Supreme Court against the ruling by the trial judge, Judge President Mr Justice Wilson Sandura, that the men's confessions are admissible as evidence.

·NATIONAL DIRECTORATE·

713 Van Erkom Building
Pretorius St., Pretoria 0002
Telefax: (012) 325-6318
Telephone: (012) 21-2135

Our ref:
Your ref:
Date:

LAWYERS
for
HUMAN
RIGHTS

Michael J Woods
PO Box 2131
Nerang East
Queensland
4211
Australia

August 16, 1991

Dear Mr Woods,

I am responding to your letter to Mrs Phyllis Naidoo, as she passed this on to us at the National Office.

We have in fact had dealings in the past with Michael Smiths family and are familiar with the case as well as with previous strategies adopted.

At this stage I am not at liberty to divulge the measures which we are taking on this issue - all I can do is assure you that we are giving this our urgent and fullest attention. It was in fact quite a coincidence that your sister approached our offices when she did, as we were working on this at the time.

All I can say is that you should not feel that this answer is in the style of " the matter you have raised is under consideration". We are working on it and will continue to do so until such time as we believe it has been satisfactorily resolved. We believe that as an independent Human Rights organisation we are well placed to intervene.

You can contact me at the above numbers at any time, or fax through if more convenient.

Yours Sincerely

Paula McBride

Paula McBride

Brian Currin (National Director), Selewe Peter Mothle (Director Research & Education), Ahmed Motala (Director Litigations), Lucreta Seafield (Director Women's Rights), Anne Skelton (Director Public Defender Programme), Laurie Pollecut (Director Publications)

269

·NATIONAL DIRECTORATE·

713 Van Erkom Building
Pretorius St., Pretoria 0002
Telefax: (012) 325-6318
Telephone: (012) 21-2135

Our ref:
Your ref:
Date:

LAWYERS
for
HUMAN
RIGHTS

Mrs W F Teakle
Queensland
Australia

26 February 1992   FAX : 0961 76 92 37 10

Dear Mrs Teakle,

Thankyou for your fax dated 23rd February 1992 .

As you may know from the families of the prisoners concerned, we
have been very involved in the process of securing the release of
political prisoners within South Africa. Arising out of this
involvement we saw the potential for the kind of prisoner
exchange discussed in the article attached to your letter [Sunday
Star 4.2.1990[.

To this end we held a number of meetings with the South African
government, the ANC and representatives of the Zimbabwean
government. It became clear to us that while this may have been
on the political agenda, the timing was not considered right by
the politicians involved. Further than that, it has been made
clear to us that if or when the timing is right, this is an issue
which will be dealt with by the politicians themselves - not by
Human Rights bodies such as ours. Under the circumstances, we
have had no option but to withdraw.

However, we remain interested and are still very much involved in
the release process here. We do not have a branch in Zimbabwe as
we are a South African organisation and as such we are not in a
position to monitor developments in that country. If we do hear
anything further, we will communicate this to you.

With thanks

Paula McBride

Paula McBride

Brian Currin (National Director), Selewe Peter Mothle (Director Research & Education), Ahmed Motala (Director Litigations). Lucretia Seafield (Director Women's Rights), Anne Skelton (Director Public Defender Programme), Laura Pollecutt (Director Publications)

SUNDAY TIMES. 25/5/97

Jailed South African spies may be home for Christmas

CHRIS BISHOP: Harare

PRESIDENT Nelson Mandela this week asked Zimbabwean president Robert Mugabe to release five South African spies.

The men have been in the Chikurubi maximum security prison for the past 10 years where they are serving life sentences for sabotage and murder.

Sources in the Zimbabwean government say the five men will be freed before the end of the year.

Kevin Woods, Philip Conjwayo, Michael Smith, Barry Bawden and Dennis Beaham took part in bombing attacks against ANC houses in Harare and a cross-border raid in which a Zimbabwean was killed.

A Zimbabwean security operative said this week: "They will be out before the end of the year. President Mugabe will take legal advice first and then that's it. They've already served 10 years here for what they did and if they are released they will then be South Africa's problem."

Political observers in Zimbabwe believe the release of the men has been made more likely by Mandela's visit.

Iden Wetherell, a political commentator, said: "I think it shows a genuine attempt by President Mandela to complete the amnesty process and to settle the past. He must also have been persuaded that the men have a story to tell."

The South African government is said to be keen on the five testifying before the Truth and Reconciliation Commission.

The Minister of Foreign Affairs, Alfred Nzo, was quoted in Harare this week as saying: "The request (for the release of the five) was made before the truth commission was established. It was purely because of the amnesty which we granted immediately after taking power. I hope they will be released."

The five, all of Zimbabwean origin, were granted South African citizenship soon after their arrest. They have been arguing for their release for more than three years, claiming that as former servants of apartheid they qualified for the general amnesty.

But there still may be resistance from within Mugabe's government to the release of the spies.

Justice Minister Emmerson Mnangagwa told Woods on a recent visit that the government would not bow to foreign pressure for their release.

The issue is likely to test the strength of the relations between South Africa and Zimbabwe, which are said to have improved following Mandela's visit.

'Commando raid leader' in leg-irons

Harare July 6th

HARARE—A man, said to be the leader of an alleged South African commando team which intended freeing 'South African agents' on trial in Zimbabwe, appeared in court in leg-irons here yesterday after being arrested in Botswana.

He is described as Charles Dennis Beahan — variously named as Behan or Beaham — 40, an alleged South African resident who gave his address as the Sandton Sun Hotel, Johannesburg.

Beahan had been arrested in 'a neighbouring country' and brought to Zimbabwe last Saturday, according to testimony in the Regional Court in Harare yesterday.

Zimbabwe did not identify the neighbouring country, but Botswana admitted last night it had arrested a 'South African intelligence agent', Charles Beaham, with the alias Henry Peter Coleman, and handed him over to Zimbabwean authorities.

Reports from Harare identified him as a British citizen. He appeared in leg-irons, and replied 'No, sir' twice when the Magistrate asked him if he had any complaints or any-thing to say.

Prosecutor Yunus Omerjee said Beahan was 'the commander of a South African commando group comprising a large number of persons' whose task had been to enter Zimbabwe surreptitiously at several different points.

He said Beahan and a colleague who drove into Zimbabwe with him at Kazungula border post on June 28 were acting on the orders of South African military intelligence.

On Monday Zimbabwe accused South Africa of attempting to free six men accused of working as agents for South Africa in an aborted operation on June 30.

Beahan listened impassively as Omerjee told Regional Magistrate Tadius Karwi that when challenged at the frontier, he and his companion 'ran off, scaled the fence at the border post, jumped into the Zambezi River and swam away from Zimbabwe'.

The pair allegedly made their way to 'a friendly neighbouring country' where Beahan was captured and returned to Zimbabwe on July 2. His partner escaped. — (Sapa-Reuter)

DR. N.D. JONKER
DCR (Lond), MBChB (Zim), FRCR (Lond), Msc (Nuc Med) (Lond)
DIAGNOSTIC RADIOLOGIST

NUCLEAR MEDICINE

TELEPHONE: 729606/7
              705571/2
              720937/8
FAX: 706551

DIAGNOSTIC IMAGING CENTRE.
Cnr LANARK / EAST ROADS
P.O.Box A1020 AVONDALE.
HARARE

DATE: 14 & 18 February 1997

NAME: Mr Kevin WOODS

EXAMINATION: Tc Myocardial Perfusion Rest & Stress

REFERRING DOCTOR: Dr I Ternouth

CLINICAL HISTORY:

Chest pain: ? Previous myocardial infarct.

FINDINGS:

The distribution of myocardial perfusion is abnormal. There is a fixed perfusion defect involving the inferior wall of the left ventricle. In addition to this, there is evidence of stress induced ischaemia within the septum of the left ventricle. This is consistent with mild stress induced ischaemia.

COMMENT :

The appearances are consistent with those of a previous inferior infarct and mild associated stress induced ischaemia within the septum.

DR N D JONKER

PRETORIA ACADEMIC HOSP \ PRETORIA AKADEMIESE HOSP
CARDIOLOGY DEPARTMENT \ DEPARTEMENT KARDIOLOGIE

Private Bag \ Privaatsak X169 , PRETORIA 0001
Telephone (012) 3542200 \ 3541180 Fax \ Faks (012) 3541895

23 February 1998

TO WHOM IT MAY CONCERN

EVALUATION OF CARDIAC EXAMINATIONS : KEVIN WOODS

This Department has been asked to review certain special examinations done on the abovementioned patient.

The patient was not seen by us , but apparently has a clinical history suggestive of angina.

The EKG seen by us was suggestive of a previous ischaemic incident to the inferior wall of the heart.

A Tc myocardial perfusion resting and stress test performed at the Diagnostic Imaging Centre in Harare , was indicative of reversible myocardial ischaemia within the septum of the heart. It also clearly showed a fixed perfusion defect of the inferior wall of the heart. We agree with the findings of Dr. Jonker in this regard.

From a clinical point of view , it is clear that not much can be done for the lesion in the inferior wall of the heart. The stress induced perfusion defect in the septum is however a different matter. It is clear that this ischaemia is reversible , i.e. can be cured by various means. The present state of clinical practice in the world dictates that this patient should undergo a coronary angiogram. This investigation will result in an exact anatomic description of the lesion and will enable the cardiologist to initiate the appropriate revascularisation therapy. Failure to initiate revascularisation will result in a long term loss of function of the heart due to ischaemic damage. This resulting long term disability will lead to progressively increasing need for medical care and thus also of costs.

DR. W. BASSON : CONSULTANT
MBChB MSc MMED(INT)

Die Staatspresident
The State President
Kaapstad · Cape Town

14 May 1993

Dear Mr Woods

Thank you for your letter dated 20 January 1993 regarding your brother, Kevin John Woods. I wish to assure you that I share you and your family's concern for the fate of your brother and those imprisoned with him in Zimbabwe.

As you are aware, your brother was originally imprisoned together with four other men, two of whom were sentenced to death. The latest information received from the lawyers acting on behalf of your brother and the other men, was received on 18 February 1992. According to the lawyers, an appeal was recently heard regarding your brother and Messrs Bawden and Smith. The result of this is expected soon but the lawyer is confident that the original sentence of 40 years imprisonment may be reduced.

I can assure you that many avenues have been explored to obtain the release of your brother. Due to the sensitivity of these proposals, I cannot furnish any details except to say that no effort on our part was spared.

During a recent visit to South Africa by a senior Zimbabwean Minister (the first official visit by a Zimbabwean Cabinet Minister to South Africa with the blessing of President Mugabe), the matter was raised by Mr Pik Botha, the Minister of Foreign Affairs and he was given the undertaking that it will be raised with President Mugabe.

I am hopeful that the present phase of negotiations in South Africa will lead us to a position where relations with Zimbabwe can be fully normalized and the plight of your brother possibly be relieved. My Trade Representative in Harare has so far not been allowed access to your brother and the other prisoners, but I have given instructions that he continue his efforts to be allowed to visit your brother.

My prayers are with you and your family during these difficult times. You can rest assured that all efforts will be made to obtain the release of your brother and the other four gentlemen imprisoned with him.

Yours sincerely

F W DE KLERK

Mr Michael Joe Woods
PO Box 2131
Nerang East

Replied 4/2/97 air mail with
proviso that it be held for Sandra
Macallister if undelivered as she said
the old boy was taken very ill on Xmas day 96.

Telephone Derby 558043

Beechwood Convent

Broadway

Derby. DE22 1AU

8 OCT 1996   England

Dear Mr Mugabe,
I was very interested to hear that you married a Catholic and in the
Catholic Church. I had a sister who went to Zimbabwe many years ago
and died there.One of her grandchildren has written to me and told me
about you.She is Sandra McAllister of 41 Station Road Observatory
Cape Town 7925. She tells me of a Kevin Woods who is undergoing life
imprisonment. I know nothing of his crime but I am asked if if I
could do something to alleviate some of the sufferings he is enduring
It is thought,no doubt that as a Monsignor and a Papal dignitary
  (I am what is called a Protonotory Apostolic) that you might take
 notice of my appeal. Especially as I am now on the edge of the grave
 I am (hold your breath) 102 years old. So,although I know little of
 the crimes this man has committed I would ask you to do what you
 alone can do to mitigate   his punishment.With congratulations on
 having made a Catholic Marriage and recalling the words of Our Lord
 Jesus Christ,blessed arethe merciful for they shall obtain mercy and
 asking the blessing of God on you and you wife I am Yours most
 sincerely

H. Wilson

(Monsignor H Wilson),

ADMINISTRATION OFFICE
Chikurubi Maximum Prison

04 FEB 1997

Private Bag 7392
Greendale, Harare

Republic of South Africa
SOUTH AFRICAN HIGH COMMISSION

P.O. Box 121
Harare
ZIMBABWE

Telex: CONSULAR: 24777 TRADE: 22332
Cable: SAHICOM
Tel: 753147/8/9, 753150/1/2

Reference..

20 December 1996

Mr R Hartley
Coghlan Welsh & Guest Chambers
P O Box 53
HARARE

Dear Mr Hartley

In acknowledgement of the letter written by Mr K Woods to the
Office of President N R Mandela, we wish to inform that the
contents of the letter has been noted. I have been requested by
the Department of Foreign Affairs to respond via your Office to
the above letter. Herewith the response to Mr Woods' letter:

QUOTE

As you are aware President Mandela and Minister Nzo, on a number
of occasions, requested the Zimbabwean authorities to consider the
release of yourself and the other four prisoners.

The ultimate decision, however, regarding your release rest with
the Zimbabwean Head of State, President RG Mugabe.

UNQUOTE

Yours sincerely,

JNK MAMABOLO
High Commissioner

SA mum over 5 held in Zimbabwe prisons

■ STAFF REPORTER

President Mandela's office yesterday refused to comment on reports of hush-hush talks with Zimbabwe to free five South African military agents held in its jails.

The men are serving sentences in a maximum security prison for murder and terrorism arising from raids against the ANC in Zimbabwe during 1987 and 1988.

Michael Smith, Barry Bawden, Kevin Woods and Philip Conjwayo attacked ANC safe houses and set off car bombs which killed a man. Briton Denis "Sammy" Behan was jailed after an aborted attempt to free the other agents.

They are serving sentences ranging from 20 to 40 years and their imprisonment has reportedly been the subject of secret diplomacy since Mandela's inauguration last year.

When approached for comment, Mandela's spokesman, Parks Mankahlana, would only say: "No comment, no comment."

SA National Defence Force senior spokesman Major-General Gert Opperman last week described the men's continued incarceration as "extremely sensitive".

The Foreign Affairs Department believes Zimbabwe is prepared to be sympathetically disposed to the men being released in terms of South Africa's indemnity programme.

Foreign Minister Alfred Nzo has asked Correctional Services Minister Sipho Mzimela to draft legislation to match Zimbabwean law which allows prisoners to be exchanged and to serve their sentences in the country of their birth. It is believed this might smooth the men's return to South Africa.

SUNDAY TIMES. 25/5/97

Jailed South African spies may be home for Christmas

CHRIS BISHOP: Harare

PRESIDENT Nelson Mandela this week asked Zimbabwean president Robert Mugabe to release five South African spies.

The men have been in the Chikurubi maximum security prison for the past 10 years where they are serving life sentences for sabotage and murder.

Sources in the Zimbabwean government say the five men will be freed before the end of the year.

Kevin Woods, Philip Conjwayo, Michael Smith, Barry Bawden and Dennis Beaham took part in bombing attacks against ANC houses in Harare and a cross-border raid in which a Zimbabwean was killed.

A Zimbabwean security operative said this week: "They will be out before the end of the year. President Mugabe will take legal advice first and then that's it. They've already served 10 years here for what they did and if they are released they will then be South Africa's problem."

Political observers in Zimbabwe believe the release of the men has been made more likely by Mandela's visit.

Iden Wetherell, a political commentator, said: "I think it shows a genuine attempt by President Mandela to complete the amnesty process and to settle the past. He must also have been persuaded that the men have a story to tell."

The South African government is said to be keen on the five testifying before the Truth and Reconciliation Commission.

The Minister of Foreign Affairs, Alfred Nzo, was quoted in Harare this week as saying: "The request (for the release of the five) was made before the truth commission was established. It was purely because of the amnesty which we granted immediately after taking power. I hope they will be released."

The five, all of Zimbabwean origin, were granted South African citizenship soon after their arrest. They have been arguing for their release for more than three years, claiming that as former servants of apartheid they qualified for the general amnesty.

But there still may be resistance from within Mugabe's government to the release of the spies.

Justice Minister Emmerson Mnangagwa told Woods on a recent visit that the government would not bow to foreign pressure for their release.

The issue is likely to test the strength of the relations between South Africa and Zimbabwe, which are said to have improved following Mandela's visit.

THE MOST REVEREND DESMOND M. TUTU, O.M.S.   D.D.   F.K.C.
ANGLICAN ARCHBISHOP EMERITUS OF CAPE TOWN

11 Lupin Crescent
Milnerton
Cape 7441
Tel: (021) 52 5821

6981 Bacela Street
Orlando West
Gauteng 1804
Tel: (011) 936 3136

3 February 1997
Dear Friends

Archbishop Tutu thanks you for your good wishes
for his speedy recovery.

He greatly appreciates your concern and caring and
the assurance of your prayers.

Yours sincerely

Lavinia Browne
Assistant to the Archbishop

Apartheid agents appeal to Mandela

BY RAPHAEL BANDA

Four former apartheid military intelligence (MI) agents jailed in Zimbabwe have made a fresh impassioned plea for President Mandela to intervene so that they can complete their lengthy prison terms in South Africa.

It is believed that South African authorities are still continuing to seek the release of the four, who were jailed in Zimbabwe 10 years ago. President Robert Mugabe last year rejected Mandela's appeal for the men to be transferred to South Africa.

Kevin Woods (45), Michael Smith (43) and Phillip Conjwayo (61) were sentenced to death in 1988 for a fatal raid on an ANC "safe house". Their sentences were later commuted to life imprisonment. They are being held at Chikurubi maximum security prison.

A fourth accused, Barry Bawden, is serving 25 years. A fifth, Briton Denis Beahan, who had been sentenced to 20 years in jail for trying to spring the other four from jail, was released last year.

"Madiba, as your swan song, I implore you to try and have us transferred to prison in South Africa. We are all legitimate SA citizens and are quite prepared to serve our sentences in SA. I am not asking to be released – that is a hopeless dream,"

Woods says in a letter on behalf of the four to Mandela dated June 11.

In his plea to Mandela, Woods describes himself and his colleagues as "former SA government MI and National Intelligence Service agents".

Presidential spokesman Parks Mankahlana said yesterday that the four men had written about 15 letters to the president's office since 1994.

The office had written back once or twice, deeming it unnecessary to reply to every letter. "It is clear the Zimbabwe government is not prepared to countenance any proposals from the South African Government," Mankahlana said.

Leon to visit SA men in Zimbabwe prison

THE Democratic Party's Tony Leon is to visit South African political prisoners Kevin John Woods and Michael Smith, jailed 12 years ago in Zimbabwe.

CAROL PATON reports that the two were given life sentences in 1988 for an anti-ANC bombing in Harare.

Leon said Woods had been writing to him since 1994. Although other political prisoners had been released, Woods and Smith had been "forgotten" in the amnesty process, he said.

Attempts by former President Nelson Mandela to persuade Zimbabwean President Robert Mugabe to release them had also failed.

The visit forms part of Leon's debut tour to Namibia, Zimbabwe and Botswana — the first official visit to neighbouring states in almost 30 years by an opposition leader.

The trip is aimed at building relationships with other opposition parties and is set to enhance Leon's image as a Southern African statesman.

"We have got to promote the concept of opposition and democracy. And no opposition party can survive in SA without knowing what is going on in the region," Leon said this week.

He has already met Botswana's President, Festus Mogae, and senior Cabinet ministers in Botswana and Namibia, as well as opposition parties, NGOs and business representatives in all three countries.

Mugabe expected to stand firm on jailed SA agents

Prisoners' future raised again but sources don't see change of mind

BY ANDREW MELDRUM
Harare

It is highly unlikely that Zimbabwean President Robert Mugabe will change his decision that Kevin Woods and his cohorts must serve out their life sentences in Zimbabwean prisons.

Mugabe's office did not respond to the question but legal sources say Mugabe is not expected to alter his often stated position on the matter.

In May 1997, when Nelson Mandela visited Zimbabwe, it is understood that the question was raised whether Zimbabwe would allow Woods and three others, found guilty of committing crimes while acting as agents for South Africa, to be transferred to serve out their terms in South African prisons. The answer was no.

The question of transferring the prisoners to South Africa dates back to 1994 when it was raised during the transition period. At that time the ANC hoped to trade the Zimbabwean prisoners for some prisoners held in South Africa. Zimbabwe refused that request also.

On both occasions President Mugabe stated categorically that because they were Zimbabwean residents and committed the crimes in

Zimbabwe they must serve their sentences in Zimbabwe.

Mugabe suggested he did not recognise the validity of their South African citizenship. He said they had been longtime British citizens resident in Zimbabwe and it appeared they only took up South African citizenship to receive protection from the apartheid government for the crimes committed in Zimbabwe.

Perhaps the strongest factor against Woods and his accomplices,

Cold-blooded killing of man counts against trio

Michael Smith and Phillip Conjwayo, was the cold-blooded nature of the killing for which they were convicted.

According to court testimony, in January 1988 the three went to a Bulawayo employment agency and hired an unemployed driver, Obert Mwanza.

They told Mwanza to drive to a house on Jungle Road in Bulawayo and hoot loudly twice to pick up some passengers. The car had been loaded with explosives and when

Mwanza hooted the h⎯⎯ ⎯e automobile exploded, kill⎯ Mwanza instantly and badly d⎯ ⎯ing the Jungle Road residen⎯ ⎯ut not causing any other fata⎯⎯⎯.

Woods was appre⎯⎯⎯d after investigators found M⎯⎯⎯'s hand in a tree. The dead m⎯⎯ fingerprints matched tho⎯⎯ at the employment agency ⎯ registered with the polic⎯ ⎯e employment agency's re⎯⎯rus of the hiring of Mwanza le⎯ ⎯he police to Woods.

Mwanza was no⎯ a South African ANC activis⎯ he was merely an unemployed driver who was sacrificed in a plot to blow up an ANC safehouse in Bulawayo.

Woods, Smith and Conjwayo were sentenced to death, but the Zimbabwe government reduced the sentences to life imprisonment.

Another case is that of Barry Bawden who is nearing the end of a 15-year sentence for carrying out a car bombing in Harare's Avondale shopping centre which seriously injured anti-apartheid campaigners Jeremy and Joan Brickhill.

A fifth prisoner was Briton Denis Beahan who was convicted of carrying out a plot to free the others from prison. Beahan was released from prison last year. – Star Foreign Service

RAPPORT, 3 DESEMBER 2000

NUUS 17

Twee van SA 'sterwend' in Zim-tronk

JOHAN EYBERS
Johannesburg

Mnr. Kevin Woods (48) en mnr. Philip Conjwayo (68), aan wie lewenslange tronkstraf in Zimbabwe opgelê is vir apartheidsmisdade, is glo sterwend weens gesondheidsprobleme en 'n gebrek aan mediese hulp.

Woods, wat saam met mnr. Mike Smith (46) as Suid-Afrikaners lewenslange tronkstraf saam met Conjwayo vir hul misdade uitdien, word in sekere geledere as die vergete grensvegters bestempel omdat hulle die enigste Suid-Afrikaanse politieke gevangenes uit die apartheidsera is wat in 'n ander land vir apartheidsmisdade in die tronk sit.

Woods ly aan hartprobleme en daar word gevrees dat Conjwayo prostaatkanker het en besig is om te sterf.

Mnr. Philip Albertyn, wat die twee mans onlangs by die Chikurubi-maksimumveilig-heidsgevangenis buite Harare besoek het, sê hy was geskok toe hy hulle sien.

"Dit was duidelik dat daar nie veel aandag aan hul welstand gegee word nie.

"Dit was veral skokkend om te sien hoe hul toestand in 'n jaar agteruit gegaan het.

"Hulle het verskeie kere om behoorlike mediese hulp gevra, maar dit word geweier."

Albertyn het gesê die Verenigde Nasies (VN) se voorskrifte oor gevangenes se behandeling word nie nagekom nie.

Dit lyk ook nie of die Suid-Afrikaanse regering genoeg druk op Zimbabwe uitoefen om iets hieraan te doen nie.

Mnr. Barry Bawden, wat saam met Woods en Conjwayo twaalf jaar tronkstraf in haglike omstandighede in die tronk uitgedien het en verlede jaar stil-stil vrygelaat is in die hoop om nie die Zimbabwiese regering te ontstel nie, het gesê dit het nou hoog tyd geword dat die Zimbabwiese regering genade toon en sy makkers bevry.

"Alles is van ons weggevat. Die laaste ding wat nou moet gebeur, is dat my vriende nou ook hul lewe verloor, terwyl diegene wat die opdragte gegee het, amnestie gekry het."

Die drie word steeds in Chikurubi aangehou, ondanks herhaalde pogings deur oudpres. Nelson Mandela en pres. Thabo Mbeki om hulle vrygelaat te kry op grond van amnestie vir politieke terreurdade wat in die apartheidsjare gepleeg is. Mugabe weier steeds botweg en hul vrylating het hoofsaaklik hul eie verantwoordelikheid geword.

Mnr. Dumisani Rasheleng, woordvoerder van die departement van buitelandse sake, het gesê die konsulaat in Zimbabwe het 'n versoek vir beter mediese behandeling van Woods ontvang.

"Die konsulaat sal hom binnekort besoek om na sy welstand te verneem en daar sal met die Zimbabwiese regering onderhandel word as gevind word dat hy nie die nodige behandeling kry nie."

jeybers@rapport.co.za

Mnr. Kevin Woods, aan wie in 1986 in Zimbabwe lewenslange tronkstraf opgelê is nadat hy, mnr. Mike Smit en mnr. Barry Bowden nege Suid-Afrikaanse kommandolede gehelp het om 'n ANC-kantoor in Harare op te blaas en om 'n voorstedelike huis naby Harare aan te val waarin ANC-vlugtelinge geskuil het.

WOODS
Truth Commission
7307/2003

KEVIN JOHN WOODS *ADDENDUM TO MY TRUTH COMMISSION APPLICATION*

Addendum to South African Pardon Application of 19th June 2002

I am a prisoner of conscience. I had no criminal motive and every aspect of my imprisonment is political – from the former South African Government, which I assisted, to the ANC which bore the brunt of the military activity that may have resulted from that assistance. This addendum is not an attempt by myself to atone for my sins. That is impossible. I simply wish to place my perspective before an impartial panel. I pulled no trigger. I placed no explosive. I operated as an accomplice, and on the fringes of a South African military service unit in Zimbabwe during the mid-1980's. I was convicted of murder as an accomplice. I was convicted of sabotage as an accomplice and likewise of possession of arms of war. These are facts that were accepted by the courts that convicted me.

I knew the military raid was to be carried out on an ANC guerrilla safe house in Bulawayo in 1988. The target was the ANC guerrilla occupants. I was in South Africa when this raid took place and therefore had absolutely no control over the operation and certainly no idea or wish that the innocent driver of the vehicle used to attack the premises would be killed. Nevertheless, I admit that I played a peripheral role in this attack by supplying intelligence regarding the safe house in Bulawayo. As per my numerous (failed) petitions for clemency, I reiterate my profound remorse for the death of that innocent person. In retrospect, I also wish to place on record my remorse for injury and any other damage suffered by anyone as a result of my activity. I was not a proponent of apartheid. It is a fact that I was living happily in a multi-racial Zimbabwe. My involvement and assistance rendered to the former South African Government was occasioned solely to try and prevent innocent people dying in the guerrilla bombing campaign in South Africa. I was sentenced to 25 years imprisonment with labour (after appeal) for the sabotage and possession of arms of war offences. Once again, I only played a peripheral and non-essential role in these crimes but nevertheless admit complicity.

I have made peace with God and now I wish to make peace with man. I am aware that the former South African President, Nelson Mandela, forgave me for the above transgressions and on numerous occasions requested my (and my two co-accused's) release. It is my belief that this incredible policy of reconciliation is still part of the new South African Government's agenda although as yet it has had no effect regarding my plight. I spent five years on death row, and now serve an indeterminate life sentence, for the death of the Bulawayo driver. There is no parole in Zimbabwe and my fate rests entirely with the executive authority of the Zimbabwean President. I have been told by the Zimbabwean Justice Minister, who recommends the release of life prisoners, that I will never be released. The reason he gives for this is that I am a serious threat to the security of Zimbabwe and also that, as a senior member of the Central Intelligence Organisation, I acted contrary to Zimbabwe Government policy in assisting the South African Government. I have no idea how my assistance to the former South African Government in its campaign against the ANC in a war that ended with the June 1990 cease-fire suddenly renders me a threat to the security of Zimbabwe. That would best be explained by the Zimbabwean Justice Minister. I did nothing that was intended to harm Zimbabwe – however, I admit that insecurity and destabilisation did occur as a result of my activity and once again, as per my failed petitions, I sincerely apologise to all who suffered. I bear no malice to Zimbabwe or its people, never have and never will.

I suffer from heart disease, have had at least one minor stroke, suffer from haemorrhoids and ulcers and possibly a prostate problem. I have a neurological problem that renders me dizzy most of each day. *I am a threat to no one.* I have no knowledge if amnesty from the South African Government will affect my incarceration in Zimbabwe but I do know, that as a South African citizen, a South African amnesty, fair and square, will give my long-suffering family and myself a margin of self-respect, a feeling of belonging to South Africa's reconciliation process, and also that most elusive emotion of all – hope.

KEVIN JOHN WOODS

Double agent's account

Part

BY BRENDAN SEERY

Sometime around June 1988, at an air strip just outside the Zimbabwean steel town of Redcliff, a nine-year-old girl was hit in the stomach by a 9mm parabellum bullet. It goes without saying that her life was changed forever.

But, sadly, shamefully, history hasn't recorded her name. We can't even say whether she lived or died, whether she fell in love, married, had children, got a job.

Why should this be? She was black, for one thing. And she undoubtedly came from a poor family. And, the stories of poor, black people in the history of southern African – particularly in the times of colonialism and post-liberation – have seldom been fully told.

Even now, 12 years after South Africa threw off the shackles of apartheid to become the last African nation to chart its own destiny, it's the white voices that often dominate the discussions about what should, or should not, constitute history.

Which is ironic, given the fact that the siren whinge of many white South Africans is that history is being "changed" daily by the perceived victors – the ANC government (and by implication, black people).

Despite that complaining, history is being reassembled by some of the so-called "losers" who, with the benefit of time, and the fact that some political winds have changed direction in the subcontinent, can now lay claim to have been on the side of the angels.

Which is why I must remember the little girl on the airstrip outside Redcliff. I must remember her and her basic human dignity. And because, as a journalist, one of my jobs is to be, as the saying goes, one of those who compiles "the first draft of history".

To leave her story untold or, worse, to have it distorted, is, for me, unconscionable.

And at the very least, her story has been ignored in the re-writing of history by one Kevin John Woods, a self-proclaimed "political prisoner" who served almost 20 years in prison in Zimbabwe. This week, he

wrote to *The Sunday Independent*, on the passing of former state president PW Botha, to say that he was sorry he had never met the "Groot Krokodil" to say thank you for the attempt to rescue him from prison in Harare in 1988.

What Woods neglected to mention, perhaps because it would have somehow soured his saintly story, was the fact that the operation to rescue him and others who had been jailed for working for the then South African Defence Force (SADF) went badly pear-shaped. Another white Zimbabwean (like Woods), a Flight Lieutenant Kane from the Zimbabwe air force, had stolen a Bell helicopter which was to have been used to take on board the prisoners after they were dramatically snatched while on their way to court in Harare from the Chikurubi Prison.

When the rescue couldn't be pulled off for some reason or other, Kane flew the chopper to the rendezvous at Redcliff air strip, where a South African Air Force Dakota transport plane was waiting, engines turning over.

Some Zimbabwean security forces apparently tried to prevent the South Africans and their Zimbabwean Fifth Columnist, Kane, from escaping. There was a shootout, and the nine-year-old girl was one of the victims.

That is what Woods wants to say thank you for.

But, brushing aside the facts of the Redcliff debacle is nothing compared to the weapons-grade rewriting of reality in which Woods, and his coterie of supporters in South Africa, have been engaged in for the past decade.

According to Woods, he was jailed by "Robert Mugabe ... for politically motivated offences committed on behalf of the apartheid era government".

The facts need to be understood by everyone who seeks to make sense of the turbulent times of the 1980s – and especially by whites, wherever they may be in southern Africa, who are outraged when their black compatriots don't always trust them wholeheartedly.

Woods was a senior officer of the Central Intelligence Organisation, which began its life in Ian Smith's regime and which continued its covert work after

# of his betrayal neglects to

Part 2 (handwritten)

A copy of the original Reuters transmission print of Kevin Woods on his conviction in Harare in 1988 and, right, Woods after his release in July this year. Woods published a posthumous thanks to PW Botha for attempting to free him in an aborted raid in the same year

PHOTOGRAPHS: HOWARD BURDITT, REUTERS; TJ LEMON

Mugabe and Zanu-PF took over in April 1980.

From that time, in 1980, right up until his arrest in early 1988, Woods – and many other whites like him in positions of trust within Mugabe's security apparatus – was playing a double game. He was working for the SADF.

According to him, he was a soldier of that organisation, doing what he infers was his patriotic duty to prevent a "communist, terrorist" organisation like the ANC ever gaining power in South Africa.

Indeed, Woods was jailed for his role in the death of a Zimbabwean citizen – again a man whose name has disappeared into the dust of history – who died when a bomb in a vehicle he was driving detonated prematurely.

Whatever else Woods was involved in on behalf of the government in Pretoria, and supposedly for the noble aspiration of fighting against communism, has never been revealed by him. It seems fairly certain, though, that, in the almost eight years he was playing double agent, there were plenty of other things he may have been involved in.

Before we ponder what other incidents he, or others he was working with, may have been involved in, let's consider the harsh reality of his situation. Between 1980 and the time of his arrest in 1988, he was never a fully attested member of the SADF, but was being paid money by Pretoria to play the double game.

Since his release earlier this year from Chikurubi (on health grounds), he has been at pains to stress that he was only ever reimbursed for his "expenses" –

mention a few details

which would underline his committed "patriotism".

He is no doubt secure in the knowledge that all the documents related to those years in SADF hands have long since been shredded so there is no way of verifying if he is telling the truth on that issue.

Suffice to say that, in the 1980s, when the annual foreign exchange in Zimbabwe "holiday allowance" was just R600 and emigrants could take less than R2 000, hard currency "forex" was tempting to many Zimbabweans.

However, the only problem for Woods on the issue of patriotism was that for eight years he was a Zimbabwean, taking money from a foreign power for aiding and abetting acts of terrorism on the soil of the country of his citizenship. That sort of conduct, by the dictionary definition, is treason – not a politically motivated struggle for any sort of freedom or justice.

Woods, and others like him, was a mercenary, prepared to turn against his homeland for money. He is correct when he says he is a South African citizen – yet this citizenship was only granted in the 1990s, years after he was jailed.

While the "rescue" attempt by PW Botha's government may have been out of loyalty to one of its "soldiers", it may also well have been launched to ensure that Woods and company did not reveal the extent of South African "destabilisation" operations in its northern neighbour.

And that destabilisation was deep and widespread. While it is true that the Nat government believed its "total strategy" was to combat the "total onslaught" from the ANC and the communist world, the reality is that there were never the ANC training camps that Pretoria feared would be set up north of the Limpopo. But, perhaps more important for the apartheid securocrats was to ensure that the uppity black man with socialist aspirations did not succeed.

And, lest it be forgotten, in 1980, that was exactly what Mugabe was doing. With a stated policy of reconciliation and investment in people, the country thrived. Education boomed, as did the economy. Go back to the records: in the early 1980s, Zimbabwe exported maize to South Africa!

From early 1981, the South Africans began interfering, having much of their dirty work done by Zimbabweans, like Woods, who were eager for the pieces of silver thrown their way.

Among others things that had a South African connection, yet which had little direct connection to the ANC in Zimbabwe:

● The blowing up of the Inkomo Barracks armoury outside Harare.

● The bombing of the Zanu-PF headquarters in downtown in Harare, in which more than 20 people died.

● The destruction of most of the frontline fighter aircraft of the Air Force of Zimbabwe in a sabotage raid on Thornhill air base.

● An attempted raid in southwestern Zimbabwe in which three SADF soldiers died in what was later described as an "unauthorised mission".

● The arming and supporting of former soldiers loyal to Joshua Nkomo. These "dissidents" made a point of targeting white farmers and missionaries.

In addition, the South African government, by backing the Renamo rebels in Mozambique, ensured that Zimbabwe's fuel supplies were choked by the destruction of the Beira-Mutare pipeline.

Then the South African Railways suddenly had no tanker cars to transport fuel northwards and the country's customs officials began delaying road fuel tankers at Beit Bridge, resulting in crippling fuel shortages across Zimbabwe.

In many of these operations, whites were involved. As this became revealed, Mugabe and Zanu-PF became increasingly distrustful of whites – something which remains to this day.

Although not the only reason behind the land grabs in Zimbabwe, it is an important catalyst that seldom, if ever, gets a mention in analysis of the current situation in that country.

When the histories of southern Africa are finally written, Woods and others like him must have an important place. This piece has been an attempt to ensure his massaging of history is not accepted unchallenged.

We owe it to the memory of that girl and thousands of others whose stories are ignored or distorted.

Section 8 (3) (a) of the Act
Sectioon 48 (1) of the Regulations

Printed by the Government Printer, Harare
Form I.F. 20

GOVERNMENT OF ZIMBABWE

IMMIGRATION ACT [*CHAPTER 4:02*]

*1. ~~NOTICE TO PERSON REFUSED LEAVE TO ENTER ZIMBABWE~~

*2. NOTICE TO PROHIBITED PERSON

To ...... KEVIN. J. WOODS ....

at ...... HARARE ....

TAKE NOTICE—

*1. That leave to enter Zimbabwe is refused in terms of—

    *(a) paragraph ( ) of subsection (3) of section 12 of the Act;

    *(b) paragraph (b) of section 17 of the Act;

    *(c) subsection (1) of section 18 of the Act

*2. That you are a prohibited person in terms of—

    *(a) paragraph (E) of subsection (1) of section 14 of the Act;

    *(b) subparagraph (iii) of paragraph (f) of subsection (1) of section 14 of the Act.

*Immigration officer to delete or complete as appropriate.

You are notified that, in terms of subsection (1) of section 21, as read with subsection (1) of section 22 of the Act, you may appeal to the nearest Magistrate's Court—

    (a) if you have been notified that leave to enter Zimbabwe has been refused, on any grounds relating to the question of whether you were properly refused leave to enter; or

    (b) if you have been notified that you are a prohibited person in terms of paragraph (a), (h) or (k) of subsection (1) of section 14 of the Act, on the grounds of identity only; or

    (c) if you have been notified that you are a prohibited person in terms of subparagraph (iii) of paragraph (f) of subsection (1) of section 14 of the Act, on the grounds of identity or on the question of whether you have been convicted of an offence specified in Part II of the First Schedule to the Act; or

    (d) if you have been notified that you are a prohibited person in terms of any other provision of subsection (1) of section 14 of the Act, on any grounds relating to the question of whether you are a prohibited person.

If you have been refused leave to enter Zimbabwe, you are not entitled to enter or remain in Zimbabwe for the purpose of noting or prosecuting your appeal, making representations to the Minister or being present at the hearing hereof, but may be represented at your appeal by a legal practitioner.

Your appeal may be noted—

    (a) if you have been refused leave to enter or are outside Zimbabwe when you receive this notice, not later than ten days, Saturdays, Sundays and public holidays excluded, after receiving this notice;

    (b) if you are in Zimbabwe when you receive this notice, not later than three days, Saturdays, Sundays and public holidays excluded, after receiving this notice;

and must be noted in Form I.F. 21 which may be obtained from any immigration officer.

The provisions of sections 49 to 59 of the Immigration Regulations, 1979, are to be adhered to in the event of the submission of an appeal.

Date: ....

Place: ....

ZIMBABWE IMMIGRATION
(A87%)
0 1 JUL 2006
HARARE IMMIGRATION
HEADQUARTERS

I hereby acknowledge receipt of this notice.

Date: ...1 JULY 2006...

Immigration Officer

Signature: ....

9TH JULY 2006   K.J. WOODS.

TO FT. FIDELIS MUKONORI
    c/o MS J. WOOD

DEAR FATHER MUKONORI,

I DO HOPE THIS WILL FIND YOU IN GOOD HEALTH.
MY FAMILY, FRIENDS, ASSOCIATES AND MOSTLY, MYSELF,
THANK YOU MOST WHOLEHEARTEDLY FOR YOUR CONCERN
AND EFFORT WHICH RESULTED IN MY RELEASE AND
SECOND CHANCE AT LIFE. I CANNOT THANK YOU ENOUGH.

PLEASE WILL YOU BE SO KIND AS TO PASS MY BEST
WISHES AND GRATITUDE ON TO HIS EXCELLENCY
PRESIDENT R. G. MUGABE?

FATHER MUKONORI, IF I CAN EVER BE OF ANY
ASSISTANCE TO YOU, IN ANY WAY POSSIBLE,
PLEASE DO NOT HESITATE TO CONTACT ME VIA
MS JULIA WOOD.

---

23 JULY 2006
THE PRESIDENT OF THE REPUBLIC OF ZIMBABWE
Cde R.G. MUGABE.

DEAR MR PRESIDENT.

PLEASE ACCEPT MY SINCERE GRATITUDE FOR YOUR
BENEVOLENCE AND MY RELEASE FROM PRISON IN
JUNE 2006.

YOURS SINCERELY

Kevin John Wood.

K.J. WOODS.

Woods should thank his lucky star

When murderer Kevin Woods was released from the so-called "notorious" Zimbabwe Chikurubi Prison looking surprisingly hale and hearty (in spite of reportedly being a very troublesome prisoner), he was given a warm welcome by much of our local media.

President Robert Mugabe had shown clemency, supported by the South African government.

Woods and his apartheid-period comrades cannot even be termed war criminals because there was no declared war, merely a brutal paramilitary total onslaught against mainly civilian communities and majority rule in frontline states.

Woods was a Zimbabwean traitor who aligned himself with South African apartheid forces to destabilise the democratically elected government in Zimbabwe and later was granted South African citizenship as a reward.

Woods's disgusting, fawning letter of support for the late "Groot Krokodil" (*The Sunday Independent*, November 5) illustrates the success of the apartheid brainwashing regimen.

Those racist murderers are still in a denialist time warp, believing they were fighting some sort of noble war, strutting around like heroes.

Our Truth and Reconciliation Commission exercise has been a dismal failure in bringing home to much of the mainstream white populace the culpability and repentance needed for that crime against humanity.

The Nuremberg trials ensured that the perpetrators of that era were brought to book, and the group guilt acknowledged so that those nations could go forward united, without their baggage.

PW Botha died on Tuesday, October 31. He was 90   PHOTOGRAPH: ADIL BRADLOW, AP

I would like to ask Woods if he supports capital punishment.

He is fortunate indeed not to have suffered that fate himself.

Woods and his ilk will not escape ignominy when grandchildren read their history books.

Brian Venter
Pretoria

6 | FORUM

THE SUNDAY INDEPENDENT NOVEMBER 5 2006

Write to Box 1014, Johannesburg 2000, or fax (011) 834-7520
E-mail: scribe@sunday.co.za

I should have thanked PW

I was jailed in Zimbabwe by Robert Mugabe for nearly 20 years for politically motivated offences committed on behalf of the apartheid era government.

I was arrested in January 1988 and PW Botha authorised a military operation to spring me from Harare's maximum security prison in May the same year. The operation to secure my freedom involved South African military and airforce personnel and equipment, and only failed due to human error.

The fact remains that PW was honourable enough to appreciate his moral responsibility towards myself, a South African secret agent, jailed on the front line. Since my release in July this year, I have seriously considered a trip to PW's home, simply to thank him for having the moral conviction to try and rescue me.

I failed to get my act together and now with PW's death, I will have to live with the regret of not making the effort to try and visit him.

We all have our cross to bear and life is replete with profound regret – I've created yet another for myself.

In sackcloth and ashes, yet with a sincere heart, I offer my profound condolences to Mr PW Botha's family.

**Kevin John Woods
Political prisoner, January 1988 – July 2006**

To Kevin,
Best wishes to a Courageous person.
Mandela

MANDELA

14. 11. 06

THE
AUTHORISED
PORTRAIT

Editorial Consultants
Mac Maharaj and Ahmed Kathrada

Narrative: Mike Nicol; Interviews: Tim Couzens, Rosalind Coward and Amina Frense
Editor: Kate Parkin; Picture Research: Gail Behrmann

————)✕(————

Wild Dog Press

in association with PQ BLACKWELL

Index